HERE'S MORGAN!

by Henry Morgan

Barricade Books, Inc.

New York, N.Y.

Published by Barricade Books Inc.
61 Fourth Avenue
New York, NY 10003

Printed in the United States of America

Library of Congress Cataloging-in-Publication Data

Morgan, Henry, 1915-
Here's Morgan! / by Henry Morgan.
        p.   cm.
    ISBN 1-56980-001-4 : $22.00
    1. Morgan, Henry, 1915-   . 2. Radio broadcasters—United States
Biography. 3. Television personalities—United States—Biography.
I. Title.
PN1991.4.M57A3   1994
791.44′028′092—dc20
    [B]   93-45406
                                                                               CIP

First Printing

Obituary of Henry Morgan
(written while alive, January, 1994)

IN CHILDHOOD:

Numerous abscesses
Heart murmur
Influenza
Whooping cough
Scarlet fever
Measles
Mumps (mumps!)
Nearsightedness

LATER:

Arthritis
Gout
Emphysema
Bursitis
Hemorrhoids
Pneumonia
Psoriasis (two years)
Lumbago
Hypertension (natch)
2 cataracts—lenses replaced
Migraines (five years)
Skin cancers. . . . five facial, eight body
Arteries replaced in both legs
Aorta replaced
7 teeth gone
Colitis (two years)
Hiatus hernia of diaphragm—AND a "normal" hernia
Skin graft on foot (June and July, '91)
One heart attack
Enlarged prostate (Nov., '92)
500 pastrami sandwiches
3,000 quarts of beer
7,000 quarts of liquor
17,250 bacon and egg breakfasts
21,000 steaks and hamburgers
1,296,000 cigarettes
2 wives.

"He was born with the gift of laughter and a sense that the world was mad."

—Rafael Sabatini

"Life is a joke and the punch line is a killer."

—Karen Sorensen Morgan

This book is dedicated to the people who made it posssible:

Dr. Bernard Gretsch
Dr. Richard A. Marks
Dr. Walter A. Wichern, Jr.
Dr. Philip Terman
Dr. A.A. Attia
Dr. C.K. Loving, Jr.
Dr. George DiGiacinto

This book is dedicated to the people who made it possible:

A WORD OR TWO BEFORE I GO

O Tempura

I was an unloved child; neither parent ever molested me.

❈ ❈ ❈ ❈

Being born is not your fault, of course. Then as time passes, and still without your active attention, without your even having noticed, you find yourself in the habit of living. Constant living leads to old age. It's in old age that you finally understand that prices really *have* been going up all the time.

This is being written during the Golden Era. Uneeda Biscuits, once a nickel a box, are now a dollar and a quarter. Baseball players, once a dimeadozen, have remade the world. An illiterate youth who bats .176 and fields like a mouse is paid three millions dollars for spending six months standing around in the sun and scratching his crotch.

You're hearing this from a man who, back in 1942-43, made one thousand dollars ($1,000.00) a week. And Pepsi-Cola hit the spot, twelve full ounces that's a lot, at five (5) cents.

But enough of sobbing about the past—even though we live at a time when the island of Grenada has been completely forgotten. Who remembers now that we fought a war there, a wonderful triumph, during the course of which the Armed Forces of the United States of America (without ANY outside help) shot and killed a Cuban workman who, the Pentagon said,

7

had ties to the Communist Party. How could we have so soon forgotten that four thousand seven hundred medals were awarded to the American heroes who were there?

Not too long ago we won another sensational victory during the course of which combined forces from countries having a total population of 500,000,000 (five hundred million) people fought and managed to beat Iraq, population, nineteen million. The United States alone spent eighty billion dollars, including carfare. For every Iraqi killed, military or civilian, the cost was three hundred and seventeen thousand dollars.

Truly, an Age of Gold.

Money is everywhere. Japan makes a lot from selling its cars here, and gives no rebates. Chrysler gives you five hundred dollars of your own money back if you buy one of theirs. The reason is that only half the Chrysler is made in Japan. The half that runs.

As I write, time has passed since the "Education President" has given way to the "Health-First Woman." At any rate, we have managed to live through the reigns of a friendly, sleepy movie actor and that of a Master of foreign policy. The policy consisted of having a phone on his desk in The Oval Office that had a direct line to King Saud . . . in case the King needed more armament to protect his desert from the spread of rampant Zionism.

As of now the United States borrows billions each year for the Space Program—an idea brought forward by the Developers' Lobby. Some of the money is raised by selling bonds to the Japanese. They have a state-of-the-art, mainframe computer which is obliged to choose, for investment purposes, between the United States and Soweto.

This is the Short List, and to hell with it.

Instead, I've just spent a lifetime at a marvelous party and I'd like to tell you about it.

1

Sex

Instead of spreading my extraordinary life-atop-the-sheets in steaming episodes throughout this pamphlet, the way it's done in vulgar books written for money, I thought it preferable to hump it all together in one vile chapter.

I slept with very few women. But I stayed awake with perhaps a hundred. Not a lot these days (or even in those days) but I often "went" with one girl for a (comparatively) long time. Compared, that is, with the notorious one-night-standers of fact and fiction. I don't remember ever bouncing around with anyone I didn't truly like. Besides, I was married about six months to my first, and twenty-five years (so far) to my second, and never cheated on either one. It's just so.

There were a few of these friendships before I married, and then there were twenty years between the legals, so it must be clear that I'm no maniac. Besides, of the hundred, most often THEY chose ME.

Me? Why? For one thing, I was shy. This led me to talk sort of defensively, but in an amusing way. Girls who liked me liked bright guys, guys who weren't pushy and who made them laugh. I was also physically very clean and I dressed nicely. In addition, I "made love" in a kind of flat-out way. Shy in the restaurant, but not so shy that she didn't suspect a romping future sometime after midnight.

Another thing. I've always vastly preferred the company of women to that of men. It probably showed, hah?

But Mr. Adorable was no big bargain, either. There were ten abortions. I always took care of the girls, but there it is. With just one exception: a lovely lady who refused that way out. She explained that she had flown East specifically in order to have my child.

As I write, my son Steve is forty. I can cheerfully state about him what my mother used to say about me. "He's wonderful. Never been on drugs or in jail." Steve, like me, is an amusing guy and he writes for a living. I'm very fond of him and regret only that he lives in California and I do not.

But let's get back to our, uh, knitting, shall we?

From what little I've read in the best-sellers it appears I was no great shakes in the intercourse tournament. If bedtime consists of a lot of "OH, Jesus! Oh, God! Now . . . uh . . . NOW!" I was either deaf or not paying attention. My partners had orgasms often enough, but they managed to keep the news from the neighbors.

For the Guinness Book of Records I should like to state that one session (admittedly when I was twenty-three) began after midnight on Friday and finished Monday morning.

Thirteen times.

You see, before there was television, people were obliged to provide their own entertainment.

This attractive Arizona redhead had heard me on her car radio when she first drove into New York. She called me at the radio station and after we met she said, "When I heard your broadcast I knew that New York was going to be fun."

And it was—for both of us, as it turned out.

By the bye, the girl ultimately married an admiral.

I sense there's a joke in here but danged if I know what it is. Sorry.

✦✦✦✦

A handsome, blond-brown haired, blue eyed, five-ten-and-a-half, useless youth was asleep. He lived with his mother and younger brother in a small apartment on the third floor of what had once been a one-family house on upper Riverside Drive in Manhattan. "Useless" would have slept late every morning but for a loud, disagreeable sound, to wit: "Go out and find a job!"

One day, while slouching around Times Square, he ran into a guy he knew. The guy said that a press agent in the Brill Building on Broadway was looking for a gag writer. The idler applied, and by fibbing got the job. "Here," the man pointed, "here's a typewriter. All you have to do is write gags that the columnists will use. Fifteen dollars a week."

I became a ghost. Mr. Fagin's clients were celebrities and restaurants, and one way he kept their names in the papers was to send in clever things that they said the night before at Sardi's or The Stork Club. Clever things that I now was to invent. It could have been a fascinating job except for one thing—I couldn't think of anything clever. I was a funny talker all right, but staring at that dirty wall in that cruddy office, all I could think of was funny things to write on dirty walls. By the end of the week I had turned in five amusing lines. Three were actually printed by a columnist on Hearst's New York *American*. One pay day Fagin told me that I wasn't worth fifteen dollars, or, for that matter, any dollars. He paid me nothing.

Then I got a job as a page boy in a radio station. It was easy because some years before, my father had bought a Stutz automobile covered in leather. (Please, just let me alone.) One day my mother drove into the public garage and parked next to—another leather-covered Stutz. She knew there were only ten in the world, so she got into a conversation with the owner of the other car and a few weeks later he hired her to sing on his independent radio station, WMCA. She worked at the going rate, which was nothing. Some time later he hired me as a page.

This job, four hours on, four hours off, four hours on, six days a week paid only eight dollars but the difference between that and my former salary was that I actually got the eight dollars.

Alas, I was one lousy pageboy. For one thing, I had the big

mouth. For another, the secretaries all had inkwells which had to be emptied, cleaned and refilled every day, or every time the girls felt like it. Sure, fountain pens had been invented but these drabs had INKWELLS. I was just a damned gopher for a clucking barnyard. And I must have mentioned it a few times because in three weeks I was fired.

We live in parlous times. It's not enough, apparently, that there are vastly too many people on the globe, that the very air reeks, that the forests are being destroyed, and election notices are printed in two languages, but precious TV time is being afforded to David Letterman.

This is a kind of memoir of other times. I say 'kind of' because all efforts of this type are melanges of foggy recollection, subtle gilding of the more unattractive facts, and a determined glossing of self-inflicted disasters.

To begin. I have many drawbacks. One of the most enduring is un-American aversion to suing. For example, there was once a TV personality-cum-newspaper columnist named Dorothy Kilgallen. When the woman died her column was given over to a short, pop-eyed putz whose talent was completely invisible. This undersized, misbegotten squirt clawed his way way to attention by attacking his obvious superiors, among them Steve Allen. Steve eventually wrote a scathing, psuedo-psychological piece about the stunted slob, but it served merely to enlarge his ego, and he went on to attack the hero of *this* book as a 'pinko'—again and again. I could have sued him, his paper and his syndicator and won millions, but it had taken me many years to get a divorce from a dreadfully infatuated wife and I couldn't possibly look at a lawyer again without doing tremendous harm to my health.

Another of my failings is a sort of stupidity, or, perhaps a bit more accurately, an unawareness, an inability to grasp most pertinencies, such as a rationale for 'being'. As a boy I had great difficulty in understanding what, to other kids, was intuitive; I had to *learn* how to operate a punchboard. If you don't know what a punchboard is then you are probably one of those reprehensible little stinkers whose life began with Ringo and ended with Elvis. This book is probably not for you. Except for the seething sex, you will be bored witless.

This is a hop skip and jump through the days before our only exports were hamburger stands. It's written from a narrow point of view. After all, the man who says, "I have climbed the mountain" actually went up a single, narrow path. He did get a good view outward, finally, but he didn't see much of the mountain.

Because of a failing memory and a snappy imagination, parts of this may be bunk. Henry Ford said that history is bunk. The only stuff he believed in was the *Protocols of the Elders of Zion*. And the personal history he left behind him was—well, he liked to boast that he was the inventor of the assembly line. That was bunk. Eli Whitney invented it. Yes, the gin man. Eli thought up the moving belt in order to facilitate the manufacture of rifles for the U.S. government for the War of 1812. He invented the military-industrial complex.

I have slept with (or, more accurately, stayed awake in bed with) a lot of women. I have also eaten a lot of food. Since millions of American men have done the same there won't be too much about the girls (you'd know the names of only about forty of them) and nothing about food.

Dr. Johnson said that no man but a blockhead ever wrote except for money.

My fingers are crossed.

2

Readers' Rest Period

Eisenhower

About twenty of us were standing in line under the eyes of the Secret Service. We had just done a show for President Eisenhower and his guests at the White House and had been told that he wanted to meet us. Soon he appeared with an aide and started to shake each person's hand and say a word or two. I was last in line. They approached and the aide said, "Mr. President, Henry Morgan."

I had a funny idea. I shook his hand and said, "Sir, I used to work for you."

The President looked a wee bit surprised.

"In the Air Force," said the great wit. The President took a step back and, half turned towards me, stage-whispered to his aide.

"Charlie," he said, "isn't this the guy on the radio that we turn off all the time in the car?"

The man nodded, took Mr. Eisenhower by the arm, guided him to his left and gestured with his arm.

"Mr. President," he said, "the bar."

Carson

I was an on-the-air guest of Johnny's about forty times in the early days and knew him, sort of. Actually, I knew Ed McSweepstakes better.

The reason was Johnny.

This was far and away the wittiest man ever to appear on a regular basis in public. The problem, if I may call it that, is that he had an extraordinarily rapid mind. He was able to think, re-think and edit before he spoke. He was shy. Even when he was at home, if the topic of himself was brought up—what he personally thought, how he truly felt, the editor awoke immediately—even when he'd been drinking a lot. And he was, to use a by-now-discredited word, insecure. An instance of this: he had a large party at which, to give an example of what 'large' means in this context, the Hubert Humphreys were the most noticeable guests. As I was leaving, an all-but-reeling Johnny pulled me aside and sort of leered. "You don't really like me, do you," he said.

I said don't be silly.

He grabbed my suitcollar and snarled at me. "Don't ever call me silly!"

The fact was that I liked him very much. Still do, but things came to an awkward end for us. A young woman named Betty Rollins interviewed me for an article on Carson she was writing for Life magazine. I had met Betty back when I first met Joanna—they were good friends. When Betty closed her notebook she said, "Off the record, what's Johnny really like?"

"Well," I said, "He's sort of cold." What I had meant to say was that he was sort of shy, but it came out wrong and that's the way she printed it.

He never spoke to me again after that.

I told his wife Joanna the "off the record" story. She asked Rollins about it and reported back to me.

"She says that you've been around too long to believe that stuff about 'off the record.'"

Miss Rollins later wrote a book called *First You Cry*.

Manny Zora

Manny was a Portygee fisherman of Provincetown. Six-foot-three, face carved out of a sixty-year old block of Portygee wood, hands just twice the size of and ten times as strong as mine. Twenty. Like many men who are powerful both inside and out, he was peaceful and kind.

One dark winter's day we were down at the P'town pier to experience the weather. The wind was at about forty knots and full of freezing rain and the bay hurled six, seven foot waves at the town. The few boats at anchor reared and whinnied at their ropes. We had to hold on to the stanchions with both fists and it was scary and thrilling. No day for fishermen.

After a bit Karen motioned with her head for me to look along to my right. A tall post stood firm and upright, fists in pockets, hat squarely, somehow, on head. It stared out through the mists at the bay. It held on to nothing and it didn't move an inch. Manny Zora.

Rudy Vallee

A wretched pop-tune singer made famous by the radio. Rudy was born in Maine and sang in a New England twang through his nose. In front of a band in a hotel, he sang through a megaphone. Although he was lousy, one could understand the words and this differentiated him from the other alley cats. He was also an unbelievable pinchpenny. At Musso Franks restaurant in Hollywood, he impressed me by ordering his "special champagne." What came to the table was a bottle of something like sick, pink grapejuice. Rudy smiled. "It's only a dollar a bottle," he crowed.

Rudy's wife always sat at a table different from his. He said that it was because he was ashamed of her English. It was Vallee who popularized a ballad that began, "Life is just a bowl of cherries . . . don't take it serious, it's too mysterious." He was famous too for his rendition of the "Maine Stein Song." When he opened the door to his house, a recording played it automatically. Every time. Every goddam time.

Eartha Kitt

A remarkable, sprightly and talented woman. Once when she was visiting England a hotel clerk told her that there was no room to be had. She is a black woman. This was the dialogue which followed the turndown:

Eartha: "Oh, by the way, I'm not black, I'm Spanish."

Room Clerk: "Oh, rilly. Say something in Spanish."

Eartha: "Adios, motherfucker."

Gloria Swanson

Someone introduced me to Gloria Swanson. She must have been about seventy but she looked just fine. Fine and, I thought, short. Very short. We shook hands and her eyes lit up and she invited me to a party for that same night. I went, knew nobody, and nobody talked to me. Including Gloria Swanson.

3

We think you are crazy
(Signed) Frank Sinatra and Ziggy Elman

❖❖❖❖

The above telegram was delivered to me at radio station WOR in New York City one day in 1940.

I'd never met Sinatra, but I knew that he was that skinny kid who sang with Tommy Dorsey's Orchestra and was one of the many, many things that make young girls scream. I first laid eyes on him in the flesh (about fifty pounds more flesh) at one of his semi-annual farewell concerts forty-six years later. I thought him marvelous.

Elman, I think, played in Dorsey's band.

When the telegram arrived I was doing a fifteen minute radio, uh, program, five evenings a week.

I had been a staff radio announcer who fooled around too much on the air, and the station had decided to give me fifteen minutes of air time once-a-week to do my fooling around in so that, in the Program Director's words, "You can get it out of your system and then go back to work."

The "program" to which the telegram had been sent was a sprightly monologic farrago interrupted every few minutes by snatches of slightly cuckoo phonograph records. The idea, if

19

that's what it was, worked, and in about a month it was aired five-nights-a-week. By the time I enlisted in order to help my country "Slap The Jap" I was making a-thousand-dollars-a-week.

Sinatra had said I was crazy. Well, yes.

So was the Army Air Corps, which it was then called. I never made it past corporal. But I must have been an interesting one because I made it to corporal on three different occasions.

4

Sometime in the 1950's the television program "I've Got a Secret" was being broadcast on a one-time basis from Hollywood. It usually originated in New York. There were two syndicated gossips stationed there, Louella Parsons, an ignorant fat lady, and a charmer, Hedda Hopper. Miss Hopper invited the cast of the TV enterprise to a party. Bill Cullen, Garry Moore, Faye Emerson and I arrived together, Garry, being the leader, rang the bell and the door was flung open by Fred Astaire. He greeted each of us by name. May I remark, "WOW!"?

It's not that I am dedicated to name-dropping, it's just that I've spent a lifetime among people who, in the main, had names that fell like stones. Besides, an autobiography has to start *somewhere, somehow,* and who better than Sinatra and Astaire? They, along with Joe DiMaggio, Fred Allen and James Thurber were heroes to me. And I like my heroes unsullied by biographers who find both pleasure and an audience by bellowing that so-and-so was a wife-beater, so-and-so was a homosexual. It is the WORK they did that is important to me. And I am enamoured of skeptics like me who have heroes. For instance:

I was having dinner at a midtown steakhouse in Manhattan with a girl I will call Joanna. There were but a few occupied tables. Suddenly, Joanna grabbed my wrist.

"Olivier!" she said.

"What?"

"Over there, by the window. Laurence Olivier!"

I am a bit reluctant to tell you that I allowed her to drag me over to where he sat with two other men. I snorted, stumbled, muttered something or other to him, and, since I was half-blinded, Jo guided me back our table.

"Did you hear that? He said 'Goodbye, Henry' to me!"

Joanna was indignant.

"What he SAID was, 'Goodbye, Joanna!'"

The blind leading the half-blind?

5

Genesis

"He's a Dzerman Dzew" my grandpa Sock would say. He'd be referring to an obvious poseur—a Russian or Polish Jew in America who was trying to pass himself off as having come from Germany. He thought it gave him 'class'. Sock had come from Odessa and he used the Russian prefix "dze" to point out that those people were faking it—they were not German Jews, they were only second class . . . like him. If they were real Deutschers he'd give them the accolade, "Cherman Chews." Sock almost always made me laugh.

According to the Bible as we know it, Sarah was about ninety years old and it had ceased to be with her after the manner of women. Therefore when she heard the Lord say that she would bear a son, she laughed. Ultimately, she did have a son and the father may have been the Lord himself—much as is said to have happened in an even more celebrated case.

Sarah's laugh is the first in recorded history. When she gave birth to a son she named him "Ytzhach"—"laughter." This Hebrew (Aramaic?) word is pronounced EETZ—HOCK! which is onomatopaeic because it's meant to sound like a short, barked laugh. In English it's "Isaac." For short, Sac. Pronounced Sock. See?

To Sac all women were beautiful. Yesterday he "met a beautiful woman at a luncheon." He saw a beautiful woman on the bus. He bumped into a beautiful woman in the hall. His dentist was married to a b. w. Sac, good-looking, blue-eyed man of medium height was ever on a skirt-alert. He wore a fresh red carnation in his buttonhole every day of his life. He always wore spats and a homburg hat. He told me he'd started doing this when he was seventeen. He read six languages but I'm sure his accent showed through five of them. For example, he told me more than once that I was too "sourcaastic".

Sac left Odessa when he was twenty-one.

In America His business card read "Isadore Lerner" but his wife called him Sac, see? So he must have been Isaac which was, apparently, his real name. Before he Americanized it. Hah?

Sac's wife's maiden name was Schultz. Sophie Schultz. Of Cherman descent. Whom he met in Odessa. A hundred or two hundred or a thousand years back their progenitors came from Spain, or, perhaps, Morocco. Greece. Canaan. Millenia before that, apparently nobody cared for the food in Ur. Mon dieu.

This is the way it happened. Sac had had it with Odessa where, according to my mother, he'd been a huge success. She never told me at what, and his history in the New World belies any possibility that this dreamer, this charming, amusing, utterly failed entrepreneur could ever have been a winner. He did have a kind of success once. In Alameda, California, he put together a kiddie revue featuring Eva ("Little Eva", of course) and her brother Ben who played an Italian organ-grinder. "Brownies in Fairyland" toured the far West and did well, so Sac dropped it. Success always went to his head and exploded. At that same time he rared back and passed a law, "No daughter of mine will be in show business." My mother obeyed it except for that brief stint on radio during the Depression and that engagement led to my getting that job on her station when I was seventeen.

Soc started a chain of grocery stores in California, sold it, and bought a steamship on the Atlantic. He was quite pleased when it didn't work out. Now in New York, he opened one of the first movie houses, a nickleodeon. He quit that, he told me, because he didn't like having to rent folding chairs from an undertaker.

Also, he said, and he truly looked me straight in the eye, he thought that movies had no future.

Soc once left the real estate business to buy an aged theater in the Bronx called Miner's Burlesque. He cleverly converted it into a loser by booking fourth-rate vaudeville acts. After he had lost the house he suggested to me that I join him in a new enterprise he'd thought up—doing away with the need for oranges. We'd ship orange juice in tank cars direct from Florida. (I never said he was a stupid man—"dreamer" was the word I used). Of course all we did about the orange juice idea was talk.

I think the only difference between him and me is that I speak five fewer languages.

Well, my mother told me that one day he saw a beautiful woman walking along an Odessa street, stopped, tipped his hat and asked her to accompany him to America. She demurred on the grounds that A) she didn't know him and B) she was married and the mother of the little girl by her side. Sac explained, in his courtly style, that she was too gorgeous for Odessa and that if her husband was any kind of a man he would already have taken her to the States. Mrs. Schultz truly was a beauty and her daughter, Manya, was one too. She looked like no one else in the entire family, which gives the story nice sturdy legs.

Mr. and Mrs. I. Lerner moved into a house in Alameda, across the Bay from San Francisco, and to keep Manya company they parented Anna, Ben and "Baby". "Baby" was my mother, Eva.

How come Alameda? Drat. Mother used to plead with me to "Go and talk with your grandfather" but she took the wrong tack. I'd know a great deal more about the family if only she'd said "DON'T go talk with your grandfather." I never did find out.

Sac had a brother Charlie who built cheap housing in Westchester, N.Y. Charlie fathered Sam, Mike and Joe. They in turn gave birth to the Lerner Shops. Joe, for lagniappe, sired Alan Jay Lerner. For Broadway Alan J. begat six [seven if you include *Gigi*] shows. He also had five wives and allegedly died broke.

Charlie also had a daughter, Beatrice, who makes her bow here only because she married a man named Ginsberg who later changed his name to Gray. This annoyed my mother, and until her death she never referred to the woman as anything but Beatrice Ginsberg Gray. "I hear that Beatrice Ginsberg Gray . . ."

* * * *

Early on, our own personal family Santa Claus gave me my first 'gift' book. The difference to a kid between a gift book and the *Book of Knowledge* which I had at home was the same as the difference between getting a set of trains and getting a bathrobe. The donor was a tiny old man with an enormous white beard, a snub nose and the brightest blue eyes in the history of the world. They are the only eyes I ever saw that could really twinkle! (There is one other set, and it belongs to Mary Ann Madden of *New York* magazine, but don't distract me.)

The tiny man's name was Nehemiah Moses Dayyan and he'd once been the Chief Rabbi of Odessa. He was also the paternal grandfather of my cousin Boris. (Boris, who as I write, is eighty two, and was once a member of the wrestling team at Harvard. Geez!)

The book the rabbi gave me was *The Breakfast of the Birds* and he took it down from a shelf in his library. There was a time when fairly ordinary people (except Soc) actually had a room with shelves of books . . . no trinkets, just books. In our family every Johnny (and Naomi) could read.

I received my book at Channuka and somebody gave me a quarter, worth, in those days, about ten dollars, and to a kid, one thousand. I always got one in my Christmas stocking too.

I had a stocking and a tree from the time I was two. For the first few years, Santa used a formula: one celluloid deer, one apple, one orange, some nuts and raisins, and the quarter. Starting at daybreak I would march the deer up and down the snowy hills of my pillow. The bed was next to a window which faced south and even on the coldest nights, the window was open an inch or two. The brand new sun hit ice crystals along

26

the sill and burst into a rainbow across the bed. The deer had a wonderful time.

One year it dawned on Santa that I was aging up in years, and he came through with a set of wind-up trains and started me on the life of a train buff. I've ridden them in the Congo, all over Europe, in Canada, Japan, Mexico . . . and in places Santa never even heard of.

Granpa always gave me a quarter at Xmas, too. As I say, his wife called him Soc, but to the rest of the family he was "Colonel." Seems he often played pinochle with General John J. Pershing. Now, Pershing's nickname was "Black Jack." I just relate these things, I don't explain 'em.

Once, when I was grown up, I gave each of three girls I was involved with a full set of luggage for Christmas. Bloomingdale's bill came, automatically, to my secretary. She had received the brown set. It happened too that she was living in my house at the time.

Worst Christmas I ever had.

∗∗∗∗

A note about Granma. Soc's wife was a handsome, elegant woman who loved to travel. She spent her summers (when Soc was doing well) in Wiesbaden, Germany, and, most important, kept a supply of Za Rex in her kitchen for me at all times. Za Rex was a colored syrup that, when mixed with water tasted like Hawaiian Punch. (George Jean Nathan despised authors who larded their work with knowledgeable references to food.)

Granma was a bad influence in other ways, too. She'd take me to the movies even on lovely afternoons if I wanted to go. If I said that green was red, she averred that it was so. I KNOW she was crazy about me because, in addition to Boris, I had this cousin Phillip, Anna's child. Granma never took Phillip anywhere. So there.

6

Daddums

You've heard of L. Ron Hubbard. He wrote science/fiction for those who had knowledge of neither. He was a thoroughly second-rate man who had the great good fortune to live in a second-rate time. By a series of curious chances one of his stories took off into the world of third-rate people and became the basis for Mr. Hubbard's great gift to the brainless, Scientology.

I have often wondered whether he may have been a descendant of Elbert Hubbard. Elbert became known, by reason of his own machinations, as "The Sage of East Aurora," a small town in upstate New York. His was the mind of the typical Chatauqua lecturer of his day—the equivalent of an Oral Roberts in ours. He sold inspiration to the normally uninspired. One of his better-known works was a short, shoddy piece called *A Message to Garcia*. This wholly fake bit of trumpery was the supposed story of a young lieutenant of the American army who, during the war with Cuba, managed, heroically, of course, to get through the Cuban lines with a message for a man named Garcia—someone who could, and did, turn what was left of the tide.

Since Elbert invented the letter, I invented the answer and herewith happily append it.

"I see your fella with letter. Nice looking fella. I give him sandwich. No understand letter.

Garcia"

Elbert's chief accomplishment was a seemingly endless set of tiny books, each measuring about three by four inches and bound in fake green leather. They were called collectively *Little Journeys* ("Into the Lives of Famous People.") One skimpy volume, for example, told everything allegedly worth knowing about George Washington. Two others did the same service for Isaac Newton and Victor Hugo. In fact any name that popped into Hubbard's dismal head was fair game. The series was sold BY subscription only, a new *Journey* to arrive every six weeks, or whenever Hubbard finished his claimed intensive research.

My father searched his soul and his wallet, which were interchangeable, and then subscribed. He knew all about Victor Hugo, of course, but he probably envisioned the itty books marshalled smartly across the coffee table, successfully subduing envious neighbors.

Poppa was a graduate of De Witt Clinton High and wrote a neat hand, the which, he once told me, was vital in getting him his first job as an adult, clerking in the Harriman Bank.

He'd been born on Attorney Street in the heart of a racially pure slum on Manhattan's Lower East Side. His parents had come from Breslau, now a part of Germany. When it was Polish it had been Wroclaw, improbably pronounced "shtetl."

My granpa was a small, slight, bald man with a tiny button for a nose. His wife was a short dumpling with a nose to match. I mention noses because my father had a honker. And while granpa's eyes were blue, father's were black.

As fathers will, mine often reminded me of how easy I had it. He had made his first way in the world by running uptown to get a packet of New York *Sun* newspapers and then running downtown to sell them. Saved a nickel each way, he did.

And he maintained that policy for the rest of his life.

He was what was called a "street angel, house devil." Poor

fella couldn't shout out his frustration at his life-insurance customers but he felt much freer to vent them around the apartment.

I had my own room, one window of which allowed me to hear the street noises—the important ones. I could tell the beginning of Fall because I heard coal rattling down the chute to the basement. Winter was when I heard the janitor's snow shovel clearing off the sidewalk.

The janitor was a Polack named Mike. My father like to shout at him too, but carefully. Mike was powerfully built. My father shouted at waiters, regardless of build. And he's the only man I ever heard of who shouted at theater ushers.

I collect Social Security and I have a few dollars put away but I still get nervous around men with loud voices.

Poppa talked, like Jackie Gleason did so many years later, about getting "steamed." He referred to his temper proudly; it was one of his prized possessions. He enjoyed displaying it to the neighbors. He had the power to build such tension in a room that I clearly remember my brother Roger in his highchair becoming more and more nervous until he finally threw up.

(As an adult, when Roger visited father he always got colitis.)

Poppa's father, Mr. Ost, was born in Breslau, Germany. Or in Wroclaw, Poland. It's the same town, but the German-Polish border has moved a lot and as of now it's Polish. When Mr. Ost, a short, pug-nosed cabinetmaker, left town in 1880 it was Germany, and that was the language he spoke.

I have a cabinet of drawers that Mr. Ost made in 1882. It's in excellent shape but has a slab of marble on top. I added that after my first wife sent it out behind my back to have it "modernized", which to her meant to sand off the mahogany finish and remove the claw feet in order to bring it to the style that was acceptable to the political left in the late Forties. I rescued it just as the man was sanding the top. Thus the marble.

Mrs. Ost was a plump woman who, after forty years in this country still had no English other than "dot's a nize baby."

My father changed his name to "von Ost" in 1914. I believe he saw a war coming and wanted to be safe from the draft. One other interesting item is that he was a member of the Teapot Dome Oil Reserve Scandal jury in the 1920's and took a bribe. To round out his portrait I offer this illuminating summary vignette. Once, in a conversation with me, he patted his wallet and said, "My best friend." We shall now leave him.

Ah, but the other side of the family! My mother's mamma was a regal lady who wore her hair (unbeknownst to her, I'm sure) in the style of the Queen Mother of England—a sort of neat, bouffant roll with a perky hat on top. What I remember about her in the hospital, dying of cancer, was her serenity. She had died once and been brought back. What was it like, Granma? "Oh . . . very quiet, very peaceful". She took a sip of water and, as was her queenly fashion, she took a napkin and dabbed lightly at the corners of her mouth. I loved her outright.

7

─────────────────

Toothy Amos

Granpa Soc had a friend who was, like him, from Odessa. His name was Louis Chalif, the Ballet Master of the Metropolitan Opera. Mr. Chalif had a school for children with ballet potential. It was on 57th Street across from Carnegie Hall.

Once each year, Mr. Chalif pranced his more promising puppets in a (to me) gloomy fete at Carnegie Hall. He packed the house with parents, friends of parents, neighbors of friends of parents, elegant riffraff and, sorrowfully, with old friends from Odessa. And relatives of old friends from Odessa. Which included me.

To begin with, I was introduced to one thousand people of whom some were alleged to be related to me. If I had actually met any of them I didn't remember it, and my parents, surrounded by the glitterati of Ashkenazic America, were annoyed to death by my constant, "No, I don't remember." I was a bemused but straightforward little pain in the ass. My father kept sotto-voce-ing me to smile, at least, but I never smiled when meeting anyone until I was fifty. To this day I don't really know why I'm supposed to be happy at meeting a stranger.

I have a literal mind. As a child I was confused no end about

33

Mary and her dumb little lamb, and by that other Mary—the one who was "contrary" (?) and who had those dopy cockleshells (?) and silver bells in her nutty garden. I got no message when Jack Horner pulled a PLUM out of a pie? J. Sprat ate no fat and his wife ate no lean, but nobody ever told me what lean was. Jack fell down and broke his crown. This little kid was a king? An owl and a pussy cat did WHAT? Rock-a-bye baby in the tree top—they put the cradle *up there*?

But they're waiting for us at the Hall. My father wasn't very important (and Soc didn't like him) so we were always seated somewhere in the back. By heaving up in my seat I could see the dancers, which was a dreadful thing to do, so I scrunched down most of the time and stared at nothing.

There was one cheery note, however. This was Amos Chalif, the adored (read "only") son. He was about six or seven the first time I saw him. He was onstage, under the Steinway. During a number he'd crawled from stage-right to his camping ground. Amos had a blond cowlick and large teeth and once ensconced, from time-to-time he'd give his well-wishers in the audience a big, toothy grin and, when he darned well felt like it, he'd leave.

These galas went on for four or five years. Sunk in my fauteuil, I'd wait for the whisper passed through the house from one delighted adult to another, "Amos!" and all of us kids would strain to see him. I never met him but I still think of him fondly.

When, years later, I moved from a penthouse on that same 57th Street, it was taken over by Mikhail Baryshnikov. From the Kyrov Ballet School in Leningrad. Not all that far from Odessa.

****

My mother seemed, at times, to learn too slowly. She would greet her husband at the door in the evening and tell him immediately what I'd done wrong during the day. I can't blame him for popping off. He told her a hundred times to let him get into the goddamn house and get his goddamn coat off *first*, but she just didn't remember.

34

The awkward part of it was that I would get beaten up before dinner and it didn't help the old appetite one bit. And *that* made Poppa mad all over again.

Sometimes pop wouldn't even make it to the apartment but would storm off to something called "The Rutgers Club." I don't know what a Rutger was but I do know that he played poker there and always lost.

Once when he should have gone to the club, he stayed home, listened to mama's complaints and broke his favorite walking stick, ebony and ivory, over me.

No doubt about it, he was a good insurance salesman and won trips from the Travelers Insurance Company to Atlantic City, to Denver, to Havana. He even took my mother along once.

He didn't drink but he smoked cigars. Big ones. Optimo Cigars. When he ran out of them at home he'd hand me a quarter and, staring at me as if this were an entirely new project and that I had the mental capacity of an omelette, he'd say, loudly, carefully and slowly, "Optimo Claros."

Then he'd add a bit *more* voice.

"OPTIMO Claros." As I put my hand on the doorknob, it was full throttle:

"REMEMBER, NOW, *OPTIMO CLAROS*! ! !"

There's a lot more, but you may get to thinking that I wasn't crazy about him and, after all, as I didn't end up as a therapist's darling, why bother?

Maybe this will cheer you up. Toots Shor, the bar owner, once went to see the movie version of *Hamlet*. Afterwards he smirked that he was probably the only person in the audience who didn't know how the story would come out.

My father also saw the movie and when asked what he thought of it said, "What the hell good was it? I already knew the story."

What's sort of amusing about all this is that Toots probably told the truth. My father did not.

Once he bought a Victrola and ten records. The *William Tell*

Overture, Cohen on the Telephone—a nice assortment. And he never bought another.

He bought an electric player-piano that came with five rolls of music, and never bought another roll, either.

I sometimes think that Clarence Day, who wrote *Life With Father,* was a genius. His father too was impossible but he came out funny in the writing.

Listen, he couldn't drive either. Too uncoordinated.

Bought a set of golf clubs. Never played. Same reason. Poppa couldn't get over the fact that the owners of the "21" Club in Manhattan had started as delicatessen people.

When one of our local deli guys opened the Brass Rail, a huge restaurant on Times Square, he'd take me to dinner there occasionally. He'd call over Max, the owner, and remind him of his, Max's, humble beginnings.

Years ago, radio announcers spoke a bit stiffly, orotundly, and always, very correctly. This led to the fairly popular putdown, "I hope all of your sons become radio announcers." When I became an announcer my father never told anyone about the terrible thing that had happened to him. Still, about every six months or so he'd ask me how a network was put together, and every six months I'd explain to him that the stations were hooked together by specially 'balanced' phone lines. Since this was his dummy-of-a-son giving the explanation, he never listened. Or, perhaps, he simply thought I didn't really know.

When I was fourteen, to the consternation of her family, my mother got a divorce. Consternation AND relief. Daddums found himself saddled with alimony and child support. Which leads to the following bit of business:

My grandmother, old Mrs. Ost, was a widow who lived in a tiny apartment on the first floor of an old building in the Bronx. Her upkeep was split among her four children and must have come to about 75¢ a day each. One day my father had a thought. Not much of a thought but it had its effect on me for the following thirty years.

"Listen," he told me, "I support my mother so you should support yours."

And this man didn't even go to college!

Truly, I was glad to be able to do it. It was no hardship either, because for years I made enough to support my mother, my ex-wife, my son by another woman, a number of lawyers, two dogs and dinner for lots of young women. Oh yes. And me.

8

We were talking about little old New York.

I was born there in 1915 B.C., Before Cholesterol. Up where I lived on the Heights there was mostly heartburn. We had no unsaturated fats, either, but some heavy peoples were to be seen once in a while. Well, look around you at the mall. The only difference between our fatties then and yours now is that your blimps wear bright red polyester.

Herman Wouk once wrote a book called *City Boy* in which he managed to lose the entire flavor of Washington Heights, one of the cradles of civilization. Our family lived there at 86 Haven Avenue which overlooked the lordly Hudson River and an unpaved Riverside Drive. Above 135th street was a dirt road because the city had run out of money, which, of course, it still does on Mondays and Thursdays.

It is a fact that most of us kids had never seen a black person. Oh, we knew about them—black people came from a place called Africa, south of here, way to hell and gone in the jungle. These people lived on berries and leprosy, and if they made it to nineteen they were et by lions.

What we had for neighbors was the middle and all-but-lower middle-class whites (no asiatics, no Latinos) and they had names like Tomadelli, Meara, Smith, Olafsen, Levy. Did you ever notice that all English butlers are named after the landscape,

39

and always in the plural? Fields, Woods, Barnes, Brooks, Rivers, Meadows?

Up the block from us a German janitor had two boys we called Hans and Fritz, named for the Katzenjammer Kids in the comics.

One day Joey Mandel came running up to me with the astonishing (to him) news that Hans and Fritz were going to make a presentation up at the empty lot on 174th. They were going to show their behinds. Today they call it "mooning." Everybody was invited.

I was uninterested.

"They're going to take down their pants and everything!" Joey the P.R. man yelled.

I was not impressed. I found anatomical studies boring, and many years later when Dr. Butterfingers, with me drugged to the hairline, replaced my aorta with seven inches of dacron, I still paid very little attention.

Joey danced around me in a frenzy while kids gathered around and Joey delighted in explaining to one and all that Henry was afraid to look at the rear ends of H & F.

The kids nudged one another and sneered at me. They made brack sounds and someone suggested that I was a sissy.

Peer pressure. I gave way. Besides, I had nothing better to do, and my mother had told me to go out and play, anyway.

We all trooped up to the open-air theater and formed a circle. After a bit the midget Huns let their pants down and, bent over like a pair of idiots, woggled from side-to-side and turned everywhere so that everybody there had house seats. Sure enough, each of them did have a keister. A can. A caboose. Most fittingly, a heinie.

Satisfied, the gang shuffled off and in a day or two all was forgotten and I was accepted as a member again.

❄ ❄ ❄ ❄

The Reed-Hills, father, mother, and children John and Mary, (really) lived on the ground floor at number 86 Haven Avenue. Mr. Reed-Hill looked precisely like a man who'd have a name

40

like that. Erect, Britishy, and Vandyked, he wore a homburg hat and had a stickpin in his tie. It was odd to hear this formal person address his wife always as "Dearie" as though it were her name, and thus the children called her Dearie, too.

John told me that he went to something called "parochial school" where he was taught by "nuns," and I asked him what that all meant. He thought awhile and then proceeded to explain it all in detail so that neither of us understood it.

John and I played Tom Mix and Tony, his horse, a lot. We'd go up the street to the same hilly lot where Hans and Fritz had bummed it and we'd play horses. We were the horses, see. We galloped up and down the mountains chasing the bad guys. When the horses needed a breather we pulled up even and trotted along talking about how things were here in the West. When, toward sundown, the first mother stuck her head out the window to call her little Susan upstairs, we knew we had to head for camp. Time to chow down.

✿ ✿ ✿ ✿

Mama had an unusually deep voice and around the house she sang what were called Negro spirituals. Those and anything that Fanny Brice sang. A lot of that time was defined for me by mama's songs . . .

"It cost me a lot . . . but there's one thing that I've got . . . It's my ma-an . . ."

✿ ✿ ✿ ✿

When I was bar-mitzvahed on my 13th birthday my aunt Blanche gave me a set of *The History of the Jews* by Graetz. They were six heavy volumes bound in leather and gilded and tooled and important and a white elephant in our apartment. I meant to read them for thirty years before I finally threw them out. I wish I had them now. Not to read, of course, but because they were excellent examples of craftpersonship. Bound by hand with bookbinders' cord, with ridges across the spine where the cords crossed over, and old rag paper and beautiful

41

colorplates, with $10 worth of gold edging and real Spanish leather!

****

I remember mama—indeed! When I met her she had hair down to her waist, dark, reddish-tinted hair with highlights of gold. She had it for the rest of her life, too, and she didn't use Enrico Fermi's Super Holder Number Seven on it, either. A good looking lady with a long, perfectly straight, handsome nose, clear skin all her life (she used only Ivory Soap and water, ladies,) merry brown eyes and a jolly disposition (which her husband managed to knock out of her—but it took him fourteen years to do it.)

She was an untaught painter in oils, and my favorite room in this world was our dining room. It had a red-tiled floor and an old-timey Spanish mission table and chairs. The walls were panelled and painted white. In the panels Eva had painted pirates and chests of gold coins and, for me, one pirate that had a parrot on his shoulder.

(Daddums belittled the hell out of it, but when guests oohed and aahed he'd manage to convey the idea that he certainly hadn't begrudged the cost.)

Mama always had help around the house. Her husband bullied the girls, but we had Maude, a nurse who had impressed my mother at the hospital where I was born, and so she was brought home to take care of me. She put up with the bullying for four years, then went off to have her own family and sent us her sister Betty, who lasted five. The producers of *I've Got a Secret*—the TV panel show I was on, surprised me on the air with my dear Betty forty years later.

After Betty left, Mother did what other ladies did—she 'broke in' new girls. In those days all maids worked 24-hours-a-day with Thursday evenings, and every-other-Sunday afternoon and evening off. They came in various colors and nationalities, but they were all slaves.

And so was Mama. Her only regular allowance was for food, and each week she was obliged to ask for it. The money was always given to her as though it were a special, one-time-only, gift. But only after a suitable interrogation, of course.

Mama did all the shopping and we ate canned food so seldom that she never got the hang of opening a tin. The can opener was a wicked device which had to be plunged into the top of the can by hitting it with the heel of your hand. Then you jockeyed it back-and-forth around the edge until you cut your finger on the opener, the can, or the cover.

The maid collaborated on doing the laundry. An enormous copper boiler was put on the stove for boiling the stuff. The kitchen sink was a huge, two-part affair which was used for scrubbing—with a washboard—and the ironing was split, since Fadder always knew if anyone other than his wife did his shirts. Which reminds me. When Popsy made a good insurance sale he would invite his wife to take a little trip to Sulka's on Fifth Avenue with him so that he could celebrate by buying a couple of the most expensive shirts in town. Sulka had a Ladies' Department too, but my mother never found that out.

Doctors say that they don't know what causes migraine headaches, but I know. It's suppressed anger. Mama had them for years—not your kind but the real kind. (I had them too, later on, and probably needn't have gone into the military but I was too grand to chicken out.)

A true migraine is like forty hangovers at once. You can't sit up, you can't turn your head, you can't stand light or sound and you hope, in a sincere way, that you will die quickly. TV panelist, author and painter Alexander King used to give himself injections of dope while explaining to me that it was Ginergen—which is used for migraines. Maybe junkies do have migraine headaches but Alex certainly never took Ginergen. He took junk.

As time went on Mama did get to be a little batty, but we solved our personal inability to see eye-to-eye by moving her to California. Actually, she'd always wanted to live there and she was pleased to have her own apartment with a little terrace looking out to the hills.

In her late sixties she contracted cancer of the intestines, which left her in a grievous state which necessitated her eating her meals precisely on time, and which also had bad effects on her heart. Therefore, when she was seventy, she went to Japan. And Mexico. And, later, to Europe.

They don't make them like that anymore, Jack.

9

I've checked around and I believe that my mother must have gone to some kind of Mamma School since a lot of what she used to say is said by other Mammas. One variant, told me by actress Kaye Ballard, is an Italian-American mother's equivalent of *my* mother's outraged "For this we have children!" Kaye's Mom would say, "For this Columbus discovered America?"

I quote:—What do you think I'm running, a restaurant?
   —Some hungry child in Europe would *love* to eat that.
   —Look at you, how you look.
   —Some day you'll thank me for this.
   —What do you *do* to get holes in it? (them)?
   —Don't make me have to come and get you.
   —Some day your face will freeze like that.
   —Don't make me get up from this chair.
   —Don't tell me again that you didn't ask to be born.
   —Go out and come in again, and don't slam the door this time.
   —I'm not here to pick up after you.
   —What do you mean she didn't give you any homework?
   —You say that again and I'll wash your mouth out with soap. (Did, too.)

—Now go back and do *behind* your ears.
—I don't care what Arnold's mother says.
—Well, you have no fever. Do you have tests today?
—You're going to get the back of my hand.
—This room is a pigsty.
—Whadda you think I'm made of, money?
—Open your mouth when you talk.
—How many times do I have to tell you?
—Go put some iodine on it. I know it burns. Now *go*.
—I simply don't know any more. I just don't know.
—No child of mine is going to . . .
—So this is the thanks I get.
—That'll be just about enough out of you.
—What do you mean, you lost it?
—Then why don't you go live at Eddy's house?
—You're not dumb, you're just lazy.
—Get me a glass of water, please, and *let it run*.
—Because I said so.
—No. You just *read* "one more chapter."
—When you're old enough.
—Put on your sweater anyway.
—You think this is a hotel?
—Just wait till your father comes home.
—I'm your mother, remember?
—You're lucky that I'm not like other mothers.

10

Somewhere along in here I was further humiliated by being sent to Miss Brown's School. A lady used to call for me every morning and walk me, hand-in-hand with a bunch of other shrimps, past my jeering pals.

The first day when it came time to play a game, Miss Brown asked the class who should be the leader. They raised their hands so I raised mine, too.

"All right, Junior [me], who do you say?"

"Me."

"Oh," she said, "you're supposed to name someone else."

I blushed. I didn't know the system. But, gosh, doc, I didn't KNOW anyone else.

That Brown was pretty good, though. When I got to P.S. 169 I knew that seven twelves were eighty-four and a lot of other nice things. They wanted to put me in the fifth grade but my mother couldn't handle it. She didn't want to be saddled with a kid who got out of grammar school at the age of ten, and out of high school at fourteen. She settled for third. I was 'skipped' a couple of grades anyway.

❖❖❖❖

At Public School 169, Wednesday was Assembly Day. At about eleven the inner walls which separated the classrooms on

47

the second floor were rolled back to create a large space where the muppets were made to congregate for an hour of spiritual uplift. Sometimes it was Music Appreciation Day. A big wind-up Victrola was wheeled in and, while Mrs. O'Hara and another gangster woman glared at the shrimpolas, scratchy noises inundated the music lovers.

Some Wednesdays we were enthralled by Recitation Hour. When it became the turn of my class, our teacher gave each of three of us stuff to memorize at home. My mother coached me. Besides the fact that I had no interest in the project whatsoever, I was and still am a very slow study, and it really stretched her patience.

At eleven on Wednesday we three *artistes* were lined up right smack in the middle of the Hall. Dr. Schmidt, the principal, sat with his white beard and two tough ladies up on a podium in back of us. They were there to judge whether or not the reciters would be allowed to live.

About four o'clock that afternoon I ran into Angela Tomadelli on Haven Avenue.

"I saw you at Assembly," she said. "I saw you but I couldn't hear you. Were you whispering. Or what?"

This was my first review. Henry von Ost Jr. was launched into Show Biz.

❊❊❊❊

I don't know what I had for dinner last night, but at 86 Haven Avenue our phone number was WAdsworth 4478. Understand, to make a telephone call, you picked up the receiver and waited until the operator said, "Number ple-uz." Then you told the number to a living, human person. All operators were alike. Each was a white, middle-aged virgin who lived with her mother and a geranium. She was paid just enough to feed the geranium—so no operator ever retired—she just dropped dead of malnutrition. If she had a canary to feed, too, they both died a little sooner.

When you needed ice for the icebox, you stopped at a little podium of wood which sat on the sidewalk at the head of a flight of steps that led to a cellar. On the podium was a pad of scratch paper and a pencil on the end of a string. You wrote down your name and address and how much ice you wanted, in pounds, and the next day Tony would arrive in a wagon, cut the required piece of ice from a large cake, pick it up with a pair of tongs, sling it on his back and walk up six flights of stairs. In August. It cost twenty cents.

The City was made up of neighborhoods. Next door to the kosher butcher was the Italian vegetable market, next door to the dairy, next door to the grocer, next door to the candy store.

At the greengrocer's, soup greens were free. So were scraps and bones for your dog and cat. Remember when pets ate what pets eat? Few readers will believe that within living memory (mine) *nobody ever bought anything whatsoever for ingestion by a dog.*

The candy store man had the worst time of it because people would pick up their newspapers from his stand outside the shop and leave the money on top of the newspaper next underneath. Bad boys used to pick the money up and walk away with it. On Sundays when the stand was full of nickels and dimes I sometimes picked up a dollar or so on my way home from Sunday school. I would then go into the store and play the slot machine with the money from the newsstand. By using the candy store man's own nickels a lucky kid could go home with a couple of bucks. When you lost . . . well, so what? The candy store man got his money, anyway. There was another newsstand in the next block. That is, if some rotten kid hadn't beaten you to it.

We stole a lot of things we didn't need, and it was exciting to outwit the poor little shopkeeper and nerve-wracking to have to think up explanations for the loot when we got it home—so, most of the time, it never got home. A person who stole could get his brains knocked out.

Here, Lieutenant, was our usual M.O.: One of the crowd would decide that we all needed Official Boy Scout knives. (There's something about having a screwdriver, bottle opener, awl, fish scaler and big knife all in one handle that drives city kids crazy.)

We'd go into a shop in broad daylight and ask to see something that we knew was kept "in the back." As soon as the wretched merchant left the room we grabbed everything in sight, stuffed it away, and when the man returned we'd examine the item and declare it unsuitable for Harold's birthday. Once I asked a jeweler to show me a tray of silver mechanical pencils for Harold's birthday, and one of the pencils stuck itself up my sleeve. Since Harold wouldn't have cared for any of them, I thanked the men and left.

To steal the Boy Scout knives we went into a store which had a lot of them, but they were all inside a case with sliding glass doors. There were three of us well-mannered, polite kids, so when the man dutifully went "in the back" for whatever, we slid the doors back and picked up ten knives. I took seven.

We even stole *Boy Scout Handbooks*. And we *were* Boy Scouts!

As a friend used to ask, "Name three Eagle Scouts who died in jail?" I couldn't then—but times have changed.

Understand, we were solid, middle-class kids who would steal *anything*. Some of us, later, got over it.

If you want to know why well-off kids steal, read *Why Well-Off Kids Steal*, by Dr. I. D. Savant.

Savant is an idiot.

✧✧✧✧

Butter was delivered to the dairy in large wooden tubs. Say you wanted a pound of sweet. The man had up-ended the tub and the big circle of butter was in the ice chest. He took a wire hoop and drew it through the butter towards himself. This left a wheel about four inches thick. From the wheel he would guess a pound out with a knife, place it on a piece of waxed paper and weigh it. He was a wizard, that one. Always came out to just about a pound. The old joke that he also weighed his thumb with it was often true . . . but his scales were probably crooked anyway.

At the grocer's you took out the list your mother had given you and handed it over to a nice man who then hopped around the shop getting the order together. He then added all the prices up in pencil on the paper bag and, with a flick of the wrist, snapped it open and piled the stuff inside.

Maybe electricity hadn't been invented yet.

And your mother could then check it all out right there on the bag. Crude, hah?

When you bought tomatoes next door, the man always picked over them, discarding the bad ones. Then he'd weigh them on a crooked scale and charged you a little less, making both sides happy.

Of course your mother could call up on the 'phone and have things delivered, but that meant giving the delivery boy a dime. It was cheaper and more healthful to send your son. "Making the boy useful," it was called.

Of all the stores my mother sent me to, the one I liked best was Butler Brothers grocery. The clerks were all young, red-cheeked Irish boys who seemed to love their work—waiting on customers. You didn't wander in Butler's—you stood at the counter and the snappy fellas turned and snatched things off the shelves. But what I fell for was the way they spoke. It was an earth-shaker. Their words were so clear, the brogue so enchanting—everything they said snapped, crackled and popped. To this day, Irish seems to me to be the true language, and what the Brits speak is a fakey corruption.

We had hardware stores. Not Houseware, hardware. You could buy a couple of nails. Not gift-wrapped, but out of a barrel. You could buy a huge battery with two-screw terminals for fifteen cents. You could buy a hinge. ONE. You could stare at hammers and saws and braces and bits. You could watch important men in overalls, men who *did* things, who could make things, buying necessary stuff.

You could buy clothes irons made of iron. (You heated them on the stove).

Milk was sold in one-quart glass bottles with a cardboard cap on the top. A man in a horse-drawn wagon drove around the neighborhood and delivered the bottles right to the door of your apartment before you woke up.

About that milk; it wasn't homogenized the way it is now—that is to say, the cream wasn't blended in so when the bottle stood for a while the cream floated to the top. In the winter this made for a funny sight. When the milk sitting outside the apartment door froze, the frozen cream was forced right out of the bottle and it stuck out a few inches from the top. It was a slightly curved white cylinder wearing the cap. It looked, I now realized . . . oh . . . never mind.

Mamma sang—

"Yo' jack a-diamons, yo' jack a-diamons . . . I know ya of old, boy I know ya of old . . ."

11

Now, before we get on with the famous gorgeous women I've bedded, let's take a further look at my own Old New York.

Every apartment house had a janitor. He couldn't be a superintendent because he had nobody to superintend. About the only worker he could boss was the man who delivered coal. The janitor sometimes told him to hold it a minute until he could get back to the basement and shift the stuff around. After firing the boilers, he fixed plumbing, retiled a bathroom, replaced washers in sinks, put up shelves, rehung doors, painted over cracks in ceilings, added cement to the sidewalk, put out the garbage cans, repaired light fixtures and made his wife a new dress.

Herb Welling the son of *our* janitor, the one who replaced Mike, built a hut in the woods back of our house. A real hut. We kids had many important meetings there.

In winter, we "borrowed" bricks from construction projects, "borrowed" potatoes from open grocery bins, "borrowed" salt from home, built fireplaces in the woods, and with all this made mickeys. A *mickey* is a potato placed in the ashes near the fire. When the outside of the mickey has burned black, and the inside is still raw, one of the older boys thoughtfully takes a stick and rolls one out on the ground and does his imitation of the Chief Justice of the Supreme Court.

"It's okay," he says.

Translation: It's time for each hardy outdoorsman to roll out his own mickey, burn his fingers, drop the damn thing two or three times, then bite gingerly into hard, hot charcoal until the center is reached, the part you stole the salt for—one cubic inch of uncooked rock. By which time we all had ice on the seats of our pants. Try it sometime when you're sitting in the snow, and tell me if it isn't one of the thrills of a lifetime.

"Mickey" was from Mac, which meant Irishman, because Irishman meant 'potatoes' . . . from the days of the potato famines in Ireland. I found that all out when I was forty-seven.

✿ ✿ ✿ ✿

There was a wonderful, long hill that ran past the Deaf and Dumb Institute, and as soon as the snow got packed down by automobiles the kids assembled from the surrounding neighborhoods and we all went belly-whopping on Dummy Hill. The rich kids had Flexible Flyers and my brother and I just had a sled. A girl just sat on her sled, like a girl. A boy picked up his sled and ran with it, at the last moment hurling it to the ground, himself on top of it stretched out prone. There was *one* girl, Ida, who did it the way the boys did and it made us all nervous. I'm afraid that none of us had heard of Girls' Rights.

Spring? Up where we lived it was marbles, stickball, one o'cat, steal-the-banner, ring-o-leavy-o, mumble-dee-peg, hooking rides on freight trains down by the river—the usual.

The way you hooked onto freights was fairly simple. The trains ran on tracks alongside the Hudson River and, once in the city, slowed down so that stupid kids like me could run and grab the bottom bar of the ladder that led to the roof of the freight car.

Only one kid in our neighborhood lost his leg doing it, too. Once on the ladder, you climbed to the roof and walked along the narrow catwalk like a real trainman, until a real trainman saw you and chased you off.

Ultimately the city got rid of the freights so that everything could be trucked in, thereby clogging the streets forever.

More Games People Played

Know about stickball, do you? Boxball? Gutterball? Steal-the-Banner? Red Rover, Red Rover?

Nah. You were born in some dumb place where there wasn't enough asphalt to justify your taking your roller skates apart and nailing a section to either end of a short, stolen two-by-four to make a scooter.

For stickball, you take a discarded broom and saw off the straw to make a bat. Some say that you had to use the handle of the janitor's snow shovel because it was oak, but in my neighborhood you made do with pine. Janitors kept their snow shovels under their beds.

The ball was a little hollow pink rubber thing that cost a dime. The owner of the bat and the owner of the ball were the team leaders. They would choose up sides from as many kids as were standing around. Now get this right. The bat owner tosses the stick into the air and the ball owner catches it as near one end as he can. The remaining space is filled in one finger at a time by each of them. The one who squeezes in the final finger gets to choose first and he picks the best player on the block. I was never chosen first, of course, as I was a mite slow when it came to running from one sewer cover to the next (bases) but I was never chosen last, either. Practically never. If a kid came upon a game already in progress he stood on the curb and mewed plaintively, "Kin I getta game?" It depended. For instance, sometimes a mother would call out the window and a kid would have to leave the field (gutter). That left an opening, see?

Boxball was played on the sidewalk with anything that could bounce up against a building wall. Each kid had a territory one-square-wide from the wall out to the curb. You hit the ball with your open hand down to the ground so that it bounced up against the wall and into another territory. The best part was when some interior kids had been eliminated and two guys were left about four or five squares apart. Boy, it was tough to be accurate!

Steal-the-Banner could have any number to a side. A handkerchief was stuck in a window grating on either side of the street. The object was to grab the opposing "banner" without getting tagged by an enemy. The most fun is when it's played in heavy traffic.

Johnny-ride-the-pony is one maneuver in a game of Knife. You take the Boy Scout knife and whirl it around your head and let go. It must stick in the ground without the handle touching. This can lead to discussion.

Immies is all the variants of shooting marbles. Marbles include glassies, aggies, steelies et al. When the marbles are in a circle (or a hole) you shoot one between your fingers to hit the enemy's immies. While you are thus engaged your opponent keeps shouting, "Knucks down, knucks down!" and this can lead to discussion.

The most important thing to have in the winter was a sled, of course, but as I mentioned before, it HAD to be a Flexible Flyer. FLEXIBLE FLYER was in large red letters down the center slat. It was better to have one that said FLEXIBLE FLYER going one way and RACER the other way. Best of all was RACER going both ways so it could be read from either side. This was known to the gang as "Hey, he's got a Racer Racer!" It must have cost too much. My old man gave me and my brother not even a plain Flexible Flyer but some silly substitute for us *both* to ride at the same time, and that was completely ridiculous. Or what's a middle class for?

"Now ain't them hard . . . tri-als . . . great trib-u-lat-tions . . . I'm bound . . . to lead dis land. Oh, I belong to the Methodiss church . . . and I'm bound . . . to lead dis land."

12

In those simple-minded days a useful son was taught to say "Yes, sir" to his Father and "No, thank you" to his Mother. I swear before God that we were trained to give up our seats to ladies in the subway and to say "Pardon me" when we bumped into somebody. It was very long ago.

If you were a reasonably good kid you might get taken on the bus to go downtown to Macy's. They were double-deckers, and in the summer there was often no roof on the upper decks. If you were lucky, you got the very front seat or the very last one, both great, and after awhile the conductor came by with a hand-held device into which you slipped a dime. He pulled a trigger, a bell rang, and the thing registered another sale. I don't know what it was called but I still wish I had one.

The bus went down Riverside Drive and a block past the Schwab mansion the bus turned left to Broadway, then to Fifth Avenue. Every few blocks along Fifth there was a traffic tower in the middle of the street, about thirty-five-feet high. A policeman sat inside monitoring the flow and manipulating red-and-green lights. As the bus passed Saint Patrick's Cathedral both the driver and the conductor crossed themselves. I didn't realize it at the time, but all bus people, trolley car people and policemen were Irish. Their wives all hired out as maids for a spell, and then they went home and had twelve children each.

I don't know why, but we always thought of the Irish as nice people. Blacks were called Negroes, though we didn't see many. They weren't the enemy. The enemy was any kid who lived on a different block. A strange kid was always ordered to leave, except in the Spring when we would allow him to stay until he'd lost all his marbles, yes, or his tops, or we beat him up. There was no malice in this: it was just that God had made one-hundred-and-seventy-first street for *us*—over as far as Broadway. Well, maybe not to Broadway but at least to Ft. Washington Avenue.

Next door to where we lived was an old stone house owned by a Mr. Springer, a recluse, who invited me inside one day to see the place. It was dark in there with antlers looming through the murk and Chinese (?) vases and bric-a-brac from around the four corners of the globe. I didn't make that up, though I still don't understand it to this day. How can a globe have four corners? The Hittites or the old Cretans or the ancient Langomorphs thought that the world was held up by a huge turtle in each corner (but aren't we over that by now?)

Mr. Springer liked my reaction to his junk and he gave me a Dutch wooden shoe (which mama painted blue). He also arranged for his Fillipino chauffeur to drive me to school every morning in his Rolls-Royce. It was one of those cars in which the chauffeur sat way up front out in the open, and I sat next to him.

The kids who saw me got pretty raucous and it became embarrassing, so each day I had the man let me out farther and farther away from P.S. 169. In a few days he was letting me out five blocks from the school. Finally, he was dropping me so near home that it just didn't make sense any more. I had to quit, so one morning I got courageous enough to explain to Mr. Springer as well as I could, and he laughed sympathetically. He'd been watching what I went through and was wondering how long I'd last.

Along in here my mother got the idea that her boys would look sensational in berets. THAT brought the other kids on the block pretty near a frenzy. My brother and I tried to explain our problems to the management but she wouldn't budge. We did what we had to do in order not to get beaten up. We'd leave the house and take off the stupid berets as soon as we were out of sight—rain, hail, blizzard or cyclone. One day after it had rained mine fell in a puddle, and it was still wet when I got home. I said that a kid had tripped me. She then asked why was my suit so dry? Some things mothers don't seem to grasp.

✤✤✤✤

They sent me to Sunday School. About a dozen of us sat in pews at one side of the temple in a kind of box and listened to dumb, boring things that made no sense at all. I had to do something until the session was over, so one morning I put my seven Boy Scout knives in a row on the railing. Mr. Bright (sic) called me into his office after class. He seemed thoughtful.

"Where did you get those knives?"

"They were presents from people, you know."

"What people?"

"Well, see, when I get to be thirteen soon, I'm going to be a Boy Scout, so relatives and, you know, people, have been giving me knives. So I'll be ready."

His head tilted to one side.

"Everybody gives you knives? How many do you have?"

"Just these see."

"Do your parents know?"

"Oh, sure." (With a little more conviction) "Oh, yes, my father and mother know. They think it's funny. They told people, you know, to stop."

I'm sure he didn't buy it, but he didn't squeal either. Nice fella.

But then the homefolks decided that I go to school and prepare to "get bar-mitvahed", as we kids said.

Why?

I mean, why? Nobody in my immediate family had even been to a synagogue during my first twelve years. And this one was orthodox, which meant that I had to memorize that portion of the Torah that I would have to read in front of the congregation on the Big Day. It meant going to HEBREW school for a couple of hours every day after regular school. Not to learn Hebrew— oh, no, just to commit the chapters by rote, without a glimmer as to what it meant. And to SING it.

Well, The Day came, I did my stuff and some friends and relatives came back to the apartment, cooed a bit, and left a few checks for me. Four hundred dollars.

My father opened a bank account . . . Henry von Ost in trust for Henry von Ost Jr. Shortly thereafter, he borrowed the money. Forever, as it turned out.

The real question that remained with me was, if I were now a man, how come I was still wearing knickers?

Knickers were baggy pants that stopped and were anchored just below the knees. They were only worn by small boys and by men who played golf. Both looked ridiculous. And, now that I was going to the High School of Commerce, I felt humiliated. A knickered nerd.

One fine day my mother crumpled and bought me my first pair of longies. Free at last, free at last! A man! Never mind for God or for a congregation of the orthodox, but for where it counted: High School.

Seeded among the drudges were two wonderful teachers at the High School of Commerce. One was a shrimpy woman, Miss Friedenthal. American History. I was such a nuisance to her that when, at the end of the term, she announced who in the glass had passed the dreaded Regent's Test, she read out the names, and mine wasn't among them. She gave me a significant look which easily translated into "Well, what did you expect, you who talked away the hours?"

She rattled some papers.

"Well, von Ost, you got one hundred."

Damn fine teacher, Miss Friedenthal.

The other was Mr. Beer, English. A stout man with black-framed glasses, he taught the hell out of it.

One day Mr. Beer asked if I'd like to go to a show on Broadway as his guest. Definitely yes. We sat in the last row of the balcony, fifty-five cents, gents. We watched *Mr. Money-*

penny, a tirade against the rich, I believe. It was by Elmer Rice, a man who wrote plays against everything.

I was about fourteen and my teacher was interested in my opinion. We agreed that it was just fine. I never told him that I thought it awfully dull. And I never told him how much I admired Morris Abel Beer.

13

The Girls in Their Bright Summer Dresses

Fanny was a girl's name. Once upon a time.

It appears to me that girls used to have lovely names that seem to have disappeared. I wonder, for instance, . . . do you know of any new baby named Faith? Hope? Mary? Why, there used to be Marcia, Iris and Daisy, Cora, Sarah and Ina.

No Tiffany.

But there were Josie, Serena, Antoinette and Myrna. Evelyn, Honoria, Ethel, Millicent.

❖❖❖❖

New York newspapers in English included the *World, Sun, Tribune, Journal, American, Herald, News, Graphic, Telegram, Telegraph, Times, Mirror* and the *Brooklyn Daily Eagle*. Late Saturday evening the newsboys (there were newsboys!) would stand on the sidewalk yelling, "Hea'yah, gitcha Sunna Noos an' Mirrah!" Sometimes when a big story broke in the middle of the week a boy would come around the neighborhood carrying an armful of an "extra" edition of a paper yelling, "Wuxtree! Wuxtree! Read all about id!"

He might be followed by the old clothes man. This fella wore two or three overcoats and as many hats as he'd already bought, one on top of another. For cash. His song was short and to the point. "I kesh! I kesh!"

✧✧✧✧

And Phyllis, Wilma and Teresa. Stella. Melanie. Charlotte. Deirdre and Clementine and Wilhelmina.

✧✧✧✧

We used to sit on a wall overlooking the newly paved Riverside Drive and call out the makes of the cars as they came toward us. Every manufacturer had a distinctive product. For instance, *any* kid could spot a Buick from four blocks away.

✧✧✧✧

Charlotte, Monique, Patricia, April, May, June, Edna, Bettina, Doris, Florence, Mignonne, Frieda, Geraldine.

✧✧✧✧

Our first radio was an Atwater-Kent. It used a 'wet' battery which had to be recharged at the store. Someone at last invented a recharger that Poppa plugged into the wall. This had to run all night but it was worth it because after the battery got its strength back, we could listen to the Happiness Boys who sang "every Friday night at eight, be sure you aren't late."

Little Jack Little was good, and so was the organist, Vaughn de Leath—a girl whose family name was von der Leith. And a brilliant media space salesman actually sold the time of day— "At the signal, it will be eight-pee-em, B-U-L-O-V-A, Bulova Watch time."

✧✧✧✧

Martha, Frances, Angeline, Eunice, Loretta, Grace, Honey and Harriet. Violet. Pamela.

✧✧✧✧

When I was five I was taken to a hospital where, I was told, my mother was having a baby. A clever lad, I walked into her room and pointed to her stomach.

"I can see the baby," I announced.

64

Mother smiled. "I've already had the baby."

This gift of saying the right thing at the right time has been with me all my life.

****

Gladys, Paulette and Edna, Nellie and Naomi, Lily and Iris, Rebecca, Neva, Isadora, Charita, Corinne, Ellen, Angela, Barbara . . .

I miss you, loves.

14

Kinaani is an Indian Word, Mayhap

My brother Roger and I (known to the world as Junior) were sent to summer camp when I was twelve and he was seven.

It cost $700 for the two of us for eight weeks. Today the same jaunt comes to about $16,000 at a comparable place, so you can see how anxious my father was to impress the neighbors . . . and how much life insurance he'd been selling.

Camp Kinaani, named after somebody's peace-pipe dream, was spread over some acreage at the confluence of the famous Songo River and the equally applauded Long Lake, three miles from the world-renowned village of Naples, in the state of Maine.

The logistics of getting there were, uh, boggling. Our parents brought us to Grand Central at the prescribed time. Our shiny new camp trunks were filled with what the pamphlet said we had to have. The official shirts and shoes came from Macy's. Each shirt, each sock, each handkerchief, each undershirt, each pair of shorts had to bear a carefully sewn-in name tag. Many were the joyous hours my mother and the maid had spent in losing their collective eyesight.

The station was a shock. Fifty camps were leaving! Thousands of little kids stood around looking brave. Hundreds of mothers were sniffling into their hankies.

We were introduced to large athletes, each of them called "Uncle." I wondered what they were all doing there.

At last we boarded the train. Roger was quite short for his age, which was lucky because we were both assigned to a lower berth and told how to lie there—his feet in my face.

In the morning, Portland, Maine, where we were all loaded onto open trucks in which we stood for the whole trip to Naples.

On the truck I made some jokes and some of the kids laughed. It's not that I was nervous—it's just that I thought it was time to start a career. It is possible that I was the first stand-up comic. At least I was the first to work a truck.

Roger, immediately nicknamed Rajah, was assigned to the Midgets, I to the Intermediates. In the following days I also became a member of Bunk Eight, then the Grey team, the Iroquois, the Mexicanos of the Sunset League, and other fine organizations.

Bunk Eight was a one-room cottage containing six Iroquois and Uncle Ave. I was brought up by Uncle Ave for three summers. He was the drama counsellor and also a fine basketball player. Most of the other Unks were Phys. Ed. majors.

Now, the food was excellent. (Visiting parents ate the same stuff we did in the same Mess Hall).

It was the custom of the camp to give the parents a cheer after lunch, and their very own kid led it. One day we were graced at mealtime with the presence of Doctor and Mrs. Weinstein. Georgie had to stand up in front of the whole world and lead an Al Al, not an airline, but the Official Kinaani Cheer. That day it went like this:

◊◊◊◊

Al! Al! Cibaides!
Socratum! Socrates!
Mithranites! Sharonites! Pelepponesus, BOOM!
Rah rah rah rah CAMP!

68

Doctor and Mrs. Weinstein! Doctor and Mrs. Weinstein!
RAYYYYYYY!
(APPLAUSE)
After which everybody left for the bunks and a half-hour lie-down. Write to your mother and father, you hear?

15

Show Time!

The gym was a two-story wood structure that housed a basketball court and a stage. A real stage, too. On Saturday nights folding chairs were set up for the two hundred-odd city kids who were spending the summer at world-renowned Camp Kinaani. Included on each evening of theatrical magic were the Directors, Dr. Kaplan and his missus; Dr. Schwartz, a real doctor, not like Dr. Kaplan; nurse Gallstone, the entire kitchen staff, and a dog.

On this particularly memorable Saturday evening the presentation is Act One of *The Last Mile,* a recent Broadway hit of the time, the entire production suggested and directed by Uncle Ave.

Just picture the powerful set: three prison cells, their heavily barred doors facing the audience. Little do the audience suspect that all is illusion! The doors (and the walls between the cells) are of cleverly painted paper and wood.

In each of the cells, a dangerous prisoner. In Cell Two, smack center-stage, "Killer" Mears, remarkably portrayed by twelve-year-old Junior von Ost, possessor of possibly the loudest voice in the entire camp. The prisoner on stage-left, the one nearest the Execution Room, none other than Harvey Leitzman, a terrifying, if thin, figure of restrained savagery.

The main thrust of Act One is the tension created by the

71

knowledge that a con is to be put to death at any minute. The prisoners discuss this at some length, being careful not to touch either the bars nor the walls.

At last, there is a stir off-stage-right and—here they come!

Two Intermediates are cleverly got up as guards. They are accompanied by heavily disguised Amos Gansbourg, a priest, and by Emil Lautenburg, the condemned man. The cortege slowly makes its way across the stage and exits toward the Execution Room.

There is a freighted pause.

Suddenly, there is a loud, humming sound and the lights go dim! The humming continues in the darkened prison. It is obvious that the Chair uses so much current that there's not enough left for the lights!

From the center cell an outraged "Killer" Mears, fighting to contain his rage, screams out,

"Whadda they trine ta do, COOK 'IM?!!"

Curtain.

Applause.

❋❋❋❋

Fifty-five years later my second wife, Karen, arranged with the Schuyler Chapins to give me a party celebrating the fiftieth anniversary of my working life. You can get the flavor of the occasion when I tell you that among the fifty guests were Walter Cronkite, the eminent British actor Emlyn Williams and, best of all, dear old "Uncle" Ave.

In the middle of mild chaos Uncle Ave handed me a small package to be opened immediately. Inside was an old Boy Scout knife and a short note to the effect that Ave had taken it away from me fifty-five years ago for wielding it "in an irresponsible manner."

Around 1947 I had bought my first real, expensive combination radio-record player from Ave's company. He used part of the profits from that sale to rebuild what came to be known as Avery Fisher Hall.

16

Palisades Park, 1928

In the Spring, a thirteen-year-old's fancy lightly turns to thoughts of Saturday, what to do with it.

Sydney or Artie or Stevie said why don't we go to Palisades Park? This was an amusement center high above the Hudson, right across the river in New Jersey.

Geez, said somebody, it ain't even open yet.

Yes, said the wise guy, it opens today.

We took the ferry (five cents) and walked up the switchback road to the Park. The main attraction there was the world's scariest roller coaster. Very tall and, given that it was up above the river by four hundred feet to begin with, when you were hauled to the top of the first drop and looked down, you fool, you looked straight into death-on-the-rocks; it was easily five or six hundred feet.

We weren't in the place five minutes before a man asked if we wanted to ride the roller coaster? We were embarrassed to admit that we only had a nickel apiece to get home on. Forget it, he said, the ride was on him.

Great day!

The four of us duly got into the car, the chain grabbed and away we went. It was, in the term of the day, nitzy.

The first drop was steep enough so that it gave the car enough momentum to enter a loop in which it travelled completely

73

upside down. After that it was merely breathtaking and then, with a few violent swoops, drops and sharp, wrenching swerves, at last we were back on the ground.

I was a nosey kid. Why, I asked the man, why he let us ride for free.

"Oh, it's the beginning of the season," he said. "We wanted to see if it's still safe."

17

Goldie, 1927

I was twelve and Yascha Bunchuk was at the Capitol Theatre on Broadway. Yascha Bunchuk was *always* at the Capitol Theatre. Major Edward Bowes was the General Manager and lived in a grand apartment upstairs, but I didn't know that then. I did know that any man who kept his military title long after the war was over, unless it was General, was a horse's foot.

During the Depression the jolly Major had a couple of hundred of his *Amateur Hour* kids touring the United States at a salary of thirty dollars a week each. When someone had the gall to ask the Major how he could justify the thousands of dollars he was making off these kids he said that he ought to get a medal instead of abuse because he was supplying jobs during the Depression.

The Major was a fixture on radio for many years and he ate young talent like a gas oven. Still, this mean man made his peace with God by leaving St. Patrick's Cathedral two million dollars—enough money to have a sandblast job and fired his secretary of twenty-six years, giving her two weeks salary as severance. They gave him a swell funeral.

So there was Yascha and his cello at the Capitol and over at the Paramount Theatre down the street we had Genial Paul Ash. I swear to God we all thought that was his real name because that's the only way we ever saw it—Genial Paul Ash.

75

(He had to leave his conducting job in Chicago when a jealous husband put a bullet in his butt.) Genial conducted the mighty Paramount Theatre orchestra and Jesse Crawford played the mighty Paramount organ. (Later, he went over to the Roxy Theatre gang.)

The thing of it was that you could go to any movie house on Broadway for thirty cents if you went before one o'clock. Promptly at one, a seven-foot doorman dressed like the Admiral of the Ocean Seas would lift the little "30 Cents Before 1 P.M." sign from its peg over the box office window and start to harangue the passersby:

"Prices are about to change in two minutes—seating on all floors without waiting—prices about to change . . ." and he'd keep that up until ten or fifteen minutes after one, or until his arm got tired.

The trick was to have lunch before one at either of the two nifty restaurants up the avenue which featured live orchestras. One band was led by Isham Jones. The other, and a better deal, we thought, was the Chinese place which offered lunch and Paul Tremayne and his Band from Lonely Acres.

We were little kids but the *idea* of lonely acres made us feel nostalgic. Nostalgic for what? Kids don't need a what. They can feel nostalgic looking at a horse.

At the Chink's you got nostalgia, soup, chicken chow mein, tea and two kumquats for thirty cents.

Many a day was filled more than adequately for seventy-five-cents. Figure: a nickel each way for the subway, thirty cents for lunch, thirty for the Paramount. The other nickel? Well, we certainly tipped the waiter, fagodsake!

I had started my theatre-going some years before at the Claremont. Saturday matinee at the Claremont, 135th and Broadway, was all kids. The big sign outside read "Ten movies—ten cents." Inside was a mix of Specially Selected Short Subjects, cartoons, and a couple of serial stories, and one Tom Mix. Our regular group consisted of Davey Shrieber, Eddy Something, Vinny Tomadello, Bronson First and Junior von Ost.

But, any day, any day, I'd take vaudeville. There was Fox's Audubon, there was Loew's Eighty-Third Street (catchy, eh?), there was one at 168th and even one theatre way up at 181st. Or even down at 116th. 8—Big Acts—8.

There were Sophie Tucker and Will Mahoney and Eva Tanguay and Benny Fields and Blossom Seely and Tess Gardella and the Tiller Girls and Cardini and Cantor-Jolson-Jessel and Belle Baker and Professor Lamberti and Long Tack Sam and Tilly Losch and Fanchon and Marco, the Builders, and dog acts, and acrobats and jugglers and, always,

8—Big Acts—8

Some of the acts weren't all that great. There was a little old broken-down movie house over on Amsterdam Avenue which had only four acts. The house was part of a circuit that gave a tiny living to people who earlier had never been in the Big Time or were on their way back down. One act in particular remains with me. This was a strongman turn. Out came an old boy of sixty, say. He had been muscular once but what showed through his bathing suit top was mostly flab. It was an old-time bathing suit with red and yellow stripes across it, and for bottoms he wore clean old chinos and there were sneakers on his feet. He bowed and then turned and gestured in a courtly but perfunctory manner and his "lovely assistant" appeared at stage left— his wife, I suppose. She was a greyhaired lady in a tutu, a sagging halter top and wrinkled black stockings. The old boy lifted various things while his assistant looked on in little-girl astonishment and appreciation. She pointed at him and she curtsied, and she smiled a dreadful smile.

The climax of the act was this: she walked offstage and returned immediately pushing a little cannon on wheels. He turned with his back to the cannon about fifteen feet away and assumed a mighty stance, legs spread and anchored, fists out before him, head bent forward. He nodded, then she touched a button on the cannon. There was a puff of smoke and a "cannon ball" made a little arc in the air and landed on the back of his neck. It stayed there for a second and then he caught it with his hands behind his back. The violin and piano, all the orchestra there was in the pit, struck up a chord, the old folks bowed, and the act was over.

I saw that act only once, and for the next fifty-five years I've hoped that some kind of God arranged for those two people to have a small chicken farm somewhere to retire to. He couldn't have been more kind.

✵✵✵✵

Cheer up! On Broadway there was Will Mahoney who danced on a huge xylophone while reading forty feet of sheet music. There was Long Tack Sam (& Co.) who strode about the stage pointing in turn to various members of his exotically costumed group of Chinese magicians. The moment he pointed to someone, a stream of water shot up from the top of that person's head. Impossible! At the climax of the turn he pointed again and this time streams of "gold" coins fell out of their mouths. Absolutely impossible!

And then there was Professor Lamberti. I think I'm going to faint. The Professor played a xylophone of normal size while, unbeknownst to him, a lovely girl walked behind him, slowly stripping. At each of her exits the audience applauded wildly—at which the professor would solemnly lay down the hammers, prance around to the front of the xylophone and take gratified bows. He was fringe-bald, wore a battered tail coat and had short pants which displayed his falling down white socks. Oh heavens, but he was gorgeous. For his finale he'd pick up four hammers between the fingers of each hand, ostentatiously display them to the house, bow, then throw away all but two and play a wild march.

—I did faint.

I'm back.

✵✵✵✵

For stand-up comics there were W.C. Fields (and his unbelievable pool table routine) and Joe Cook, Fred Allen, J.C. Flippen, and Frank Fay. And Burns & Allen.

Listen, I've been asked to describe another thing that Will Mahoney did and I'd like to have a whack at it.

He got down off the xylophone and started an ordinary kind of clog tap—but he couldn't keep his balance; he started to lean to his left, then he started to fall. He kept dancing and falling, further and further until, just as he was about to hit the floor, he reached the proscenium and grabbed it in the nick of time. Hauling himself upright, he started to clog again, suddenly realizing to his horror that now he was beginning to fall the other way, to his right. Nervously, he estimated the distance he had to go before he could grasp the proscenium at stage right—it was too far! He'd never make it in time! Bravely clogging on, tilting further and further, he quick-wittedly, but with infinite labor, got his jacket off and managed to fold it into a cushion for his head. He *had* to fall! The audience was hysterical, the suspense was incredible. My pants were wet. Mahoney clogged and puffed like a steam engine, his arms stretched out like those of a drowning man reaching for the life preserver, purpose forgotten—and then, oh, incredible! with one-fifth of a second to go, he reached the wall! And then, slowly, inevitably—he slid the last foot to the floor.

—I just fainted again.

I'm back

❖❖❖❖

Joe Frisco, a pantomimist, had the greatest 'entrance' in vaudeville. The stage was dark. A spotlight hit stage right.

Suddenly, a running figure hit the spot which followed him as he ran . . . and the spot kept traveling but the figure suddenly disappeared! He had run into the space between the black curtains but the spotlight kept going. Believe me, the effect was like magic.

❖❖❖❖

Funny, but honestly I'm so shy that my happiest days were as a monologist on radio, where no one could see me but my engineer—I wouldn't allow any one else in the control room because it upset me to be looked at while I worked. So how come I always wanted to be in vaudeville? It's because I'm a living dichotomy—I'm an introspective person who likes to appear in public.

Garrison Keillor, the country humorist, got a lot of mileage out of the word 'shy.' If I may say so, he never had a clue.

As a kid, teen-ager, adult and middle-aged man I always had difficulty in entering a room with people in it. Including a room with my own parents in it.

In my teens I found The Answer. Two or three shots of anything at all and I could at least make it inside without slithering along the wall.

During fifteen years of summer theatre, I never once went on stage sober. I even drank when I was a monologist on radio. I was on panel shows: Paar, Carson, Merv—all of them. Not drunk, mind you, but not sober, either.

For the duration of my first marriage, I was loaded. Gad, I *must* have been. For many years, I happily guzzled my way around Manhattan. I contributed to the profits of Toots Shor, Dinty Moore's, the Formerly Club, Chumley's, Jimmy Ryan's, Costello's—oh, anyplace that was open. And if it was open till four ayem, so much the better. Gallagher's comes to mind, the Absinthe House, the Palm. Pietro's. And no matter which place it was, I knew I'd find guys to talk with. Newspaper, theatre and radio guys. Robert Preston at Sardi's until closing, then down the street to the German's.

The German was an amusing guy. Down the block from him at the Picadilly Lounge was Morty and Artie Nevins and their cousin: The Three Suns Trio that broadcast every evening. During the months of trouble with ASCAP—ASCAP controlled the copyright on most music—radio people couldn't use the standard tunes of the day and had to resort to long arrangements of uncopyrighted material, Morty had an arrangement of the Anvil Chorus that took eleven minutes, and he played it on every broadcast. After work one night he strolled into the German's.

The proprietor asked the crowd for quiet and got it.

"Ladies und chentlemen," he announced, "I introduce you to Morty Neffins, leader of der vun-toon-bant!"

18

The Formerly Club.

During Prohibition there was a speakeasy about five steps from the New York *Tribune*. One dim bulb marked the doorway. The place was owned by a man named Bleek, pronounced Blake. He called his enterprise Bleek's Club.

Shortly after Repeal, an illuminated sign was erected over the doorway. It read:

Bleek's Tavern
(Formerly Club)

Stanley Walker was the editor of the *Tribune*. Dick Maney was the most puissant of theatre press agents. So much so that the *Times* often printed his handouts just the way he wrote them.

Maney, Walker and I liked to sit at 'our' table in the small hours and play the Match Game for drinks. Often, after four, we'd be joined by Heinrich the bartender. Poor guy, win or lose, he had to make the drinks.

I was obliged by my then fiancée's father to journey to Hartford in order to get some instruction from a priest about Catholicism. Poppa was a Papal Knight and had agreed to our marriage if I would make the trip. I put up the usual outsider's questions and was awarded the usual answers. You know—can you see the wind? No, but you believe in it, don't you?, etc.

But, along with the philosopher Heine, I didn't think that any Jew could believe in the divinity of another Jew.

Well, her poppa had believed he had done right by me, anyway. The fact was that I hadn't done right by his daughter. It was in the Formerly Club that I proposed. She knew my motive and turned me down. I was so upset that I had to excuse myself, go out to the sidewalk and throw up.

Whether it was because of relief or because of guilt I still don't know. It's a question for a psychiatrist, and since they're known as being able and willing to testify for *either* side. . . .

✿ ✿ ✿ ✿

Sudden thought: I just realized why I wanted to be in show biz. Remember Soc's production of "Brownies in Fairyland"? It's all genetics—of course!

And so we come to Mamma's woman friend, Goldie. Goldie was Florenz Ziegfeld's personal secretary. Mr. Ziegfeld was an implausible and impossible man (for one thing, he never knew what his Broadway productions cost, and he didn't care). He needed a plausible and possible person to be a buffer between him and the world of practicality, ergo: Goldie.

Flo, by the by, didn't understand comedians and he didn't like them, but he'd hire a Will Rogers or an Eddie Cantor because they held the front-center stage "in-one" long enough for scene changes and for the Ziegfeld girls to get into even more lavish costumes. It should be explained that "showgirl" in those days didn't mean a girl in a show—it meant 'a girl who shows'—an elegant young lady, usually quite tall, who did nothing but walk slowly and gracefully across the stage in fifteen hundred dollars worth of plumes. The shorter girls who did the dancing were called 'ponies.'

Goldie knew of my theatre lust and one day she gave me a ticket to a Saturday matinee of *Show Boat*.

At this point a cannon should go off. A twelve-year-old boy entered Heaven, fourth-row, center-aisle. Charles Winninger and Edna May Oliver. Charles Winninger staggering across the stage shouting, "Hap—pee New Year!" a dozen times, while fourth-row center aisle fell out of his seat each time.

Helen Morgan. Omigod. She even did one number sitting on the piano, which, I knew, she did in nightclubs, whatever *they* were. And Jules Bledsoe sang "Old Man River", and when he came to ". . . tired of livin' and scared o' dyin'", I believed every syllable.

After the show Goldie came to find me and took me up in the private elevator to the great man's office and his collection of elephants and then, best of all, through the special door into his private box, high up in the back of the theatre.

"You can hear every word up here," Goldie said. "He doesn't like the comedians, but he insists that, as long as they have to be on the stage anyway, they should be heard."

(Many years later I saw George S. Kaufman "directing" from the last row of the orchestra with his back to the stage. Whatever became of actors you could hear without microphones?)

And then Goldie told me Ziegfeld's secret—or one of them.

A group of his backers, hoping against hope to get some return on their investment, came to Ziggy one day and complained that he clothed his chorus girls in silk underwear.

"But why, Ziggy? Nobody will know they're wearing silk underwear."

"Wrong," he said, "the girls will know."

19

1929 and 1930. Harrisburg, Pa.

At New York's High School of Commerce I learned touch-typing and humility; I was reasonably happy there, but after two years my mother decided to send me to the Harrisburg Academy in Pennsylvania. Since she knew nobody in Harrisburg, or even in Pennsylvania, I have no idea as to where she got the idea, and I still don't know why we invaded Grenada, but sobeit.

The Academy turned out to be a handsome grouping of, no-fooling, ivy-covered red brick buildings arranged around a quadrangle and separated by a two-lane road from the Susquehanna River. It had begun turning out little sojers in 1789, the same year that George Washington left the service and took up politics.

My two years there weren't a total loss. For instance, in the smoking room on the top floor of my dorm, I learned to inhale. I also learned how to play poker at night with a blanket over the transom so that the housemaster, on seeing the blanket, would think that the lone boy in there was composing odes.

Oh, it wasn't a military school any more . . . the only thing left was "walking guard". This was a punishment for anything at all and was done in the afternoons between school and dinner.

87

You (I) walked up and down the gravel walkway in front of your dorm, not speaking to anyone until your time was up. If you (I) managed to save up enough punishment you (I) continued walking on Saturday. And Sunday, after church. Still, I managed to play right guard on the football team and, later, to play on the water polo team until I drowned a few times. (I played goalie. As the first move of the game the other team pushes the rival goalie underwater and tries to kick him to death.)

The "Masters" were, with one exception, very pale, thin, sad and mostly earnest. The exception was Mr. Drew. He was odd, we knew. "Queer", we said, and "fruit", we said, but such were the dear, dear times that we teenagers didn't know what the words meant. All we knew was that he minced about and did little-girl things with his hands . . . but if he had a sex life we didn't know what it was.

Mr. Drew read the Bible portion in Assembly when Headmaster Dr. Brown didn't. He did it with great emotion and a kind of theatrical conviction. He must have known that we didn't follow a word of it, we just *watched him.* He waved his arms, his eyes burned, blue sparks shot out of them, his voice squeaked and trembled. He was simply awful. We all liked him: he was a very nice man.

Like me, he had come to the Academy from New York City and he felt that that gave us a footing. Once, being particularly roguish and direct, he said, "We've got to get together over the holiday. I'll call you and we'll do the Drive, stinkin'."

It makes me sad now. He meant that he and I would cruise Riverside Drive and look for sailors. He surely knew I had no idea of what he was talking about, he probably just wanted to say that he liked me.

Others on the staff were pale Mr. Demaree, teacher of French. Pale Mr. (Shadow) Glen, Master of my dorm, married to (pale) Lady Tintail; "Snowball" Smith, pale, short, bald, stupid—teacher manqué of trig; Mr. Bayard, pale, skinny stinker from Maine who ate pistachio nuts in class and taught German and bigotry; Mr. Dahl, healthy-looking!, jolly, excellent teacher of geometry, and some teachers who just weren't memorable at all.

Coach Miller ran the gym and taught tennis, football, water polo, track and field, baseball, basketball, mumbletepeg, boxing, handball and whatever else Dr. Brown could find for a man who owned his own whistle.

Thirty-five years later I was starring in a play in summer theatre at the Playhouse in Dennis, Massachusetts. After the show a gentleman and his wife were waiting for me backstage. "Coach!" I hollered. I'm smiling now as I remember how pleased we all were.

I wrote "I will not talk in class" a little under two million times during my stay in Harrisburg. This was always done after three o'clock when I was supposed to be out on the field playing right guard. I almost made All-State just the same, but it's hard to remember the signals when you've spent most of your practice hours practicing penmanship.

The way we got drunk on Saturday nights was this. (These were Prohibition years, mind you). Downtown, there was a small saloon in the basement of the State Capitol. The Building that housed the Government of the State of Pennsylvania. The saloon had an inside entrance which I never saw, and an outside entrance lit by a single, naked bulb. Wayne Porter, the Gibson brothers and I were the only teens allowed in ("'Sall right, they're Academy kids") and that's where we drank needle beer. This is ordinary beer which is amplified by advancing the tap all the way, thus allowing a 'needle' of real ether to shoot into the glass.

Afterwards, we rang the buzzer of a private house two blocks away. A shadowy figure stood at the top of the stairs. "Oh, Academy," it said. The man came halfway down the stairs and handed Wayne a half-pint of gin and Wayne gave him fifty cents. The four of us would then take our jewels over to the ice-cream parlor on Main Street and order four ginger ales.

You may think that a half-pint of gin may not stretch very far but after needle beer it works all right. The Gibson brothers would make their way to Cherry Alley while Wayne and I sat on the cement steps that led down to the river and talked about real things.

We were obliged to be back by the last streetcar at eleven. Invariably we missed it and had to take a taxi. After Wayne had thrown up we went inside and were checked in by kindly, flabby Mr. Tebbets. Late again, same speech again. His sparkly glasses flashed.

"I see we have two miscreants who have decided to return to the fold. And where, may I ask, is the Gibson twosome?"

We just shrugged. We knew that he knew, he knew that we knew, and the three of us just sighed and upheld the honor of the Harrisburg Academy.

Homer

H.L. Mencken mentions somewhere that Homer Rodeheaver used to be kappelmeister (song leader) for Billy Sunday, the Jimmy Swaggart-Falwell-Bakker of the early 1900's.

This same Rodeheaver used to appear at assembly in Harrisburg twice a year. At each appearance he'd sing and play his trombone. His best number (loudest) had these lyrics:
There's a rainbow shining somewhere,
Far across the northern SEA,
There's a rainbow shining somewhere,
Which someday will shine for MEEEE.
(Big trombone sounds.)

The fact that the words don't mean anything is unimportant. What is important is that the other day, 58 years after having heard the silly thing for the last time, I came across the name of the lyricist.Miss Ina Dugley Ogdon. She also wrote *Brighten the Corner Where You Are*. At least I understand that one. Sort of.

✱✱✱✱

Each Spring a declamation contest was held, a sort of oratorical bout which meant a great deal to everybody at the Academy. You picked something you wanted to memorize, and then on the great day you stood before the whole student body and a flock of guests and spellbound them with, in my case. Poe's *The Telltale Heart*.

The judges were Dr. Brown and two ministers . . . people in the spellbinding trade. Don't go 'way, this is interesting because I won the gold medal.

What makes it interesting is that second place went to Arthur E. Brown, Jr.

The headmaster's son.

Less than a year later I became a radio announcer.

The River

During my last winter at school the Susquehanna River froze over and the surface was smooth enough to skate on. After classes one day we laid out a classy hockey rink. Tin cans were the four corners and small rocks marked the goals.

The ice, the air and the sky were all white and grey, the far shore of the river a darker grey inked in by a thumb. We skated in a misty half-world which stretched about a mile wide, and as long as forever.

There were Charlie Peck and I from New York, Albert Zenke from Oil City, the Bodmer brothers from Venezuela and a couple of boys from Harrisburg. There were three Bodmers and each of them was named Luis. They all used their middle names, Dios be praised.

By the by, one of the Latins at the Academy, Jaime "Blank" (even now I suppose I could be sued) was such a quiet boy that I felt a bit of pity for him and we became friends. Once I asked him what he intended to do when he got back to Venezuela. His eyes woke up. Become President, he said. Build roads and schools, he said, and help the people. He was earnest and he glowed in a kind of mystic aura.

Of course he became President (or this would be a stupid interruption) and the last I heard of him, some years back, he had left his country by request and was living in Miami with several millions of dollars from the Venezuela Treasury. I was old enough by then to be only mildly dumbfounded.

And now may we play ice hockey?

The two team captains bent over the puck and together they counted. On THREE! they thrashed about 'til one of them managed to hit the thing away. This was called "passing." After a lot of skittering about (none of us could skate a damn but we had enormous energy) somebody got "possession." Somebody collided into him and the two of them heaved and grunted their way down the river while the others stood around (mainly on their ankles) and screamed advice.

There was a little island in the middle of the river, and one time two of the wrestlers, another fellow and I, got around behind it. Exhausted at last, we agreed to pick up the puck and start ankling back. Alas, the others, freezing in their boredom, had gone ashore.

No music, no scent brings back those days, but the sight of the skating rink at Rockefeller Center does. Sometimes I pause for a minute or two and watch the poor, hemmed-in people making their dismal, unnatural rounds in dreadful surroundings. None of them will ever tangle with Luis (Pepe) Bodmer on the beautiful broad stretches of the frozen Susquehanna, happily skittering through the pearly afternoon, ice, air and sky, all of a color, and with nothing to do but play until dark.

20

Somewhere Above David Letterman's Theatre

Since Mr. Letterman had yet to be born, the theater at Broadway and 53rd Street, at the time of which we sing, presented real entertainment. On two floors above it were the studios for two radio stations, WMCA and WPCH.

WMCA had been christened when it was housed in the McAlpin Hotel. WPCH had been in the Park Central Hotel. See? Many stations were named for something or other; WGN Chicago stood for World's Greatest Newspaper: it was owned by the Chicago *Tribune*; WOW Cincinnati, Woodmen of the World; KSTP was for St. Paul, and on and on.

How the little monster became a page boy has been recounted. How he became an announcer is even more gripping.

There was a dramatized news program on WMCA called *Five-Star Final*, a cheap pseudo-imitation of *The March of Time*, a celebrated major network show. *Five-Star Final* was written and directed by a cheap, pseudo-imitation person who called himself Charles Martin. His company were paid thirty-dollars-a-week each, and it included Garson Kanin, Alice Frost, Sam Levene, George Tobias and Martin Gabel.

One day Mr. Martin needed an extra voice and hollered at the kid setting up the folding chairs. Could he read? This kid had been a not inconsiderable theatrical personage at Camp Kinaani. He now became, at the same eight-dollars-a-week for being the page he still was, a kind of utility infielder.

Soon thereafter the management discovered that the page boy-actor was really a pain in the ass and, as I mentioned earlier, fired him.

On the way out I passed a WMCA studio inside of which someone was auditioning to become an announcer. I asked the Chief Announcer, one A.L. Alexander, could I audition too?

This guy was a piece of work. He was a twenty-seven year nearsighted low pile of flab who had studied for the rabbinate. He was unable to say 'hello' without spewing two tablespoons of saliva. The program he most enjoyed introducing was *Tom Noonan's Bowery Mission* which was broadcast every Sunday from some hall downtown, but Alex did his introductions from the radio station. These grew fatter and more oleaginous as time went on. It was, after all, his only pulpit. He was Heaven's Troubador and God never had it so good. Alexander's Supreme Moment came, I believe, on the day he said, in referring to the studio he was sitting in, "We speak to you this glorious afternoon from within the confines of the broadcast enclosure."

Anyway, fatty agreed, warily, to let me audition.

There were no subtle announcers then—nor ever. Loud and clear, Loud and Clear. I was born Loud and had learned Clear from my California-born mother, so a funny thing happened to me on my way to the breadline. When I left the confines of the broadcast enclosure, Alex offered me eighteen-big-ones-per to be L&C.

There was no union in those days and my hours were from two in the afternoon until I finished announcing dance bands up in Harlem at three ayem. There were nightclubs such as the Cotton Club and the Ubangi which had all-Black shows that were wildly received by the all-White audiences. No Blacks were admitted.

How you like them apples?

Alex, née Fishbein, thought my name inappropriate, so I took one from the bouncer at Harlem's Savoy Ballroom. "The Home of Happy Feet." He was a friendly, decent guy named Niles Morgan.

Years later I ran into Donald Flamm, the man who had owned WMCA. I asked him why he hadn't publicized me in those days as the youngest staff announcer in the country?

"No need to," he said. "You were swell-headed enough without it."

Nineteen thirty-two wasn't a very good year. I was fired, re-hired and fired again. And about thirty years later I realized that I had learned something from that experience, viz: If you're going to be bounced around, try to get it over with while you still have the strength.

21

1932 Radio

Before we get to the names of the famous women with whom I spent days and nights in bed, a word about early radio.

It was all live. Whatever could be thrown at the human ear, radio threw. Live. Now. At, as some of our cruder poseurs would say, this moment in time.

All day, every day, the WMCA radio station depended on underpaid or not-paid-at-all people to show up. We had no tapes, no recordings. If an act was a no-show, the announcer assigned to the spot was obliged to reach for the ever-ready book of poetry and take off. (One man who did this particular well, a certain David Ross, actually was given his own *Poet's Corner.*)

The alternative was to go out to the reception room to see if the stand-by pianist was actually by-standing. In the case of WMCA, this was a woman named Fern Scull.

Some things stay with you.

If Fern was there, she was dragged into the studio and introduced as "our person of melody."

Miss Fern Scull was married to a man who was named and talked like Vladimir something. He was our contact with the opening night of the Radio City Music Hall. Announcer Tom

Coates and Fern and I waited for him and he came home around midnight. How was it, Vladimir?

"Too beeg. Too goddamn beeg. I seet in middle. I am half-way between avvryting. I don't see nottink, I don't hear nottink. I say Music Hall . . . sheet."

That's one way I can remember it was in 1932.

One of our regulars was an irritating woman who called herself Miss Charm. No kidding. She spent most of the day selling advertising for her own show. She'd dart in and read a half-hour of commercials, interlarded with fake beauty hints. She was always followed in the same studio by an unpaid Polish polka band who financed *themselves* by selling spots to various Polish advertisers.

The band was obliged to come in while Miss Charm was babbling and set-up—horns, fiddles, basses and music stands. Charm had a cut-off button which she used to enlightening effect. She would stab the button and address the Poles: "Shut up, you dirty Polack sons-of-bitches or I'll tear your balls off!" was more or less her usual form of greeting. Then she'd press the button and dispense additional charm.

One of the studios contained a built-in organ and two built-in organists. Thin, pale, effeminate Mr. Robinson, one, who despised rotund, bald, effeminate Elmo Russ, the other. They never spoke to each other, nor, for that matter, to me.

The station maintained a staff which included Jack Filman, a man who did the hockey games wearing an Adam fedora, and Angelo Palange, a kind of utility fake-excitement announcer who did the usual sports blather that still exists today. Wearing an Adam hat. Adam sponsored everything of a sports nature and it was considered good policy to keep the product on hand—or on head—at all times.

We announcers wrote our own copy or ad-libbed, if we felt up to it. Since the day was endless and the programs covered everything from Mozart to politics to oddball baritones singing *The Road to Mandalay* and *The Hills of Duna,* an education of sorts was thrust on us.

Occasionally it was necessary to leave the studio to do what was called a "remote" and some of them were, indeed. I was obliged to journey down to the offices of the New York *Daily Mirror*, a dreary Hearst tabloid, in order to announce the appearance of one Nick Kenny, a singularly inept columnist and broadcaster.

Mister Kenny's appeal was to the un-lettered. He wrote his own poems, one of which was entitled, *The Synagogue in the Pines*. His grasp exceeded his reach, but not by much. It should be mentioned that when Nick grabbed at a piece of his dreadful doggerel, his brother Charley would leap to his feet and play a fiddle accompaniment. The only tune he knew was *I Love You Truly* and it always fit in just dandy.

Brief scene: My regular three o'clock piano duo on Wednesdays. The gentleman, Mr. Arbrnga, a mittel-Europa-type with a tan homburg, walking stick, fawn gloves, velvet collar on his coat—all worn, worn, worn. The lady, Madame Arlatti, heavily made up, veil on hat, heavy velvet-seeming coat down to the floor, big, soft old eyes. They played terrible duets on the same piano and we all knew they were terrible because they hadn't been able to afford a place for rehearsal in years. They were elegant and old and dusty. And after each "concert," Madam Arlatti would produce from someplace in all the folds of her endless clothings a small bag of European candies and offer them, shyly, to me, and the radio engineers, and anyone who happened by. Mr. Arbrnga meanwhile stood to one side, carefully putting on his gloves. It took him about five minutes. Then, with shy smiles and much bowing, they would leave. They were the only entertainers Mr. Flamm paid: $5 a broadcast.

At WMCA, NOTHING was over after the fat lady sang. The fat lady was a sort of soprano named Margarita Padula and I think she was paid carfare, but I'm not sure. Fat lady did I say? When she made her entrance into the reception room it looked like the front end of Cleopatra's barge nosing up to the dock.

Another permanent member was tenor "Smiling" Jerry Baker. Smiley, nee Giovanni Seggia, always wore an Adam hat, the homburg pushed to the back of his head. While he was singing, too. The hat folks paid for his program, or maybe just a mention on it.

The head of the sales department, Mr. Neri also, wore an Adam hat. A homburg. Usually on the back of his head.

There was Jack F. who announced the hockey games from Madison Square Garden—which wasn't on Madison Square in those days either. Jack was so knowledgeable that he saw and talked about every single thing that happened: he had to rip right along in order to cover every whoosh, click, buffet and bang and, in order to talk fast enough, he had to use a low monotone. During a championship game he talked even faster and lower. It was quite soothing. I don't know what he did other than the hockey games but I saw him at the station a couple of times. As I mentioned before, he wore an Adam hat. Uh-huh, Homburg.

Came spring, and a couple of aircraft crashed in the Atlantic. I was sent down to the offices of the *Daily Mirror* to be on hand for the next one so I could, hah-hah, cover it. This was very strange because there was a kid already there, Nick Kenny's assistant, who did the news every day right from his desk. As a matter of fact, my station there was a chair on the other side of his desk. From the moment I sat down in that chair until this very day during peaceful years not one plane has flopped into the Atlantic.

I don't recall exactly what shenanigans I came up with at that time but, finally, I did manage to get fired again. Maybe it wasn't shenanigans, maybe it was just that no planes fell down. Maybe the station just forgot that I worked there. Maybe I just forgot to keep going to the *Daily Mirror*. I dunno. I forget.

22

Lonely as a Goddam Cloud

I wandered through those early '30s years in a mist. The Great Depression didn't get to me much except in winter. I saw the men in three-piece suits selling apples on the street on upended fruit crates, but I couldn't spare a nickel. During the early years of the Depression, I had a hole in my right shoe and a skimpy topcoat that was about as breeze-proof as the cardboard shanty town huts in the lots along Riverside Drive.

Once I ran into a fellow who said "they" were auditioning at CBS. I trudged over, won the job and the next night I was reading the news at six, with Ted Husing as my announcer. The next morning "they" called and said I was to have a special, special audition that afternoon. I showed up an hour late and the man told me sternly that a Mr. Paley had been waiting but now it was too late. I shrugged. Mr. Paley, whoever he was, had his problems—I had mine. One of them was that I had now worked one (1) program and was back on the street. Mr. Paley owned CBS.

I had read about the WPA, the Works Progress Administration, and thought it could use looking into. It seems that the President, Franklin Delano Roosevelt, a man born into wealth and position, yet who seemed to be quite intelligent, had expressed compassion for the poor. He was somewhat different from, let us choose at random, Ronald Reagan, a man who had

101

been born without position or money or intelligence, and who had no interest in the poor whatsoever except to relieve them of the burden of Government aid.

I signed up with the WPA (Work Progress Administration). There was also a CCC (Civilian Conservation Corps.) a project put together by someone in Roosevelt's Cabinet and it might work today, too. Unemployed people of all ages signed on with the Government itself. Young kids without any background of employment were sent into the forests to cut trails, build retaining walls, etc. People were assigned to the kind of work which seemed to match whatever background they claimed.

For twenty-six dollars a week, because of my background (I had been fired as a radio announcer), the WPA made me teacher of a class "in radio."

It is still an embarrassment.

Here was a ninny of nineteen who met twice-a-week at the 23rd Street "Y" with about two dozen hungry adults; I was to "teach" them how to get into radio.

These tired people sat on decrepit wooden folding chairs, some around a long table and some back against the walls of a dusty brown room.

I am haunted still by the strained faces, the shabby clothes. They'd bend forward to listen, silent. What could I tell them? *I* couldn't get a job. They never asked me about that. So earnest were they as they listened to me, a shoeless shoemaker.

Bouncing Again

This time it was a radio station in Brooklyn that was owned by a rabbi who did all the commercials . . . in Yiddish. He ad-libbed them, too. The only words I remember from him are "groysen oisvald" which seemed to show up in everything he did. I asked him about it. "Big, ah, big, ah, big ASSORTED" he said.

One day the WPA noticed that I'd stopped "teaching," and unfairly tossed me off their payroll. That fall I rooted for Roosevelt.

The station had one 'remote' broadcast, a weekly fiesta from the World Clothing Exchange Store. The program consisted of the festivities which followed the FREE weddings given by the management to lucky brides who had bought their outfits there.

The "studio" was a medium-sized windowless room throughly draped in what seemed to be brown burlap. There was no air other than what the guests breathed onto the refreshments. Someone banged away at an old upright piano while mein host, Mr. Mowgelewski (owner of the establishment), offered macaroons for kisses, bartering with the bride.

Mr. M, a heavy, heavy man, did his one big joke once during every broadcast. He'd grab the microphone and announce that Irving, his son, was playing the piano with his "putz." Yes, that's what it means.

The other big do on the station was *Professor Wagner's Kiddie School.* Wagner was a short, puffy, red-haired fellow with the vacant blue eyes of a man who gave up long ago. After just four group lessons, which cost fifty cents apiece, the Professor would let your very own child sing on the radio. The mothers, their laps piled high with their kids' coats, gloves and scarves did their best to supply applause. Right after the broadcast they'd rush to phone grandma to make sure it had really been on the air. As far as I could tell, they were always pleased.

One day the rabbi stopped me in the hall.

"You Jewish?"

"Yes."

"You sure? You don't look it."

On a stack from Bibles.

Entre 'Acte

They were mad for me in Brooklyn, but on the days when I was supposed to sign the station on in the early morning, I was always, always late.

Canned.

Next stop, Philadelphia. Tell you how in a minute. But first I tried for a job at the class network, NBC. After the audition Pat

Kelly, the chief announcer, offered me a job in Cleveland. He said it would help me to get the hang of what NBC is like. "Then, maybe . . ."

Cleveland. Cleveland Ohio, yet. I pictured myself living in a tepee on the edge of the prairie. Mr. Kelly was kind but adamant. So . . . well, Philadelphia was at least a much shorter train ride. Listen, when your parsnips need buttering you get off your fundament and down to fundamentals.

Such as (ACH!) Philadelphia.

'33 and Philadelphia

These days old Brotherly Love is rather dismal but in the thirties it was a hotbed of somnolence. Friends, that town had died and there was simply no interest on anyone's part in attending the wake.

How I got there affords an illustration of an amusing point—that radio then was run by the same varieties of brainpower that make the decisions in TV today. Let's say that the movers and shakers were, uh, insecure. Oh, let's get it over with and say that many of them were imbeciles.

For example.

One day after I had left Brooklyn by request I won an audition at CBS, N.Y. My job was to be standby in case Norman Brokenshire forgot to leave the bar at "21" in time to announce the Chesterfield program. The idea was to have somebody ready who sounded like him. I didn't, so I won the job. But I didn't show up that evening because on my way out of the building I had noticed on the bulletin board that Broke's standby for that very night was David Ross. I went home and listened to the program and was only mildly surprised to hear the voice of Paul Douglas. He, by the by, was the same fellow who hollered into an open grand piano—

"BUCK . . . RODDGGGERS . . . IN THE TWENTY FIFTH . . . CENNNTURY!"

The open piano created a nice, hollow sound.

That's the same Paul Douglas who was in *Born Yesterday*

104

with Judy Holliday. Judy, fresh from her years with the "Revuers" (with Comden and Green) was a highly intelligent, sad sort of girl. I knew her a little and never had even a clue as to her thinking—but the sadness was evident. At least to me.

Anyway, my one-nighter for Brokenshire over, I turned up at CBS for still another audition. This was for number two on my wish list (NBC was number one)—a staff job at the only slightly less important entity—The Columbia Broadcasting System.

I won. And I lost.

What I won was a job. But it was at the CBS affiliate in Philadelphia.

23

I saw the radio station from the train as it pulled into the Market Street station. Yeah, I know. I know—there IS no Market Street Station. But there WAS. Believe me. I'm older than you.

My new boss was a slightly puffy bald guy who called himself Stan Lee Broza. His son led a band and called himself Elliot Lawrence. Okay. I called myself Henry Morgan.

This town was a dog. For instance, Sunday movies were forbidden. I kid you seldom. No movies, no bars no singin' no dancin'. Two drugstores were open in case of emergency but they were DRUG (in the old fashioned sense) drug stores. No sodas. No magazines. No greeting cards. No cigarettes. In the whole town not a mall, not a ball, not a hall. A pall, yes.

One thing DID happen on Sundays. I lived in a large room two blocks from the station with another announcer, Fred Lang. He was a pleasant enough fellow but odd. He was teen-age gawky for a man in his twenties; he had a raw-boned, cowboy-look about him. Of German descent, he had blue eyes and an old-time "prairie" kind of face. About six-feet, he looked like a hick in a business suit. His thinking was hick-ey, too. He thought small-town thoughts. He had a small-town face.

Well sir, each and every Sunday morning Fred would string a clothesline across the room, then take his radio apart and string the parts on the line. I never asked him why. I didn't want to know.

Daily breakfast at Horn and Hardart was a dime—a nickel for two rolls, a nickel for coffee.

For the benefit of two-hundred-and-fifty-million Americans who don't know, Horn and Hardart was a small chain of mechanical restaurants that had been invented in Germany. (The first one that was going to be imported went down at sea and they had to buy another). Each was a large room full of square white marble tables. It was all but surrounded by walls of little windows on hinges. Behind each window was food on a plate. One dropped a coin or two into a slot and that released a catch so that the hinged window could be swung open and the plate taken out. If you put your head against the wall and sighted along it, you sometimes found a window that stuck out a little because its latch hadn't caught and you could just reach in and grab whatever was in it. The big joke in Philadelphia was this: "At Horn and Hardart the other day I put a slug in the slot and guess what came out? The manager!"

Well, you know . . . Philadelphia.

Dinner was another triumph of mechanics, a place called Linton's. Up on the wall behind a long counter was a slab of push-buttons. You looked at the menu and then told the counterman the number of what you wanted, he pushed a button and after a while your order came out of the kitchen on an endless belt that paralleled the counter. The food was terrible but it was fun watching the man try to get the plates off the belt before they got to the end and crashed to the floor.

Sex, at last!

The night girl at the WCAU switchboard was the only possibility at the station, so we became passionate lovers. Not in my room, because we tried that once and the landlady was at the door in a little under a minute. She made a speech, too. No, what we did was use the little alcove off the girl's living room at home. It took fifty minutes by subway to get there but it must have been worth it—even though her father was ALWAYS reading the paper in the living room and the alcove had no door.

This limited us to a kind of subdued thrashing around on a narrow day-bed kind of thing. With our clothes on, of course. Even kept on my tie. I'm not positive, but I think we took our shoes off.

Know why we broke up? She found out she was a year older than I. D'you think I can sell this to the movies?

There was also a girl singer who liked my interpretation of wilding. Fully clothed, we pawed and kissed on the back seat of a friend's car while he drove around at night looking for something to do. I'm not kidding—he just drove around. Oh, I know this heaving and grunting sells no books, but I'm doing the best I can. Or, rather, the best I was able to do at that time. In Philadelphia.

By the by, in the singer repertory was a number called *Rock and Roll (Your Blues Away)*. Yes, in the thirties. H'mm.

❖❖❖❖

Two more stories and we can leave town. WCAU's house orchestra was led by five-foot-two Jan Savitt. He had to stand on a crate so that the back rows could see him. But this anecdote isn't about Jan, it's about his music librarian. George the Polack. George kept the files and when the band went on the road he brought along all the musicians' parts—the stuff he laid out for them every day at the studio.

One day Mr. Savitt decided that George was more of a trial than he was worth and he fired him. But George was back in two days. His filing system and all his records were in Polish.

I was the sign-off guy at the station and the only thing I could think of to do late at night was to go into Fred Lang's little studio when he was reading the news on the air and put the trash basket under his table and set fire to it.

Broke him up every time.

At night all the programs emanated from the network studios in New York or Hollywood, and often the engineer and I were alone in the building. I spent a lot of time riding up and down

109

in the elevator. It had a loud speaker in it and every so often I'd get out just in time to get into the little room and say at the appropriate station breaks, "WCAU, Philadelphia." Well, one evening as I was enjoying a particularly exhilarating journey, the elevator stuck. Nobody read the late news. Nobody signed off. Even so I think I could have kept my job but there was one other little thing that happened. The other little thing was that I wanted to prove that nobody listened to the Missing Person's report, which was read at one ayem, immediately before sign-off, so one morning I included among the missing one Dr. Levy—the man who owned the station.

I forgot to tell you that Stan Lee Broza had a bad stutter—so much so that it took him a half-hour to fire me. Even then it was kind of sweet because he ended with, "when you leave the b-b-building p-p-please wait for my w-wife. She'll be d-d-driving around the b-block, so when sh-she goes by tell her I'll be down in a f-few min-minutes."

I did, too.

24

Duluth, Minnesota

I know a lot about Duluth and its sister town, Superior, Wisconsin. I was an announcer there for about a year. This was because of Tom Coates, an announcer I knew. My second day home in New York after the Philadelphia story, I ran into him. He suggested that I make a recording and send it to Walter Bridges at the only station in Duluth—where Tom had worked in the past. I did, and said in my note that I'd work for forty dollars a week.

Bridges confirmed by wiring that he would pay me one-hundred-sixty-dollars a month. It was almost a year after I got there that I realized the ignorant country boy had gypped me out of four-weeks-pay-a-year.

Our hero arrived in Iron Ore Country busted. Between trains in Chicago he had wanted to kill time and, thinking to go to a place where a man of many worlds could have a light snack and some good jazz, he jumped into a taxi and said, "Say, driver, where does a guy go in this town to have some fun?"

He drove him to a whorehouse.

Hell, when our hero entered the apartment he knew enough to go right to the slot machine. He knew what to do with a nickel as well as the next class act.

111

When, in two minutes, the girls filed in and sat down in their nighties, he knew enough not to stare at them like some hick.

When the madam asked him to choose, he said, "What the hell, let's have TWO girls."

In the coat-closet-with-bed the girls asked him what he'd like to do?

Oh, he said, why don't you make love to each other.

The thin, plain young things sat on the bed and one of them sort of tentatively fingered her crotch through the skimpy cloth. The other one just stared at her.

Our hero tried small talk.

Very small talk.

In what he figured was about an hour there was a knock at the door. He asked what it meant. One of the girls told him.

"It means you've had ten minutes. You have five more."

He thought it over.

"Nah," he said. "I've had enough. Let's go."

Hell. Know what I mean?

Hell.

25

Living With a Superior Undertaker

The Spalding Hotel in Duluth must have been built just before the railroad arrived. From across the street it looked like a faded postcard in an old family album. Inside, in the lobby, there were old stuffed chairs holding old stuffed men, one spittoon apiece.

Along one wall was the first or second of Mr. Otis's successes, a jittery metal cage with a skinny old man in it. The thing worked on a counterbalance. A vertical cable ran through the cab. The skinny old guy wore a leather glove and to get the thing started he grabbed the cable and heaved. He and I slowly, slowly creaked up to the fifth floor, the top, where station WEBC was. The whole aura was of something left over from another era—which it was—except for one thing, a "thing" that took the newly arrived sport from the East by surprise.

A sparkling blonde at the reception desk.

Frances Holmes was thirty-three, she later confided, and I was twenty, but she didn't care and I managed to adjust. I was apparently, as they would say back home, a real goddamit. It seems that Frances had recently left her most recent escort, a handsome State Senator. Later on I saw him around town a couple of times wearing jodhpurs and leading his two Great

Danes. A hard act to follow—but I'd been called and I'd been chosen. Frances had, like me, a talent for adjustment.

Before bedtime rolls around, a bit of geography.

Duluth, Minnesota and Superior, Wisconsin are separated by a tiny river. WEBC was the only radio station in the entire area and it had studios in both Duluth and Superior. I was assigned to Superior and I lived there at the world-famous Androy Hotel.

Two weeks after my arrival in Indian Territory, Frances decided that the time for dithering was over. She borrowed a small suite at the Spalding in Duluth from a friend and, on a December's night, phoned me at the Androy in Superior. There was a bus, she said, but the trip would take only about twenty minutes by taxi.

Two small problems:

(1) I had no money, and (2) I was still a virgin.

The hotel kindly lent me a few dollars. They took care of (1) but as for (2) I didn't know what I was supposed to think about, so on the way I stopped the cab at three or four bars and invited the driver inside to help me think. I drank the local favorite, whiskey with beer chasers, "boilermakers."

Frances was dressed in a silky jacket-and-pants outfit with little, if anything, underneath. She took my coat, sat me down and left the room. In a few minutes she reappeared with an enormous club sandwich on a plate. I stared at it, breathed a little, took a big bite, and threw up.

Wa Wa

Which reminds me of another heart-stopping tale of debauchery. This was back in Manhattan. For those newcomers to reading, the word is pronounced de-baw'chery. Just think of bawd, a strumpet—one who works in a bagnio.

The woman I now present you was, however, no harlot. She was Janet, the nice young, divorced mother of an eight-year-old boy. She was a busty thing with an amazing sense of hospitality. It just so happens that, in her one-bedroom apartment, the boy had the bedroom. The large double bed was in the living room.

Her apartment house was immediately across the street from an elegant restaurant called the Barberry Room. It had an elegant bar and some elegant customers. At times I would leave the bar, cross the street and spend an hour or so in the living room with almost-always-available Janet.

At about seven of an evening I rang her bell and was informed that this, alas, was an unfortunate time of year. After her door gently closed, I sobbed, turned around and pushed the elevator bell.

In the small cab stood a not-unattractive woman powdering her nose. Now, with gentlemen like me, hope does not spring eternal. On the other hand, neither doth it jump on a bus and hurtle off to Newark.

The young woman eyed me over her powder puff.

"You're thinking about asking me for a date, aren't you?" she said.

We elegant types are easily struck dumb, but this was one of the easier times. I phumphered.

"You've probably heard of my father" she continued. "He owns the Latin Quarter." (A well-known nighttime dive.)

Phumpher.

The elevator landed, we emerged and started walking up the street toward Fifth Avenue.

"Well, my name is Barbara Walters. I'm having dinner over there in that building. My hosts own a Rolls-Royce."

And she crossed the street.

It's not at all odd that, in a city like New York, I never saw her again in the, ah, flesh, that is.

But Back To My Knitting

The studio in Superior took up half of the top floor of a kind of slightly enlarged two-story barn on Main Street. The other half was a Chinese restaurant. Downstairs under us was a store; soda fountain, ribbons, tires, rakes, fishing rods, paper towels— the usual. No drugs though because there was a real drugstore (but no soda fountain) in the Androy Hotel.

115

The man who ran that one had a green rubber mat on the counter—lots of the stores did. When you bought something he'd suggest that you play him double-or-nothing for it. He'd roll dice onto the mat out of a lipped leather cup. If you rolled higher, it was a "horse" on him. Two out of three horses was a winner.

Anyway, the "studio" was upstairs over the oddball shop. Next door to the same building, if I may use the term, was Gately's Ladies' Fashion. And over Gately's was the placed where you could go and eat Chinky.

The two carpenters who had hammered all this marvelous assortment together were, in real life, the "O.K. Builders." Their names were Olafsen and Kraglund. Okay?

Walter Bridges was manager and part-owner of the station. The Weyerhauser Lumber Company owned a piece, a man who owned the Duluth newspaper had a piece, and the sales manager was in on it, too.

Mr. Bridges was a farmer without a farm. (The 'engineer' in Superior, Earl Svensen, was a farmer *with* a farm.) Bridges was about forty. His hair stood almost straight up. He talked 'country' and when he wanted to make a point his eyebrows shot up and he popped his eyes. They didn't pop like snide old William F. Buckley's but like those of a nice guy who was simply asking, "do you get the point?"

The secretary in the Superior office was a middle-aged fake-redheaded woman who was unique. She was the absolute dumbest son-of-a-bitch I have ever known. Her own job was to type out the program schedule for the following day. To do this, she would type with two fingers for five or six minutes, then pick up her handbag and go to the john, or downstairs to the drugstore, or to visit her friend who worked in the dress shop. To do the schedule took her from eight-thirty in the morning until six-thirty at night. Sometimes seven. Eight.

One day I had it with this dumpy moron. I went into the office to tell Mr. Bridges. He heard me out, laughed, then popped his eyes and explained the intricacies of the problem. The vapid klutz was his sister-in-law.

But the Nice Man really laughed.

My job was to announce most of whatever originated in Superior and this included the nightly reading of the news. Now this part can be (is) pretty dull, so you can skip the next page or two and get to the incredible sexy stuff, OR, you can learn a bit of HISTORY.

There was a tiny room next to the only studio which had once been a plain wooden room (which was still a plain wooden room, but with the windows boarded up). The tiny cubicle was three-feet-by-four-and-a-half. On a kind of shelf were two turntables for 78 records, six switches and no space. Right above it was a control panel with twenty pushbuttons in On-and-Off pairs. Through the undoored doorway was a small closet which contained two LP turntables mounted on wooden bases that brought them up to the height of a workbench.

Okay. It's five minutes to seven o'clock "AND THE NEWS!" First you set up the transcriptions in the closet on the right, making sure that each needle is a turn-and-a-half before the sound begins. You have to do this to give the tables time to get up to speed, see? Now you set up records on the 78 tables and open the dial on your left to whichever table will start first. Wait! Some of the 2 feet wide transcriptions start INSIDE instead of OUTSIDE so you run back to check. Suddenly through the speaker you hear the announcer in Duluth say, "And here's the news." You punch up the SUPERIOR button and begin reading—from a copy of the Duluth newspaper which is on a rack in front of you. Towards the end of the second item you start one of the 78 turntables and keep your finger on the record. At the end of the item, you let go of the record and punch yourself OFF and turn the dial open.

The record stops, you punch yourself ON, turn the switch off and while you read the next item you figure out when to start the transcription (you have to leave time for that turn-and-a-half before the needle gets to the SOUND). Meanwhile, you have to set up the next 78 while being sure to turn the big dial the other way for the other turntable.

At this point you get your finger ready for button number

eight because a two-voice live commercial is coming up and the 8-button brings in the other voice—from Duluth. While you are sweating through this you are simultaneously setting up the next 78, making sure the arrow on the big dial is in the right place, starting the record but keeping a finger on it so it doesn't turn too soon.

It was only for fifteen-minutes-a-night but it was better than trying to sell used cars. (Coming up.) The only other person who could do this job had taught it to me, and then was fired.

❖ ❖ ❖ ❖

Fat men, they say, are jolly. If there's any truth in that assumption then I knew the world's only round-the-clock depressed fat man. Earl (lots of Earls in the Territory) Anderson was obliged to write ALL the local commercials. He sat at his typewriter from nine-to-seven, forever. The first time I went out for a beer with him I mentioned, in some context or other, the word "sale." Earl put down his drink and with great seriousness he said, "Don't ever use that word in my presence again."

The "studios" were two doors down from world-famous Gately's, the clothing store, outside of which I conducted my probing sidewalk interview in the dead of winter on an empty street by interviewing myself. (True)

Next to Gately's was the fairly new Androy Hotel where my room-and-bath was thirty dollars a month. The maitre-d' of the ground floor dining room wore a dinner jacket in the evening, so there. And the hotel entrance was fifty-eight feet from the stairway that led to the radio station, and if you've ever spent a winter in Superior you know what a bargain I had.

Counting both Duluth and Superior there were twelve announcers and it was generally conceded that I was the loudest, so in a couple of months I was named "Chief." No money changed hands—all it meant was that if anyone had to be fired, I'd be the heavy. Mr. Bridges couldn't bring himself to do the dirty so not long after my arrival he thought up a way out. He realized that nobody on the staff really liked me anyway—I

118

was a hotshot from New York AND a pain in the ass—so he made me Chief, and everything worked out just fine.

Superior was just like the Yukon but with more drinking places. A local law said that the saloons had to be separated from one another by walls, and so they were. There were 26 on Main Street.

The winter I was there the temperature never got up as high as zero all through January, so it was a good thing that in the usual blizzard a drinker didn't have to fight more than ten feet to get to the next bar. One of my favorites was run by the man whose name was writ large on the sign outside.

HY KALONEK

Yep.

25

Sam Lurie's 'Good Luck Cafe' was the night spot of Superior, Wisconsin. This broken down wooden dump offered the deck hands from the ore boats, the coal shovellers from the railroads and the impoverished travelling salesmen—GAMBLING.

Downstairs was a crummy bar and, on the other side of a skinny partition, a, har har, restaurant. Upstairs was a crap table and a roulette wheel. The innate charm of the establishment was that it was entirely illegal. The unlicensed bar was illegal. The gambling was illegal. The food in the restaurant should have been sent to jail. And it was well-known that Sam Lurie's brother made illegal wooden coins, including fabled wooden nickels. (This was in the Depression years and many communities had been obliged to turn to wood coins and locally printed paper money.) Sam's brother had no licence for the stuff he turned out, and the locals referred to him as the "illegal illegal."

The two croupiers upstairs wore dinner jackets. Minimum bet, gentlemen, fifty cents.

One night my date and I drank up the two dollars I had on me at the time. I borrowed a dollar from the girl, clumped upstairs, threw the entire dollar on the table and rolled two sevens in a row. I quit, swaggered down the steps and sat down.

✦✦✦✦

One evening I was illegally standing at the illegal bar (even if it had been legal, I was only twenty)—standing shoulder-to-shoulder in a dense mob, when a guy about five places to my left looked over at me and announced to the House, "I don't like his face." He said it again. And then again.

I looked in his direction and all I could see of him was his pock-marked face bent over a beer.

He said it again.

I am not much of a warrior but it got to where I'd had it up to here. I shoved away from the bar, took a few steps, grabbed the man's shoulder, pulled him around and smacked him in the face. He fell to the floor.

Two guys lunged for me but a very large man grabbed them and rapidly explained that from where I'd been standing, and especially in that crowd, I couldn't possibly have seen that the guy was on crutches.

By and large my luck at the Good Luck Cafe was pretty good.

(Years later I was sitting with a girl at the short end of the bar of the Blue Angel night club in New York. I was facing the girl so that my back was to two men who were around the bend at right angles to us. One of them recognized me and behind my back started making insulting remarks about me to his friend. Slur after slur. It became intolerable. I whirled around and grabbed him right through the top of his shirt collar. My girl pulled at me and at the same moment the bartender reached over and held the other fellow. For one thing, I had grabbed the wrong guy.)

By and large my luck at the Blue Angel was pretty good too. In love, anyway.

✵✵✵✵

I'd heard of Indian Sadie but didn't know anything about her until two of the boys in the WEBC house band invited me to meet her one Saturday night. Earl Nykvist and Toivo Pederson assured me that we'd have a good time. It was their custom once a week to get drunk, spend time at a sauna, throw themselves into the snow, get dressed and then go to Indian Sadie's. Toivo was a hulking, blond heap, pleasant but kind of dopey; Earl looked pretty much like him, but was bright and funny and I looked forward to the expedition.

The sauna was old-world style; a kind of hut with a built-in bench, a small pile of stones on top of a fire and a bucket of water to throw on the stones. It damn near killed me. But the roll in the snow! It felt great!

Indian Sadie, as I was surprised to find out but I'm sure you know, ran a whorehouse.

This was no time for foolishness. Like a regular fella, I chose a girl and took her upstairs. She sat down on the bed, I sat on the chair and we had a nice talk. Earl and Toivo never knew.

I don't think Sadie knew (or cared) either but she got one of the two dollars out of it.

For me, the talk didn't come cheap.

✺✺✺✺

Somewhere along in here two of our announcers quit or died, or something, and Mr. Bridges asked me if I had any ideas. Yes, I did. Former WEBC announcer my old roommate, Fred Lang, was tired of Philadelphia, so I sent for him.

26

What Was the Depression Really Like? Don't Ask.

Johnny Frazier, a fella who worked for the Chevrolet dealer, wanted to sell me a new car. All it would cost me was twenty-five dollars a month. When I said I could only afford fifteen, he arranged for me to live where he did, at Mrs. Leraan's house.

Her two kids had grown up and moved out and that left two bedrooms vacant upstairs and Johnny lived in one and I rented the other at a clear savings each month of ten dollars. For five-a-week I had the cleanest, neatest, quietest, loveliest three-windowed corner bedroom I have even seen. But I never bought a car. Where would I go in all that snow?

Mrs. Leraan, a Swedish lady, cleaned the house herself of course—every single day. All of it. On Monday she did the washing too. On Tuesday she had the ladies in for coffee and cake. On Wednesday, Ladies' Aid, and so forth, all through the week. When I came in at night she was always knitting or sewing and said I must be tired and should eat a little something—which she jumped up to prepare. She was about sixty-five. She imbued me with the feeling that everything Swedish was wonderful. (Except lutefish. I had it once in a diner. Ugh. Don't ever do it.)

I met *Mister* Leraan only once because he was always taking care of business. Which was very good. People were hungry and thin, and in that climate three or four froze to death every week. He was an undertaker.

I say that business for Mr. Leraan was good but there was a catch to it. Because of the below-freezing weather no graves could be dug, and he was obliged to store the bodies till Spring—which in those parts came about the end of June. Besides, money was so tight that he had to both store and bury on spec, as it were.

Nobody could afford to buy a new Chevrolet, either, so Johnny Frazier spent most of time going around to the tired houses and the beat-up farms trying to collect payments from folks who had bought cars years before. From many of them he couldn't get even two dollars a week.

Sometimes when I got back to the house at night I'd find Johnny, a rugged, handsome, football-player type, sitting on the edge of his bed and crying. He'd talk to me about how dreadful it was to do what his boss made him do—threaten people with jail. People who were on the verge of starving. My God, how he detested his job.

Fred Lang, my old roomie from Philadelphia, now with the station, developed a kind of tic. He had a program on which he used records, the old '78's, and when he didn't like one, he'd break it—loudly, on the air. He had also developed a personality new to me—a kind of general, all-around kookiness and it all finally came to a head. Mr. Bridges told me I had to fire him.

By this time Fred really hated his job, despised Duluth and was delighted to go. I handed him his check, he shook my hand, grabbed one of the better looking secretaries by the arm and they hopped the train to Chicago. Inside of a week he had a job at WGN and a wife.

And he shows up again in this saga in about three months.

Tom Coates wasn't working out too well either. He was constantly auditioning for "alcoholic." He had moved to a hotel down the street from me and bought a big Philco radio so that he could listen to the opera on Saturday afternoons. Two spinsters lived in the room next door and on Saturdays, it seemed to him, they made a lot of noise in order to bother him, so he decided to teach them a lesson. Tom set fire to his bed—and boasted of it. This was too much. Mr. Bridge put his foot down, on me, Tom must go.

And I, his friend, had to do the dirty.

Unlike Fred, Tom won't appear in these pages again. As a boy he had sung with the choir at St. Bartholomew's in New York, and as an adult he had a magnificent baritone speaking voice. He was a brilliant man, talented and sensitive. When the war came he enlisted, graduated first in his class at Officers' Candidate School and then shot himself.

Dear Tom. I have known eight suicides, including three who had AIDS, and each of them was a victim of his own amplified awareness of the world's injustices, its lunacies, its horrors.

Well, perhaps this will cheer you up a bit. One reads about people who, when upset or in disagreement about something or other, "snort". Tom was the only person I have ever known who actually could and did—and LOUD!. I don't mean a refined clearing of the throat, I mean a raucous, rattling blast of wind through the nose that could clear the leaves out of a driveway.

Icumen In?

The snow finally let up, so it must have been around the middle of June. Sure enough, one day a tremulous sun wavered into the sky. Mr. Bridges saw it and spoke to me, saying that I had a vacation coming. Fine! I figured to go to New York and see my Mamma.

First, I packed my trunk and left it in Superior with one of our announcers, Louis. Louis was on odd choice, in a way. He was married and had a small daughter, but he had the peculiar habit of dressing up as a soldier in a uniform he'd scrounged somewhere and going to Duluth to pick up girls. The only two people who knew about this were me and his wife. Still, he had a lease on his house and a steady job at the station, so . . .

I left the trunk because I had a . . . feeling. For one thing, I'd SEEN Superior. I had tried the local hat trick dozens of times and had never made it. And I never heard of anyone who

127

did, either. The object of the game was to have, in one night, a beer at every bar on Main Street.

I'd eaten lutefish. Once.

I'd watched the local baseball team play. Once.

I'd overheard ONE amusing, short conversation. It was between two guys in a bar. They were gabbing away about a friend of theirs who was about to get married.

One: "So . . . Ivar is going to marry that Sophie, you know."

Two: "Jah, sure."

One: "But Sophie is de biggest hoor in Fond du Lac."

Pause. Then.

Two: "Well, but Fond du Lac is very small town."

◦◦◦◦

I went to New York and saw mamma, and that done, I hopped up to Boston to see how Fred Lang was doing. He'd left Chicago. What came to pass there seems unlikely, I suppose, but this is an exact account: as I walked into WNAC, Fred was standing in the lobby talking to someone. He saw me and his eyes popped but he didn't say hello. He said, "Hey! They need another announcer here!"

And so they did, and so they did.

I sent for my trunk.

Louis did not fail me.

27

Beantown

I spent two years in Boston and they can be covered nicely in a few notes so that we can hurry on to the good stuff.

There were a lot of announcers at the station, but the standouts were:

Andy Hotz
Seymour Klotz
Roland Winters
Fred Lang
Me.

The original names of Winters and Lang were Winternitz and Langenheim. So when we put them all together we had the law firm, "Hotz, Klotz, Winternitz, Langenheim and von Ost."

One of the other announcers was Tristram Coffin. Thought you should know.

Seymour Klotz, by the by, went to New York and became Danny Seymour, the beloved announcer of the *Ma Perkins* soap opera.

Tris Coffin went to Hollywood and, last I heard, became a cowboy actor.

Roland Winters went to Broadway, in Hollywood, he followed Warner Oland as Charlie Chan.

I was the regular announcer for the mayor, James Michael Curley, a doll, thief, con artist—and everlovin' friend of the voters, most of whom loved him back.

Across the street from the station was a bar, the "Home Plate." Twice each evening there was entertainment—an Irish tenor who sang all fifteen of the songs he knew. I can sing "Does Your Mother Come from Novy? [Nova Scotia]," "Over at Southy and Thurd (On da Boolyvard)," "How Drunk Was He?," "Go Away Ye Great Big Jay" (A sly reference to the P.P.A., the Protestant Protective Association)—and eleven more.

All right. One evening Hizzoner showed up at WNAC with his gang for a political broadcast and was met by Larry Doyle, the station salesman of political air time. Pols were obliged to pay up front, in cash. Larry raised an eyebrow at the Mayor, and Mr. Curley pointed to one of his retinue. The man whirled, ran across the street to the Home Plate and was back in a trice with the stuff. It had come right out of the cash register. He handed the thirty-five dollars to Mr. Doyle and the Mayor and I went into the studio.

✿✿✿✿

Father McNeill, a Jebby, was another of my regulars. This gentleman (like every other Jesuit I ever met) was a charming, extremely knowledgeable, well-spoken person. He also was a seismologist but his Sunday radio talks were answers to lay people's questions about the Church.

One Sunday it was the day before Christmas. When we left the studio Father McNeill stopped in the hall, held back the flap of his briefcase and told me to look inside.

"Go ahead," he said, "it's for you."

A carton of Camels!

The dear man.

✿✿✿✿

130 ·

The sorriest lesson I learned in Boston came from a short conversation with Vinnie, a handsome announcer. He had just come back from the broadcast of one of the town's Elite Events, the horse show. How did it go, Vinnie?

"I was standing in the arena right next to the boxes. There was a girl there, that girl was the most beautiful thing I guess I've ever seen."

"Hey, did you talk to her?"

"Well, no. Uh. Well, see, she's a brahmin, I guess you'd say, and I, well, uh, I'm Irish."

Some years later Vinnie became the president of the local chapter of AFRA, the union I had helped to organize. There's no "T" in it because there was no television. Time do move, don't it?

One more. A retired catcher for the Boston Bees used to take me to the game once in a while. Jack Onslow was a gone-to-paunch, shambly sort of guy, and we'd get in through a side gate for nothing because the keeper was another old timer. We'd sit in the bleachers a mile behind the pitcher and Jack would amuse me by calling the next pitch. Never missed. I finally asked him about this.

"Oh. Well, I steal the signals from the catcher."

In case you're new around here the catcher signals from a crouch, mostly by moving his free hand around in the neighborhood of his crotch. We were almost a city block away from him. And Jack was sixty-eight years old and didn't wear glasses.

What can I tell you?

* * * *

Last one, absolutely. How I managed to get fired.

One day I found a pamphlet on my desk. It said that Suffolk Law School was offering, for the last time, to admit to its night school students who were only high school graduates. LOOK! I said to Vinnie. LOOK! I said to Bill O'Connell. So we all went downtown to Suffolk Law, right next to the State House, and signed up.

Some weeks later those two told me that they had known all

about the pamphlet but hadn't told me "because we knew that if you thought it was YOUR idea, you'd sell it to US. Otherwise you'd just argue about it." How true.

The flaw was that I was a night-shift announcer. Therefore, on school nights I would assign all my work to other announcers and then go to class.

After a month or two, Mr. Linus, the boss, sent for me. He explained clearly, and then even more clearly, that We are Not Paying You to Give Your Jobs to Other Announcers. But it was two weeks before midterms and I just HAD to take them. (In order to get back to the station before I was missed I did the four-hour exam in ninety minutes, but somehow I passed.)

I had lost a lot of my enthusiasm for the school, however. On one of the weekly tests I had received a mark of 60. I had gone to the instructor to find out why. Did I have the right rule of law? Yes. Was my reasoning correct? Yes. Then why only 60? "Because," he said, "it was overturned on appeal."

In short, ladies and germs, this klutz expected a student with only the facts of the original case to go on, to know what happened when it was appealed!

I figured I was well out of that one, Tallu.

Still, it was too much for Linus. He merely added up my recent offenses to a list of others that it would only excite you to read about, and, sort of regretfully, I felt, canned me.

****

I sent a wire to my former boss in Duluth, Mr. Bridges. He wired back: "Have no opening right now but will pay you forty a week until I do."

That is one of the things in my life that I am most proud of.

Anyway, I went to see my Linus, my newly ex-boss, and asked him to lend me fifty dollars so that I could get to Duluth. He did.

Bye-bye time. The landlord agreed to accept my furniture in lieu of rent and I was on my way. And first, since I had to go through New York anyway, I thought I'd drop in and see my Mamma.

28

Mamma was fine.

Before I left New York it seemed that it would be nice to look up an old pal or two, so I went to WOR to say howdy to Harry Carlson, a buddy from WMCA days.

Friends, before the Living God that made me what I am about to relate is true, and may help to explain why people like me have to duck questions like, "What drove you? What made you do thus-and-thus?"

I found Harry, and as we started to chew the gristle a chubby young man walked into the room. He looked at me briefly and then came the whacker. "Are you an announcer?"

How can anyone LOOK like a radio announcer? Whatever the look, I, evidently, looked it. This guy auditioned me immediately, and my new salary was forty-five a week.

One program I did regularly might be of interest to some New Yorkers. I was the boy who introduced *Captain Tim Healy's Stamp Club*. Captain Healy was the father of a son who was to become President of the New York Public Library.

Often I was assigned to one thing or another at the New York World's Fair of 1939. It was there I learned about closing bars at night. My guide was Ed Fitzgerald who, with his wife Pegeen was a fixture in radio for many years. Pegeen, a dear lady, was never along with us.

Nineteen thirty-nine was far more than the World's Fair. In fact, one important part of the world was missing. There were great pavilions for the leading nations of the Western world. And a huge one for Russia.

There was none for Germany.

President Roosevelt was on record. "I hate war," he said. Many times. And all America, or almost all, applauded.

If you don't believe that an era ended then, consider this. I make no apology whatsoever for pointing to a strange fact as a kind of proof that the world, as we knew it, was over. In 1939 the following movies were playing in the movie houses:

Wuthering Heights. Goodbye, Mr. Chips. Stagecoach. Dark Victory. Love Affair. Ninotchka. Mr. Smith Goes to Washington. The Wizard of Oz. Of Mice and Men. Union Pacific. Gunga Din. Gone With the Wind.

✧✧✧✧

Sometime in the early forties the manager of WOR, a Mr. Seebach, son of a Presbyterian minister, called me in and said that I was kidding around too much on the air. He offered me a fifteen minute spot on Saturday mornings to "get it out of your system." That in time became fifteen minutes six-nights-a-week at 6:45. Well, I had a wonderful time getting my system cleansed, and quit the announcing staff. The "program" sold out and by the time I enlisted I was making a thousand dollars a week.I didn't know what to do with it so I put most of it in the bank.

The "program" was kind of weird. It began with a theme song, *For He's a Jolly Good Fellow*, because every program had one. Then I would start with "Hello, anybody, here's Morgan." I said that because the big noise of the day was one Kate Smith, a fat girl who started HER show with a condescending, "Hello, everybody. . . .". I, on the other hand, was happy if ANYbody listened in.

From that point on it was a shambles. I played bits of oddball records that I'd buy second-hand from grungy little shops along Sixth Avenue for a dime each. We used so many by Spike Jones that he began sending me new ones before they hit the market. I say 'we' because the records were put on the turntables by my engineer, Sam. I said "Play it, Sam" long before Bogart allegedly did. (It *wasn't* 'play it *again*', you know.)

❖❖❖❖

History note: Sam was Samuel Morse, a direct descendant of Samuel Finley Breese Morse—the inventor of the Atlantic cable.

❖❖❖❖

In between the records there were monologues. They were meant to be funny and sometimes they actually were.

Then there were the commercials. I couldn't abide reading the junk the clients provided so I ad-libbed them in kind of breezy, off-handed fashion that sometimes bordered on the insulting. Listeners liked it, though, and something happened then that I don't think has happened since, either on radio or TV, viz, the audience *paid attention* to the commercials. One of the clients was Adler Shoes. When they started with me they had two stores and inside of a year they had fourteen.

Well, as the fella says, "He who tooteth not his own horn doth not get it tooted."

Incidentally, the shoes were called "Adler Elevator shoes" and the slogan was, "Now you can be taller than she is."

Could YOU do that with a straight face?

You can't win 'em all, as you know. For instance, Life Savers was an advertiser. One night I said that they were mulcting the public because when you got home and opened the package you found that the centers had been drilled out. I claimed that if the manufacturer would give me all those centers, I would market them as "Morgan's Mint Middles" and say no more about it.

The manufacturer was a man named John Noble. He took umbrage at my use of the word "mulct". He cancelled.

Years later at a Christmas party at the Blue Network of NBC, which Mr. Noble had recently bought, he came up to me and

135

said, "Morgan, I'm still not sure that your way of advertising is wrong."

I'm still not sure either.

At the end of each show I would give the weather forecast. Here are a few:

("For New York City and vicinity")—

—High winds followed by high skirts followed by me.

—Falling barometer followed by a loud crash.

—Snow, followed by little boys with sleds.

Now comes the good parts. Not long after the Saturday quarter-hour started one of the married guys on the staff said that he knew a girl who wanted to meet me. We arranged to have a drink at a nearby restaurant and in he came with a willowy, a wee-bit horse-faced young woman who seemed to be both intelligent and amiable.

Her name was Margo and all of a sudden she got to me. What she did was to take out a small vanity case, open it for the use of the mirror, and paint her lips with a tiny brush. I found that enchanting. In a few days Margo became the first girl I actually slept (stayed awake) with. She was a dear thing and, I imagine, for me it was about time. I was twenty-five.

In these days of free condoms for fourteen-year-olds that is probably a surprising statement. Well, I'm sorry for today's kids. They have the "pleasure" of instant gratification. Too bad, because there is no pleasure in having something to which you've never looked forward to. Poor things, they'll never know what mystery is, what apprehension is, what it is to tingle. Perhaps worst of all, they'll never even know what it is to wonder, even for a minute, "can this be love? Is this IT?" No, I'm not corny, or whatever todays's jargon for 'corny' is. Young men like me hadn't heard of Political Correctness. We didn't need it because to us, women weren't sex objects. They were embodiments of fascination.

Fascinatress Number Two. A girl calls me at the station after a broadcast. She's new in town, she says, and, giggle, she'll probably call me again. In a week she does and we make an arrangement. We meet at her apartment with her roommate present. O, tempora! And mores, too!

But, I had another girl. Two, in fact. One was Lenore Lemon, one of the major forces on the city's night-club-cum-Toots-Shor's-and-other-"in"-restaurants-circuit. Then there was a girl who was introduced to me by Lenore's AUNT. The girl was Joan Smith and she deserves a whole book. A slender, ravishing blonde, she was the virginal darling of every photographer on *Life* magazine. She lived with her father and mother in a railroad flat which was loaded on Sundays with *Life* guys, *Time* guys, guy guys.

Her father was a transplanted South Boston Irishman. Six-foot-three, on Sundays he lay on the five-foot couch with his legs over the end, doing the *Times* crossword. As the men swirled by he'd say, "twinty five acrosh . . . capital of New Jersey." One of the fellas would say, "Trenton"—upon which old Smith would snarl, "Hell. I sortinly knew THAT one!"

Joan introduced me to Provincetown, Massachusetts, one of the delights of New England. Its backbone is the descendants of fishermen who came from Portugal long ago for the teeming cod and then, some of them apparently just abandoned ship. They are fishermen, many of them, to this day.

Now, all Portagee fishermen have nicknames, and one day I asked about a fella called "Keys." It seems that when Keys was a little boy his grandfather, a retired fisherman who had come from the old country, would sit sunning on a bench in front of Town Hall. When he'd espy his grandson toddling down the street he'd fling open his arms and yell, "Come! Come kees grandpa!"

❖ ❖ ❖ ❖

There was a wharf in Provincetown that had been converted into a strip of five self-contained rental units . . . tiny kitchen, shower, the works. Joan and I had one for a while at the end of the wharf with views of the Bay in three directions.

Joan took me to meet an old friend of hers, Mary Heaton

Vorse. Mrs. Vorse, besides being a well-known writer, was the mother of someone I already knew, Joel O'Brien.

***

One sunshiny day in June Joan and I went walking on the oceanside beach. It is a glorious place even now because there's nothing man-made anywhere on or near it. Nobody goes there because it's not a 'town' beach—just a few miles of God. After a bit she said that we were where she had once walked as a younger girl and to which she had always wanted to come back. We took off our skimpy clothes, stretched out on a towel and made love to the sound of gentle wavelets lapping across the sun-warmed sand. Then we walked hand-in-hand into the welcoming sea.

***

That was the lull before the storm.

***

My show had been extended to the whole Mutual network, and late in the year, Hawaii was added. It had been on in Honolulu only one week when Lion Beer bought it. Unfortunately, that same week the program reached the ears of some Nipponese spies. Their English was poor, and they thought it was in code; the next week the station was bombed. Even Pearl Harbor got hit.

Not long thereafter I enlisted in what was known as the Army Air Corps. I wanted to get even with those foreigners for what they had done to my program.

29

Yo, Rocco!

My friend Joel O'Brien and I persuaded our respective draft boards that we belonged in the Army Air Corps. Joel and I had joined forces while working on *26 by Corwin*, a radio series written by a genius of the medium, Norman Corwin.

With the fate of our nation in our hands, we heroes decided that we needed more physical strength, so we joined a gym on Eighth Avenue for workouts under the direction of its owner, a serious, heavily accented German. This fella, not a Jewish German but a German-German would strengthen us so we could kill Germans. He had only one other customer working out on the Tuesdays and Fridays when Joel and I showed up, classical violinist Yehudi Menuhin. We never spoke with him. Or was it the other way 'round?

On a cold and bedraggled day in February, Joel and I, together with about twenty others, boarded a New Jersey-bound train. We were off to flying school, we were all in civvies, so to make it clear to the world just what was going on, about ten of the young gentlemen were wearing white silk scarves carelessly thrown around their necks. Ten Clark Gables.

These were odd circumstances. Just as Army recruits were training without rifles, we were going in without uniforms and, most strange, without salaries—but we were actually in the Service. The reason seemed to be that the "regular" airfields were too crowded and we were going to a civilian-run "contract" school.

Civilian? Oh, yes indeed. Our destination was Blairstown, New Jersey, a hamlet not far from the Delaware Water Gap, if that's any help to you. (It wasn't to us). But the best was yet to come.

At Blairstown we were transferred to a bus for the short trip to IT. From the road we saw IT. A big sign announced our final destination. We were to spend two months at

ROCCO'S VILLA SUNSET

This turned out to be a kind of summer resort for down-at-the-heel pleasure seekers who wanted to get away from it all for a one-night-stand. The main structure was a two-story frame building with no insulation. We were put two-in-a-room with a double bed in each, along a narrow corridor that contained a dozen rooms and one (1) bathroom; a closet containing tub, washbasin and toilet. The main floor was the dining room. Dining, ha ha ha.

A small outbuilding was the classroom and an old barn was the hangar. Yes, there actually were five small Piper Cub aircraft on the grounds. The landing field was, well, a field.

Yes, there was a Rocco, too. Joel made friends with him after discovering that there was an unheated (what the hell, NOTHING was heated at Rocco's, including the food, most of the time) little bar. J, a master salesman, wangled us into it on Saturday nights, and we and Rocco would have a quiet, slightly boozy, frozen fiesta, mostly on the house.

The very first time in our room Joel tried to seal out freezing February, but he overdid it and broke the glass. For the rest of our stay we slept in the room fully dressed, including our overcoats.

Actually, this was good preparation for flying lessons because every morning we had to chop the wheels of the Piper Cubs out of the ice. You don't think the barn was heated, do you? And it was great fun for the guy who stood on ice while, by hand, he heaved the propeller around to get the engine started. If he slipped when it caught, the prop would cut his head off. Well SOMEBODY had to stop the Germans.

They gave me a Sunday off and I took the train to New York. I drove somebody's car back—but not all the way. There was a blizzard and the engine died around midnight. There was no traffic on the road and, after a while, no road. No matter. The car died on me, anyway.

About four in the morning a horn honked behind me. It was a milk truck. The guy couldn't see where the edges of the road were, so I stood on the running board with a flashlight and guided him into the next town where we found a garage.

At sunup they sent a tow truck, picked up the car, fixed the pump, and off I went. But I had caught a violent cold, which provided such coughing fits that Rocco let me have a vacant room so that Joel could get some sleep. The coughing fit tore some ligaments in my chest. I had it taped up, and that's the way I took my final flight test.

We all passed, had a teensy 'banquet', hurled Rocco a farewell and went back to New York. Pilots. Sort of. It seems there was a problem. The next school, the one for larger, fighting planes, wasn't ready yet. Joel went home to his wife and I moved into the Royalton Hotel. What money I'd saved I'd split between my mother and father, except for a few hundred still in the bank. No sweat, really, but I was back in the air, sort of, with no plane.

At the Royalton I became friends with a man who lived there, a humorist named Robert Benchley. I also met a girl named Isobel Gibbs. One of these was to become the light of my life. The other, darkness. Hint: I did not marry Mr. Benchley.

30

Old Hotel. I Mean, Old.

The Royalton was and is right across the street from the Algonquin. At a cost of Godknowswhat it has been modernized, handsome-ized and expensive-ized—but you would have loved it the other way.

The concierge, key-hander, fixer, and gossip-in-chief was "Red," a bald man. He told me, "When they come through that front door, I don't care if it's a guy with his own grandmother, I know why they're here."

Well, not always, he didn't.

Just behind the front desk was a telephone switchboard manned, uh, womanned, by a reasonably attractive person of, say, forty. Her name was Dottie.

One day two men came to the desk and asked Dottie to see if Peanuts was in? She called Peanuts on the phone, then turned to the two men.

"Who shall I say is calling?"

One of the men said "Snag and Rags."

This is true. They had all been in Minsky's Burlesque, Peanuts Bone, Rags Ragland and Snag Werris.

Robert Benchley lived in two jumbled rooms, and across the top of the door to the bedroom was a painted sign about two feet high,

MR. Benchley, please.

143

Dottie at the switchboard acted as a buffer for him. I was having a drink with him one early evening when his phone rang. He listened and then said, "No, thank you." Then he explained to me that when Dottie wasn't sure about a caller she'd put the person on 'hold' and let him know the name first to see how he felt about it. His "no, thank you" was a message to Dottie—that she should say "he's not in."

I tell you this so that the rest of this story will make sense. (It is done wrong in a book about Mr. Benchley by an ex-friend of mine who pretends that she knew him.)

We had a few more drinks and Mr. B said, with a tiny stab at a leer, that he had an important date later on. After dinner he said he would take the lady to a room he had reserved at the Plaza.

By the time I left him, he was drunk.

Two days later we were having a small one and I asked how his date had turned out.

"I'm not sure," he said. "When you left here I guess I'd had a few, and you know I don't remember anything at all about the rest of the evening. I DID wake up in the Plaza, though. Twin beds. I was sort of curious so I got up and looked at the person in the other bed. It was Dottie."

I have to get this in somewheres and this is as good a place as any. I knew not only Benchley, but also James Thurber and S.J. Perelman. I mention this because, after all, I have to keep my wits about me.

Back To Earth

You can believe this or not. One day at the Royalton I received a call from someone who said he was a General in the Army Air Corps. He told me to report to a field where I was to train to be a pilot in one of those little planes which act as spotters for cannon fire. While at Rocco's I had heard from my vastly well-informed classmates that spotter guys got killed, on average, in about six minutes.

I told the general I wouldn't go. He threatened. He said I

would be put in the stockade. Or, worse, I'd have to take basic training. And that's how I got to Fort Dix, New Jersey. And from there I was assigned to basic. It was a two-day train trip to the Army Air Force's basic training site in Miami Beach, Florida. Certainly better than the stockade. Since it was still winter it was even an improvement over the Royalton. As for the Villa Sunset . . . !

Joel had meanwhile cleverly arranged to get out of the Air Force and into the Coast Guard, figuring he'd be assigned to sail up and down off Cape Cod, where he had a permanent home with his mother. Well, he had announced to the powers that be that he was a cameraman; they gave him a camera and put him on a small boat to England.

On the Beach we lived in what had been real hotels—two to a room, two beds, one bathroom. Rocco would have thought he'd died and been misdirected to a Jewish heaven. (Jews believe in God but not in a heaven. Rocco would have screwed up again.)

In a short time, because I knew left from right, and because I had a very loud voice, I was made a temporary drill sergeant.

In my off-time I volunteered to 'entertain' at hospitals because I had a funny idea: I would stand in the aisle of a ward and undo the top button of my army jacket. Thus, I would announce, I was "out of uniform" (technically true). Of course I ad-libbed some more anti-military stuff, and the poor, wounded bastards laughed like hell. I assure you, there are few things I despaired of more in my life than seeing mangled nineteen-year-old boys—some with vital part's missing,—laughing.

A tough master sergeant left over from WWI called me in. He said he'd heard I was working nights at the hospitals. Yes, I was.

"Okay," said the old boy, "I'm gonna give you this."

It was a Class-A pass. I could now go anywhere, any time. So one day I went downtown to the Arthur Murray Dance Studio to see my old New York friend, Arthur. The only person there was a singularly attractive girl whom I promptly invited to come across the street with me for a Coca-Cola.

Three nights later I was wandering around with her and remembered that my uncle, Sam Lerner, had a beach house about a mile away, so we wandered over. Once inside, . . . well, that's sort of the story except for the fact that where that beach house was is now the Fontainbleau Hotel. And lots of the same kind of thing goes on there now, too.

✿ ✿ ✿ ✿

Under the direction of Sergeant Draper Lewis (remember his name, please), a couple of other guys and I were flown to Key West to do a show for a Navy unit. Now I, as a civilian on the radio just a year or so back, had a fine time taking apart the pretensions of my own commercial sponsors. I'd throw out their ad copy and ad-lib. In the course of doing this I made fun of ordinary commercials and had myself a ball. But listeners liked it (remember my ribbing of Adler Elevator Shoes—all faintly ridiculous, but with an underlying truth which actually sold a lot of shoes?) As I mentioned, some sponsors bought the idea, some did not. The ones that did not of course cancelled out.

I repeat that information to explain, sort of, my general attitude toward bosses. At the Key West show I was the MC. When I walked out on stage I saw that the first five rows were all brass—the crews were in the back. Oh, boy! Five whole rows of sponsors! I started gently by looking directly at THEM and asking, how come they were here? They had money, I told them they had prestige—why weren't they off the base and in town, getting drunk as usual?

The gobs in back roared.

Then, a little more pointedly (if possible), I asked how come they were down front while the "help" had to sit in the back. I'm sure it didn't amuse them very much that I was from a different service AND a Private besides. But I tell you, old buddy, the 'help' yelled and screamed so long and so loud that it looked as though we might have to cancel the rest of the show.

Not long after that some twenty-year-old lieutenant who had been going through lists of men who had taken aptitude-intelligence tests called me into his office. "Private Morgan," the squirt said, "I've seen your test results. You qualify for a lot of things. What we need right now is aerial gunners, so I'm sending you to Texas."

Laredo, Texas. I QUALIFIED for Laredo, Texas, for chrissakes.

31

Deep, Deep in the Heart Of

Laredo, that mother, is on the Rio Grande. It is hot, Mexican-Spanish and dusty.

I was in a barracks with the high-class youths who were good enough to be in the high-class Army Air Force—high-class, except they were, for some godless reason, mostly southerners. Now to a Yank like me, just the way those people sounded when they talked proved they were ignorant. On my first day one of them held up an imaginary gun and said with a leer, "Ah'll just git up in a plane and kill them Krauts with ma li'l ol' squirrel raafle."

I could not stand being in a war with people like that. I took it for a week and then went to the Commanding Officer and said I had to leave for another field—any other field. He said that while he thought it over I could drive a truck and haul stuff around the base all night and sleep in the daytime. Which I did.

Tell you how I *knew* I'd get out of that place. The day came when I was due for a pass to go to town. The number on it was 467. My last home address in New York had been 467 Central Park West. Lotto!

It was Sunday, and once in town, two other wannabe's and I walked across the bridge into Nuevo Laredo, Mexico. We hadn't known that the whole town was a whorehouse, but that's the way it was, my dear. So we went to a bar and had a beer. A nice, pretty whorelady—oops! I mean a nice, pretty whoreperson and I got to talking in busted English and she said I was a nice fella. Would I like to go to the cemetery with her next Sunday? At least I thought that's what she'd said, so the next Sunday I went back to the same bar and there she was with a girlfriend and a horse-drawn wagon. The wagon was open but covered with a canvas which had a fringe all around. A surrey, indeed.

She drove to a cemetery, all right, chatting away with her friend, and once there she put some flowers on a grave. On the way back to the wagon she and the friend suddenly squatted and peed, and then we all returned to the surrey. She asked me to drive back to and through the town. The whooping and whistling of troops along the route made my day.

✤✤✤✤

Is there an explanation for any of this? No. I just tell 'em as they happened, doc.

✤✤✤✤

I hated Laredo so much that I finally wangled a hearing with the base commander. I said, "I don't belong here." He said, "I don't belong here either. I'm an expert in field artillery." He, it turned out, was a West Pointer, and they WERE different This nice, bright man questioned me for about half an hour and then he made a swell decision. He would arrange to have me declared "temperamentally unsuited" to be an aerial gunner.

Two days later I was on a train to California.

32

The Country Club

Santa Ana was a small place. It was all but surrounded by orange groves and the town itself smelled just wonderful. Truly. And I wasn't assigned to the Air Base at all, but to a radio unit—one of the odder creations of the War Department. The unit's "mission" was to create programs, done by servicemen, for CIVILIANS, and that's what it did. It was housed in an old brick building.

On the outside, chiseled in stone over the entrance was: Odd Fellows Hall. I certainly wish, on behalf of you, the reader, that I had made that up, but no. Odd? let me tell you what happened when I walked into the Captain's office and laid my travel orders on his desk. A thirty-ish, slightly puffy bald man with glasses, he had been a hay-and-feed dealer in Texas. He looked at the papers, looked out the window, then sighed.

"Tell you what, Morgan. I have to think about how we're going to use you. It will take a couple of days. So meanwhile, why don't you go up to Hollywood. See me when you get back."

My war, and welcome to it. Indeed.

It got kooky-er. When I got back they announced that I was a writer-actor. Then I was introduced to one of the oddest of oddfellows, another Captain who didn't even live in Santa Ana.

He drove in twice-a-week from his home in Hollywood, where he lived with his wife.

The man's name was Frederick Brisson. In real life he was the son of a Danish-American entertainer, and sonny had become an actor's agent. He was a fairly ignorant man with empty blue eyes and, I believe, a head to match. To me, the strangest bit of his story was that he was married to a beautiful, unusually intelligent woman, one of the leading movie stars of the day, Rosalind Russell. We called Brisson "The Lizard of Roz."

I made a friend, a bright, amusing ne'er-do-well named Jack Forker. Jack was in the unit as an actor. We would booze together and some of those instructive hours were spent in a local restaurant called The Town House. The lady who owned the place had a cook and four black waiters. Every Friday was payday for them, and Jack and I would be there for the payoff. After the last guests had cleared out the tables and chairs were moved back to create an open space on the carpet. The owner, the waiters and Jack and I then shot craps until either the waiters went broke or the owner did. Since they were all serious and Jack and I were not, on the whole we did pretty well, Once or twice we had drinks and dinner on the house, as it were. And it were, indeed.

I've said that Brisson was a monkey. Well, not entirely. Twice during my time in Santa Ana the good man paid visits to Washington. Each time he returned with a raise-in-grade, so that by the time I left this goony franchise he was a bird colonel.

There was a full orchestra in this nut house, and it had a conductor . . . oh, mother. The man had been an organist on a midwest radio station. That was his entire background. The exigencies of his position were such that this overstuffed goofball usually conducted nothing more than a never-ending search for more gin. No one ever saw this man more than half sober. The group he headed contained about sixty of the best draftable musicians in the country, including Ruggiero Ricci and Felix Slatkin, the father of today's up-and-coming conductor, Leonard. When actual conducting had to be done, Felix did it.

When we had to do a dramatization of any kind that required females, Rosalind would send down volunteers from among the actresses she knew, and one of these was a girl named Virginia. She and I became friends and I often spent time in her home in Hollywood, together with her husband Looie who played bass fiddle in the Coast Guard Orchestra, conducted by Rudy Vallee. Since Virginia didn't much care for Looie, I spent a lot of time with her when Looie didn't.

One day on Hollywood Boulevard I was stopped by a movie hero of the day, Dick Powell. He announced that he had just turned fifty. He slapped his midriff and said, "Fifty, man. I don't have to hold my stomach in any more." A bit more talk and this dear, dear man decided that as a Corporal I wasn't getting enough money, so I should become a writer for his radio show.

And I did.

It wasn't my only outside writing, though. Back at Base Lunatic was a Major who has grown children now, so he is Major Nameless. He had me write funny dialogue by the hour (for no money) on the grounds that I shouldn't worry, it would be used. He never told me that where it WAS used was on the Burns & Allen radio show for which he had been a writer—and still was.

Oh. One of the lieutenants at Unit Oddball was Rudy Valee's lawyer.

Mykes yer think, donut?

One of our actors was Lee J. Cobb. Lee never had to take what was referred to as Physical Training. This process took place out-of-doors on a baseball diamond. The reason Lee was excused from this labor was that he had convinced the base doctor that he, Lee, was "allergic to dust."

After a time I had a nice thing going. I had a lovely room in a private home with space in back for my car. My car? Oh. A fella named Mike Shore had invented a campaign for a local car dealer whom he tagged, on large billboards, "Mad Man" Muntz. "He buys high and sells low." The huge cartoon on the billboards was of Muntz as Crazy Napoleon. Muntz did so well that he loaned Mike a convertible for me—with gas ration stamps! I used it to go visit Virginia. And, on one great day, to go to the Garden of Allah Villas in Hollywood to have a few with my hero from back home, Robert Benchley. He was entertaining character actor Charles Ruggles at the time. What a day!

✸✸✸✸

One more.

One of the announcers at the unit had been 'important' in Hollywood. He must have been because his girlfriend was swimming star Esther Williams. One hot day the three of us were driving along and she said she thought it would be a good idea to stop and have a beer.

It was and we did.

As we were leaving the roadside bar a fella at a small table in the back called out, "Esther! Esther Williams! Nobody will believe me!"

Esther turned and went back to the man's table. She signed her autograph for him and then—and then she pulled down the top of her dress—under which was nothing. Well, not nothing, I mean there was no clothing of any kind.

Back in the car we asked her why she had done it. "Oh," she said, "the guy said that nobody would believe him. I just wanted to help the guy out. I made sure that nobody WOULD."

When the war ended I managed to get into a real, true Army nut hospital, and from there it was a hop skip jump back to the, uh, sanity of New York City.

33

More Babble Babble

I am doing the fifteen minute thing again, only now it's on what is called the Blue Network of NBC—shortly to become ABC. A pleasant, well-spoken young blue-eyed gent stops me in the hall one evening. He works at something-or-other for the network, says he likes my show, and could he come watch me do it? His name is Schuyler Chapin (CHAY-pin) and—hold on to your seat for a forty-year leap—a while back my second wife Karen and I became the godparents of one of his grandchildren.

In between these two events Schuyler had become lots of things, one of which was General Manager of the Metropolitan Opera Company of New York. He also spent years as the advisor and friend and trustee of Leonard Bernstein. He always did like talent.

Let's leap backwards.

The network Program Director comes to me and says that there is no future in doing fifteen minutes alone: what I need is a half-hour with a cast, an orchestra, a singer—and why? Because everybody's doing it, that's why.

What did I need with all that trouble? I was making a grand-a-week again, I had no boss, no agent, no employees, no problems.

Well, ONE problem.

I'd become a husband.

The lucky girl was Isobel Gibbs, my wife #1. I'd met her at the Royalton (remember?) and we'd corresponded a bit when I was in the service. For the immortal ceremony we'd flown from L.A. to Las Vegas with two friends of hers as witnesses. As we flew over the desert the little plane suddenly banked and the pilot pointed to the ground. "That's where Carole Lombard crashed," he said. Much later I realized that he'd probably been trying to tell me something.

The peculiar thing is that I had once called Joan Smith from Santa Ana and asked her to come out and marry me. When I called back later to hedge, she'd said that if I didn't go through with it she'd join the Red Cross. I didn't, and she did. In a military hospital in Italy, she met an American soldier and later married him. That marriage turned out to be a disaster, too.

Anyway, here I am putting together a half-hour radio show. From NBC I got my orchestra leader, Bernie Green. Then I hired the nucleus of a "company"—Arnold Stang, Art Carney, Pert Kelton and Betty Garde. I wrote the first show and then scurried around to get some help. Over time the writers included Joseph Stein, Norman Barasch, and Herman Wouk. Yes. Herman Wouk.

Joe sat at my feet, and then wrote *Fiddler on the Roof.* Herman listened even more carefully and then came up with some of the finest books of our time. In *The Caine Mutiny* I was the model for Captain Queeg.

Years later Herman told me a dreadful story. It seems that some of the horrid possibilities of the time had made him fearful about the futures of his two children, and he had moved to Cuernavaca, Mexico. He and his family were there only a short time before one of the youngsters fell into the pool and drowned. "As a deeply religious man," Herman said, "I should have understood and believed the Biblical injunction—there is no hiding place." He then immediately moved back to the States.

❖❖❖❖

A potential sponsor for the radio show invited my wife and me to his home in Connecticut for the weekend. A bit later on he bought the show. I ran home to the hotel to break the wonderful news to my bride—that I was at the top of my profession.

"He bought it!" I almost yelled.

She looked up from her magazine.

Pause.

"He's a fascist," she said.

Fascist, no. Boozer, yes. The owner of the Schick Razor Company was an unhappy man. Although newly married to a pleasant, younger woman (he was in his late fifties) he'd call me at home two or three times a week to sit and drink with him in the King Cole Room of the St. Regis Hotel. He was brilliant, but something was tearing him apart and he told me he started each day with a tumbler of scotch. At the St. Regis the waiter would automatically keep filling his glass with liquor which he spaced out with gulps from a bottle of Pepto Bismol which he kept at his elbow.

The poor guy died in a year or so. One night I was invited to join announcer Ben Grauer and his wife Melanie Kahane for dinner. They'd asked me not to bring anyone as they had arranged a blind date for me. Yep, the widow.

✧✧✧✧

In time it became necessary to switch the program over to television. One day Art Carney came to see me.

"Hen, I'd like to go with you to television."

"Art," I said in a kindly way, "You're a great comic—with your *voice*, but TV uses a lot of body language, see—and well, television's not for you."

Carney has since denied this, but it's true. It's also true that I felt sorry for him, and did allow him to appear on the show.

Who says I'm not a nice guy?

✧✧✧✧

One day network management called me in to tell me that my two writers had been reported to them by the F.B.I. as Communist Party members. I said that if any Party poop showed up on the program they could fire me. I was being either noble or nitwitty because I didn't happen to notice some letters on the office wall that spelled out MENE MENE TEKEL.

✿ ✿ ✿ ✿

Blacklisting had to wait a bit. First job was to finish with *So This is New York,* a movie I starred in, based on a Ring Lardner story. Everybody was in it, including old friend Rudy Vallee who, one evening, invited me and the bride to dinner at his house, an aerie in the Hollywood Hills.

Isobel was upset by the grandeur of the place, and asked Vallee, with some bitterness, why he, a bandleader, was "entitled" to such a palace?

The evening was, of course, a bummer. The following day Rudy called to advise me that my wife was not only a "radical" but a dangerous one, to boot.

I doubted then as I do now that she was dangerous. She was light-headed, perhaps, and overestimative of her ability to handle the problems implicit in the running of a successful society. All her information came from friends whose conversation leaned sharply away from their relatively high incomes, which, apparently, they found to be embarrassing in a world that harbored poor peoples. Their chosen method of being helpful was to attend meetings at one another's homes and discuss the problems of the hungry hordes after dinner. I am not trying to be amusing—it's what they really did. A Party member was usually invited to lead the discussions.

I was apolitical. To some that meant either that I was stupid or "inner-directed"—which meant according to them that I didn't care about my fellow man.

What I really didn't care about was the four or five of her friends who later became known as the "Hollywood Ten."

My politics consisted of voting.

Eva Lerner, 18, would be aston- ished to know that someday an author will call her "Momma."

The author.

Author (standing) ignores Eva and his cute brother, Roger.

WINS MEDAL

EARLY HISTORY OF ACADEMY IS TOLD AT DINNER

The history of the Harrisburg Academy since its founding in 1784 was told last night at the annual father and son banquet at the Harrisburg Academy by A. Boyd Hamilton, representative of the sixth generation of the Hamilton family to attend the school.

The school which will celebrate its sesqui-centennial in 1934 met at first in the home of John Harris, founder of the city. In 1786 a subscription was started for the support of the school. John Harris gave the income from his ferry across the river and about eighty persons contributed 100 "old Pennsylvania pounds."

The Academy moved from the Harris homestead a site which is now Capitol Park. Later it occupied the Maclay mansion at Front and South streets before becoming established at its present site. It is hoped that it will be possible to build a new chapel facing the River drive before 1934.

E. Z. Wallower, oldest living alumnus of the school with William Pearson, and Thomas T. Wierman were honor—

Mr. Wallower, in a brief address, said that students did not graduate in the days when he attended the school. "I went to work on a newspaper, which was a college education in itself," he said.

Evans Is Toastmaster

Berne H. Evans was toastmaster. Brief greetings were given by Henry M. Gross, on behalf of the board of

—Photo By Essinger.

HENRY VON OST, JR.

Henry von Ost, member of the Greek debating team at the Harrisburg Academy which won the twenty-first annual debate with the Roman team of the school yesterday afternoon, was awarded the Edward J. Stackpole, Sr. gold medal. The Greek team, which received the Edward J. Stackpole, Sr. cup debated the affirmative side of the question, "That the Colleges of the United States Grant Scholarships For Athletic Ability," included with von Ost, John G. Palen, Raymond F. Zwiebel, and Leslie D. Hammer, alternate.

The Roman team consisted of

No plans, but . . .

ARRRGH!

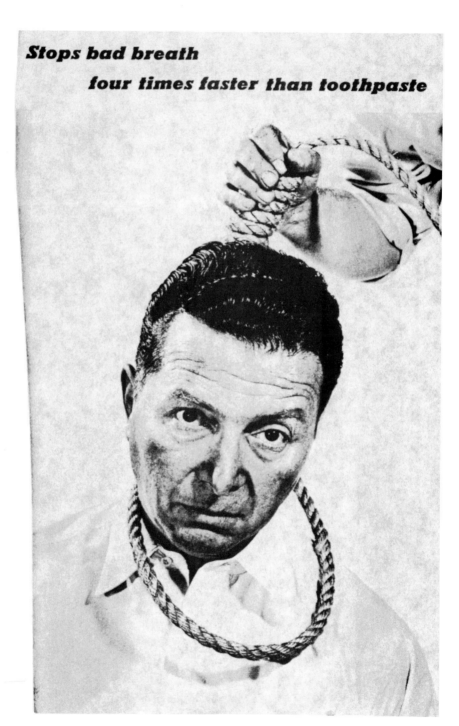

Stops bad breath
   four times faster than toothpaste

An early attempt to bite the hand that feeds him.

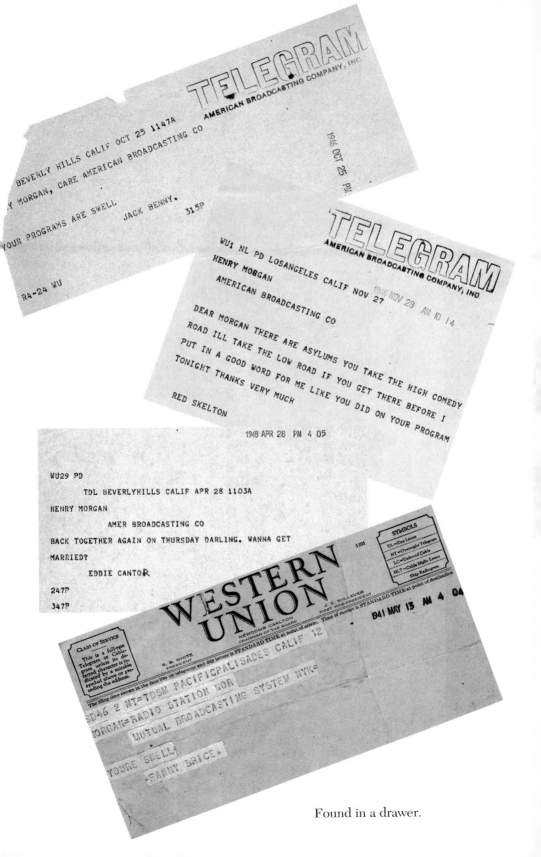

TELEGRAM
AMERICAN BROADCASTING COMPANY, INC

BEVERLY HILLS CALIF OCT 25 1147A

Y MORGAN, CARE AMERICAN BROADCASTING CO

YOUR PROGRAMS ARE SWELL   JACK BENNY.   315P

1946 OCT 25   PM

R4-24 WU

TELEGRAM
AMERICAN BROADCASTING COMPANY, INC

WU1 NL PD LOSANGELES CALIF NOV 27

HENRY MORGAN

AMERICAN BROADCASTING CO

1946 NOV 28 AM 10 14

DEAR MORGAN THERE ARE ASYLUMS YOU TAKE THE HIGH COMEDY

ROAD ILL TAKE THE LOW ROAD IF YOU GET THERE BEFORE I

PUT IN A GOOD WORD FOR ME LIKE YOU DID ON YOUR PROGRAM

TONIGHT THANKS VERY MUCH

RED SKELTON

1948 APR 28 PM 4 05

WU29 PD

    TDL BEVERLYHILLS CALIF APR 28 1103A

HENRY MORGAN

    AMER BROADCASTING CO

BACK TOGETHER AGAIN ON THURSDAY DARLING. WANNA GET

MARRIED?

    EDDIE CANTOR

247P

347P

WESTERN
UNION

NEWCOMB CARLTON
CHAIRMAN OF THE BOARD

J. C. WILLEVER
FIRST VICE-PRESIDENT

1941 MAY 13 AM 4 04

1201

SYMBOLS

DL =Day Letter

NT =Overnight Telegram

LC =Deferred Cable

NLT =Cable Night Letter

    Ship Radiogram

CLASS OF SERVICE

This is a full-rate
Telegram or Cable-
gram unless its de-
ferred character is in-
dicated by a suitable
symbol above or pre-
ceding the address.

R. B. WHITE
PRESIDENT

The filing time shown in the date line on telegrams and day letters is STANDARD TIME at point of origin. Time of receipt is STANDARD TIME at point of destination

SD46 2 NT=TDSM PACIFICPALISADES CALIF 12

MORGAN=RADIO STATION WOR

    MUTUAL BROADCASTING SYSTEM NYK=

YOURE SWELL

=FANNY BRICE.

Found in a drawer.

Movie: *So This is New York*. In 1993, *The New York Times*' ace
critic Vincent Canby told me, in Sardi's, that he had liked it. He
had kept this secret for forty years.

Eleanor R. The greatest woman of my time.

Karen S. Morgan. The greatest woman of . . . well, it's a tough call.
(Not really, darling.)

Politics with a capital 'P' seemed to me to be the province of people who like that sort of thing. These days, however, I feel that Politics is closely intertwined with everything else that constitutes a personality, and I cut my cloth accordingly.

Lionel Trilling once wrote that he believed that the reason for so many intellectuals having become Party members in the Thirties and Forties was that they envisioned a world run by "reason and virtue." Those I met in Hollywood were not intellectuals and *they'd* become members out of a peculiar mixture of social awareness and guilt.

For my part, in those days I didn't know:

A) What "fascist" meant.

B) Which side Franco was on.

C) What socialism was.

If I thought about Communism at all I imagined it was probably a step up for peasants who, I'd been told, lived in mud huts before the Revolution, but now enjoyed nine square meters of concrete for every three families.

I had always known that Herbert Hoover had single-handedly ruined the United States of America, but I didn't know how he'd managed to do it.

I knew that the country had recovered under Roosevelt, but I assumed it would have anyway under Don Ameche, Mrs. Lindbergh or Fats Waller.

That's what I mean by 'apolitical.'

So This is New York finally ground to a halt and we all returned to New York. My bride joined a Monday night "class" and also found a new psychoanalyst. A woman named Stella Chess.

Lest it be thought that the bride and I spatted like foolish urchins caught up in the besotted fumblings of young love— that we were tender simpletons who groped and tottered and soughed in the twirlings of young love: Not so.

Item: The new Mrs. had moved in with me to my two enormous rooms in a solid old hotel. The bedroom had a small terrace overlooking Central Park.

I came 'home' one evening and the desk clerk handed me the

159

key to a 'newer' suite. The madam had decided, without any consultation, without hint nor clue, to move. In the middle of the afternoon she had chosen a SMALLER, redecorated two-room, low-ceilinged arrangement that faced a building across the street. I still remember the stiffness of the fake-leather, yellow couch. Inside me, I raged.

Item: When we moved into an east side upper duplex which I had found, we had two bedrooms upstairs, one of which I had thought to make into an office for me and my writers. I came home one evening to find that she had managed to paper our bedroom in pink with an overlay of white 'lace.' When I had the temerity to suggest that I slept in that room, too, she announced that it was *her* room. I was free to decorate "your office" any way I chose. It may be of interest to note that she flatly refused to do anything to clean the all-but-unfurnished apartment. "I," she announced, "am not a maid."

The bathrooms were cleaned by me. The maid.

Item: Without notice, Mrs. Decorator sent out my dear old solid mahogany Governor Winthrop desk to be scraped and refinished in "blonde" and the pigeonholes painted GREEN. The legs had been removed and it sat with its poor bottom flat on the floor. It was ashamed to look at me.

Item: One day when I was out trying to keep off the dole, she sent out a mahogany chest of drawers, which had been made by my paternal grandfather in 1884, to be scraped down and refinished in the same terrifying style as the desk. By means of terrible threats I found out where it had been taken and managed to rescue it just as the craftsman started to sand down its top. I have it to this day, its poor lacerated scalp disguised by a wig of brownish marble.

Item: When I was making *So This Is New York* we lived at the Beverly Hills Hotel in a rather expensive suite. I came home from work one evening and the desk clerk handed me the key—to a whole bungalow! Miss America had decided, without consulting even her analyst, that she needed a grander place in which to entertain her LA-based family.

Item: I discovered that she had never learned to cook.

Item: (God, this is tiresome)—back in New York, immediately after my radio show was sold, she announced that she needed a fur coat. I explained that we had no money yet and brought in my accountant to show her the books. Would she mind starting off with something of wool? The Big Star's wife went out and found a little number in beaver that cost one thousand five hundred dollars. In 1946!

Item: (Puff puff)—in L. A. she had bought a 'picture' hat. In a fatuous attempt to be an understanding husband I said she looked nice in it. She promptly went back to the joyful dealer and bought ELEVEN more.

34

Is Icumen In

This is a bit out of order, time-wise, but if you can stand it I can.

One day in the late Forties an agent called out of nowhere and asked if I was interested in doing summer stock. Someone had offered me a job at the Westport County Playhouse in Connecticut to star in *The Man Who Came to Dinner.* I had just finished *So This is New York*, and since it was the end of June the radio show was over for the season.

We showed up in Westport for rehearsals. "We," because Mrs. Morgan had announced that *she* would play the part of "the girl." I hadn't known that she was an actress, and, as things worked out, she wasn't. I believe, from the manner in which she read her lines to "the boy" that she thought he was her analyst.

Still, for the week, we sold out all but two seats. The only person ever to sell more at that theater was Tallulah Bankhead.

Which says a great deal about the power of radio in them days. At any rate, the agent now thought it would be a good idea for me to go into summer theater for real.

I did it for most of fifteen summers.

Loved it.

Evidently.

"Theater" is a euphemism for "barn"—which is what most of the playhouses had been.

In the winter, barn managers would get together in New York and lay out their schedules. Various plays, mostly slightly-used Broadway comedies, went into rehearsal during the last week of June.

Cast and director would meet in disgraceful old "studios" in odd corners of the city. They were hot and filthy, and no matter where they were a band with five drummers rehearsed next door, while tap-dancers worked overhead.

A stage is outlined in chalk, two kitchen chairs are set up for furniture, and we are ready.

First, everybody sits in a circle and reads the thing aloud. It is dreadful.

The director and his assistants have a whispered meeting in a corner. It is about the Baghavad Gita and Woodrow Wilson's Fourteen Points, and takes twenty minutes.

During the conclave, most of the cast scratches and yawns while some of the rougher members attempt to start a conversation with the Big Radio Star. Finally the director calls "Places please for Act One."

We have one week in which to learn what the original cast learned in six. Opening night is, after all, July first.

I did summer theater on-and-off for fifteen years. The last play was *The Odd Couple*, in which my opposing actor was a man named Jesse White. You know Jesse White. From TV. He's the man who doesn't fix the Maytag washer.

I taught him everything he knows.

* * * *

Things happened out in the woods.

We were doing a week in Ellitch's Gardens, a dreamy old place in Denver. (I *know* that Denver isn't in New England. Can't you sit still for a minute?)

Suzanne was the girl in the company and asked me if I'd like to go see her uncle's bell collection. Of course not—but, on second thought, what *does* one do in Denver?

He lived thirty miles out in the mountains. The little old son-of-a-gun had three thousand (3,000) goddam bells, too. One that I wanted to steal was a seamless iron globe the size of a baseball. When you jiggled it, a pretty bell rang inside. It had belonged to Houdini.

When we left we promptly got lost on a string of narrow roads. Close to nowhere, suddenly we came across a house with an old, flaking restaurant sign on it and went inside.

Eerie.

We sat for twenty minutes in the empty dining room and at last an elderly slattern flapped in.

"We're starving . . . but just bacon and eggs and coffee, please."

Forty minutes later she served ruined bacon and eggs and truly abominable coffee.

We ate what we could and called her.

"How much do I owe you?"

"Oh, nuthin."

"I, uh, don't understand. I mean, this is a restaurant . . ."

"Oh, no. Hasn't been a restaurant for thirty years. This is just my house."

The old darling couldn't let a couple of nice kids starve.

✴✴✴✴

There was a fat man in vaudeville named Herb Williams whose act was a talk on the glory of bells. He loved them. Every time an offstage bell rang, he would kneel laboriously and recite part of Poe's *The Bells.*

It became harder and harder for him to kneel, and it took longer and longer each time. The highlight of the act came when the offstage bell clanged yet again.

The old guy heaved and puffed. He backed, he filled, he sweated. He reached around pitiably for the floor. He cried. He and the audience both knew he'd never make it.

The bell rang one more time.

He shook his head, slowly and sadly.

"Oh," he moaned. "Oh them goddam bells."

✴✴✴✴

165

This one is for actors. One summer I went out in *Seven Year Itch*, a funny play with a large cast, and each theater owner hired his own people. In nine weeks I played with nine directors, nine Girl-Upstairses, nine wives, nine of everything.

Thank you, fellow Equity members. Only you will understand.

It is said that someone once asked John Barrymore if, in his opinion, Romeo had slept with Juliet?

"All I know," he said, "is that in *my* company he *always* did."

In my companies, sometimes. But not during those nine weeks!

The managers treated the actors very well. One Sunday we arrived in Fitchburg, Mass. and Guy Palmerton, the owner-manager, came out on the lawn to assign living quarters.

In two minutes my leading lady came hurtling across the grass.

"Listen. My God, I can't live in a place like that!"

Palmerton clapped his hands and his stage manager came running.

"Get Miss Dowd whatever she wants. Change the rugs, change the draperies, change the furniture. Whatever she wants."

We were left alone.

"Those bitches," he said, "Aren't they too marvelous? All winter they live like rats in some Greenwich Village holes. The minute they get a summer job, dear Christ, they have to live like Shebas."

One summer we played an odd place called "L'Hommedieux's" half-way between Buffalo and Toronto. It was part restaurant, part playhouse, part resort, part dog. It has since, glory be, burned down. But we were a couple of years too soon.

We were doing a dreadly beast called *The Remarkable Mr. Pennypacker*. Twice-a-week I would ask the juvenile why he always froze on stage when, as his father, I bawled him out?

"Well," he said, "I'm not an actor, I'm a playwright. And anyway, when you bawl me out I have the feeling that you mean it."

166

A nice tribute. One day the guy's girlfriend showed up and re-directed him. It was unbelievable, impossible—but he was even worse than before.

"May I meet your girlfriend, this lady you tell me knows all about the theater?"

Holy cats! The girl had been my ingenue two years before! She was the worst would-be actress in the entire history of the theater, all the way back to the Greeks. She and I had been in some comedy or other when, one night, trying to put some humor in the piece, I elaborated on the family business of trying to put a bracelet on her wrist. It got a laugh.

"You know," she said, ONSTAGE, OUT LOUD, "that's a funny piece of business."

And now SHE was straightening out my juvenile.

One fine day they married. Time went by, and it turned out that SHE was the writer. One of her books, about a woman photographer, became a best-seller.

One year summer stock producer John Kennely called me to play Sakini, the oriental translator in *Teahouse of the August Moon*.

By nature I'm not much of an oriental, so I got the bright idea of asking Hal Holbrook to introduce me to David Wayne, who had 'created' the part. Hal was working with David at the Circle in The Square Theater in Greenwich Village. We walked into the dressing room and Hal made the introductions.

David never bothered to turn around. He faced his mirror and looked at our reflections. He seemed impassive. Well, snotty, really.

"What did you want to talk to me about?"

I felt like kicking him in the nose. I fought the impulse and won. By a nose. I took another breath.

"Well, it may sound odd, but I've been asked to play Sakini for a couple of weeks. I thought the producer was crazy but Bobby Lewis [director of the original company] once asked me to go on the road with it, so I thought I might get away with it. I saw you in the original and you were marvelous—but I can't

167

seem to remember how much of a dialect you used, or if you used any at all."

David turned slightly from the mirror to make a face at a friend of his. Then through the mirror he looked back at me.

"Well," he said coldly, "you can hardly expect me to tell you in five minutes what I've learned in twenty-five years in the theatre."

Hal and I mumbled our way out of the room. Out on the avenue Hal shook his head sadly.

"Funny," he said. "The other night as I left David's dressing room Jason Robards was coming along the hall, and he said, 'What were you doing in that mean old man's dressing room?' and I, well, I just didn't understand it then. Now I guess I do."

Hold for a year or two so that I can get to another major disappointment; the failure of the John Kennely production of *Teahouse of the August Moon.* This carefully thought out and expensively mounted production flopped because of a dismal oaf, one Ty Hardin. Kennely had hired me because he thought I could sell tickets. He also hired Ty because he'd seen him once in a movie. On a horse.

❖❖❖❖

One foggy night in London Joanna (of whom more later) exclaimed, "There's Cliff Robertson across the street!" No sense in arguing with her. Jo could see a celebrity through two feet of lead. We crossed over.

"Whatcha been doing?" says Cliff.

I told him I'd just closed in *Teahouse* with Ty Hardin, and it had been a mess.

"Hardin! C'mon, here's a pub. C'mon in, I'll tell you about *that one.*"

We closed that pub and I never got to tell my story. Cliff had been on a picture with the cowboy and the memories he had are not fit to print. (Libel laws, you know?)

Actually, I was able to slide *one* in. There is a scene in the play in which an old man tells the lieutenant (Hardin) why there is desperate need for a teahouse in the area. It has to do with the

168

fact that the old gentleman wants to be sure of going to heaven, and it's quite touching.

When we came to that scene on the third night of opening week, as the man started the explanation, Hardin walked away from him and sat down!

I had to be careful of him—he had co-star billing. I asked him why he'd done it.

"Whaaee? Whaaee? [Disdainfully] Because I'd heerd it all befoa, thas whaae."

The theatre manager took him on and lost. Like many of his kind, he couldn't be insulted, instructed, reasoned with—nothing. Cowboy to the end, his head was full of manure.

It should be said that the producer had put everything possible into this production including a, for the most part, Japanese cast. Everything was done as it had been in the original including the Jeep on stage, the live goat, etc. etc.

It was awful having to play in this with a man who ruined, not only the play, but also my income. I worked on percentage, you see, and after Hardin's opening night reviews (mine were just fine) nobody came.

As of this writing, the horseman lives somewhere in the South and is a leading Fundamentalist activist. If someone happens to read to him from this account, and he feels he should take some sort of action, I shall be happy to read to him the reviews he received. They are in a vault.

35

Simone

We were playing at the Cocoanut Grove Theater in Coral Gables, Florida and I roomed in the 'Winchell Suite' at the Roney Plaza Hotel in Miami Beach. (It was run then by the parents of David Schine, the rotten kid who became the partner of that other rotten kid, Roy Cohn. They worked for that additional rotten kid, the junior Senator from Wisconsin, Joe McCarthy.) Mother Schine was the only woman I ever heard of whose given name was Iphegenia.

Neal Lang, the manager of the Roney, invited me to a cocktail party—they had them in them days—and I became entranced by a pretty girl who dragged a silver fox fur along the floor wherever she walked. Her name was Simone de Greve. She spoke in a low, almost throaty voice in an English accent tinged with the barest suggestion of French. She had soft, curly dark hair and she was built like the girl on the cover of the *Sports Illustrated,* swimsuit edition.

We shall see more of her.

I certainly did.

Neal Lang was ambitious and I was to meet him again when he managed the Edgewater Beach Hotel in Chicago, where we became friends, and that job had led him to the Roosevelt Hotel in New York.

Let's change tenses. Neal is general manager of the Roosevelt and with his wife Suivy (Neal calls her that because he thinks it's French for 'follow me' and he's darn near right) is living it up.

The Roosevelt, New Year's Eve! Guy Lombardo! Geraldine, a beauty from Troy, New York, is my date. She is a tall, slightly plump, dark-haired, blue-eyed Irish-type—the type they put on travel brochures. A gorgeous smile, a fine sense of humor. Her father back in Troy is an undertaker. And, I was to discover, a fine, jolly one at that.

There is another, older couple when we slither into the Langs' elegant suite, and they will be with us for the evening.

We have a number of drinks.

The other couple loosens. He is an industrialist.

We drink to that. We are to have dinner in the ballroom at midnight, and we drink to that, too.

The six of us lurch down to dinner.

Since Neal is the General Manager, why, naturally his table is occupied by strangers. It take the maitre d' half-an-hour to get them to move—while we all have a couple at the bar.

We celebrate getting to our rightful places with a round or two and, since it took forever to get served, we managed to kill the time in a way you're probably tired of reading about.

The industrialist is so drunk that he likes me a lot. He suddenly says, "You know what my company needs on its Board? You. We could pay you only twenty-five thousand to start, but you have to come to just four or five meetings a year."

I was happy as hell. Here was a man of wisdom who saw through the shallow entertainer and discerned the fine brain hiding inside.

I accepted.

We had a drink on it.

By now I was thoroughly soused. Dripping. Booze ran out of my fingertips. I realized that though the strange man across the table was my benefactor, he wasn't terribly interesting. I turned to the strange lady next to me and, in a low voice, a whisper, I thought, asked "who is that bore over there?"

"My husband."

With admirable logic I figured it was time to leave. I made a phone call, sent Geraldine home in the rented limo, the car came back and, at three ayem I picked up *Dorothy* at her house and we went to an after-hours place I knew.

I ran into Dorothy on the street about thirty years later.

"Happy New Year," I said.

She still looked great.

"Happy New Year," she said.

After some calm consideration it seems to me that I was, in some ways, a sonofabitch.

Now, where was Simone during all this? Well, my lawyer had told me that she must move out because Isobel would use her to make more trouble. More than what I couldn't imagine, but, ignoring the fact that I believed my lawyer to be an imbecile, I put Simone in a nice hotel.

Later I made everything up to her by taking her to Cuba. I've said that we were playing at Coral Gables. I haven't said that my 'juvenile' was Alan Alda.

The bad thing about Alan Alda is that there is no bad thing about Alan Alda. I spent a good part of every day for an entire summer with him. Do you know, in his spare time he would take the cast into any available space—under a tree, perhaps, and they'd spend hours doing improvisations, learning more of their trade. I know, I know, there must be *something* wrong with the guy—it's just that I never found what it was. Too bad. It's so much more fun to write about stinkers.

Oh, the play was *King of Hearts*, and I was quite bad in it. In the fall of that year a lady sitting next to me in Sardi's turned and said, "You were out in *King of Hearts* this summer. What did you think of it?"

I explained that I couldn't manage to play a charmer, which was indicated, because the guy's lines made him out a bastard.

The lady sighed and said, "You know, everybody who's played it says the same thing. Oh, my name is Jean Kerr. I wrote it."

The leading lady in this section is still Simone. I'll fill you in a bit more.

She had been married to a Dutchman, one de Greve, and had come to Miami Beach, gotten a job, and paid for her own divorce.

Paid for her own divorce! Who would not be mad for a woman like that!

And three days after I was back in New York I received from her a package of the dirty laundry I'd left in my Roney closet.

Simone had cemented the contract.

I sent for her and installed her in the duplex as my secretary. (She actually *was*, among other things, a secretary.)

Her background was the usual. Her father had been an American fight-promoter; she'd gone to Catholic school in Amsterdam where an uncle was curator of the Reichsmuseum; spent a year as a governess to the children of the ruler of Sumatra (she showed me a diamond watch with his face painted on it—a small thank you) and had married de Greve in a fit of pique. De Greve was a mineralologist by trade—so it must have been a fit of *something*.

Before the question arises in your mind—why didn't we get married? the answer is quite simple: Isobel and I had a legal separation, but she refused to get a divorce. It may seem odd to you but at that time a respectable man never sued; it was thought to be indecent. I was respectably employed in radio, and it just couldn't be done. Isobel flatly refused to sue *me* for some six years . . . and at that, I had to sign away my life to get shed of her. Which, of course, I was never really to be. The only real guffaw I've ever had because of this woman was occasioned by the fact that when, because of her, I was blacklisted and therefore without a job, she sued me for back alimony!

See what I mean by *practicing* the avoidance of depression?

When, a few years later, Simone finally met and married Mr. Right, it was to an American diplomat named, so help me God, Miles Standish.

Meanwhile, I said, I took her to Cuba. This was before

Castro, at a time when the place was run by a dear friend of the United States, one Fulgencio Batista, a thieving dictator.

We stayed at the Kawama Club at Veradero Beach—it was a small, fantasy-kind of place many miles from Havana.

I say 'fantasy' because, when one of the waiters took us to the house where he lived, we saw enough poverty—dirty, rotten, killing poverty—to make it clear to me, later on, why Castro had such an easy time taking over.

It wasn't just the waiter's home, which wasn't all that bad. I mean, they had an electrical refrigerator. It didn't work (the Kawama Club had thrown it out). It was on the front porch. The house had no electricity, anyway. The fridge was there as a showpiece much as you might leave your Rolls-Royce in the driveway.

There was a yard out back where Dad (the entire family 'lived' in this wretched place) kept old used tires, broken boxes, exhausted dogs, shards of glass and his collection of crushed weeds.

The neighbors had nothing at all.

A day or so before we were to leave, a fellow at NBC managed to find me by phone. He had what he thought was an urgent message.

"You've got to come back right away! Somebody just published a book called *Red Channels*, and you're in it! Ben [Grauer, my announcer] is in it, too!"

"So? What about it?"

"Well, it's a list of Communists!"

"Who cares? I'm no Communist. Everybody knows that."

I said goodbye to him and forgot about it.

You know something? Well, of course you do, but I didn't. I didn't know that in addition to being a son-of-a-bitch I also had an excellent claim to being a horse's ass.

(Fade to black)

* * * * *

(Fade back in on Bank Account)

I had about eight or nine thousand dollars. I was off the air temporarily (I thought). Simone and I had a talk. It probably is

175

more exact to say that I gave a talk. I explained that, though she, Simone, had lived in the Netherlands, England, France and Sumatra, I'd spent three days in Quebec.

It brought tears to her eyes.

Therefore, I said, it was only right that she mind the house while I went to Europe.

She threw her arms around my neck in gratitude.

Now, when I'd worked in Boston I'd become friends with Frank Crennan, one of the radio engineers. We'd kept in touch even during the years when, as a tech-rep for Philco, he'd been stationed in a lot of Europe and the Far East. Also, since he was one of the few people who could install and operate radar systems, during WWII he'd been on duty in both the Navy and the Air Force . . . on loan, sort of, from Philco.

I thought Frank would be a great guide so I sent him a wire inviting him to come along at his own expense. After all, *I* was buying the car. Yep, I arranged for a cute little British number, a Hillman-Minx, to be delivered to Paris. It looked like a miniature Rolls-Royce town car.

A nice young man at the American Automobile Association laid out a trip from Paris through France, Monaco, Spain, Italy and Switzerland and back to Paris. I wasn't a member of the AAA but he gave me what amounted to a small book which had every kilometer of the journey marked, and he made all the hotel reservations; Frank arrived in Manhattan. I kissed Simone goodbye, and off we flew, Air France.

Propeller plane, ladies and gents. Propeller.

Please, not to worry. I'm not going to take you foot-by-foot over the ten weeks that followed, but I must tell you about the plane's first stop, Gander, Newfoundland.

As we started our descent into a tight, blind fog, I noticed that Frank was sweating. His hands were really white-knuckled.

"C'mon," I asked, "what are you so nervous about? They have GCA [Ground Control Approach—a new radar gimmick] here."

"Yeah, I know. I know they have it. I . . . I installed it."

176

Finally, Paris! I stepped off the plane, looked around the airport and saw, gee whiz! a big bunch of bombers, the American flag painted on them bigger than all hell and gone, big and shiny and beautiful.

I cried.

If that has never happened to you I guess, now, it never will. And then, Paris itself.

Each generation thinks that it had the best of times and that 'today' is a crock. Well, we really *had* hit it just right, and it will never again be the way it was. For a very simple reason. In 1950, Frank and I had Paris practically to ourselves. There were only a handful of Americans, a couple of Englishmen and a few French people from out-of-town.

I've been back many times, but have finally given up. For one thing, when you're fairly young and unencumbered, there's a romance waiting behind every tree . . . Also, as time went on, Paris (and the rest of Europe—and even, as we found out last year—even Acapulco and Leningrad) is bursting with South Americans, North Americans, Germans—you name them, there they are. Especially Germans.)

But we had Paris all to ourselves. We had it all. What a marvelous idea to ask Frank along. He was and still is what I call a "professional tourist", and *he* taught *me*.

Small hint. When you hear of something that is "only for tourists," be sure to go there. If I hadn't learned that right off I wouldn't have seen the Folies Bergere, Montmartre by day and Montmartre by night (from the rickety and therefore forbidden) roof of the oldest moulin in town, courtesy of Frank's old pal Robert. (He had fifty old pals named Robert, thank goodness), I wouldn't have had my necktie cut off by a fascinating woman who owned a joint on the Left Bank, etc. etc.

Probably wouldn't have had lunch with the manager (Robert?) of the Eiffel Tower in the my-God-what-a-view restaurant there, either.

One night in the lobby of the Georges Cinque I ran into Eddie Cantor and his pleasant wife, Ida. He asked where I'd been all day.

"Oh, I dunno. I went to the flea market, took a trip on the

177

river, had lunch in a wine cellar and dinner at the 'Table du Roi,' seen the nekkid ladies at a place called 'Eve'—and now I'm going to snap at a brandy."

Eddie looked at Ida sadly.

"How many times have we been here?"

"Oh, six or seven."

He turned to me.

"And you know what we've seen? Three restaurants and this hotel."

Of course. He never had Frank with him.

Once, around midnight, on our way to Les Halles, we stopped off in the garden of the Palais Royale. A nightingale sang.

Yes, I kept a diary on the trip. *A nightingale sang*.

We went to Les Halles every morning at about three. That's where the farmers came in with the fresh produce and piled it into pyramids and rectangles and diamonds and flowers. Then the buyers would arrive from the restaurants and hotels. They would sniff and heft, thump and pinch and then argue prices.

By six ayem the top quality stuff was gone. The secret of French cooking was right there . . . all the elements had been in the ground the day before. Or in the sea, or on the trees. The market itself swirled and yawped, buyers and sellers haggled and threatened, the carts and trucks backed, filled and honked and it was bedlam on top of bedlam and it was grand.

And every morning we finished our tour of the wonderful bars of Les Halles at Le Chien Qui Fume. A small, wild restaurant, it catered to the market workers. The thirty-cent bowl of onion soup, like none other on earth, the cheese ribboning down our chins, the . . . ah, forget it. Les Halles, one of the most remarkable, the most enjoyable venues in the world, was torn down by de Gaulle. He was a fine man who shaped history for the better, but in this one case, the hell with him.

I promised not to go over the territory foot-by-foot and I won't, but may I offer you a few notes I kept?

At a gas station:

H.M. "Parlez vous Anglais?"

Man: "A few."

I am looking at an impressive building that seems to be fairly new. I point to it and ask a Frenchman what it is named?

"Marshall Plan," he says.

Professional party giver Elsa Maxwell, an old friend, introduces me to the Duke and Duchess of Windsor. She tells them she knows my mother.

They are not amused.

****

Frank took me on his special trip through the Louvre. Like the back of his hand. Venus de Milo, Winged Victory, the Mona Lisa.

Twenty five minutes. Nothing to it.

More notes:

A sign in French at the entrance to the great cathedral at Chartres.

> *NO SHORTS. NO DÉCOLLETE.*
> *THIS IS A CHURCH, NOT A MUSEUM.*

We ad-libbed a left-turn in Vouvray and, by Georges, a vineyard appeared and the old guy took us through the wine caves. They were four hundred years old, carved out of soft stone. We passed a workman who methodically grasped the bottles, two-at-a-time and gave them each a quarter-turn. That's all he did, and the owner said that for the past thirty-one years. That was all he *ever* did.

Spain

Little houses like cell blocks, all bearing big painted dictator Franco slogans.

The fields are worked by old women wearing black.

Burgos.

Noisy as a city in China.

In the countryside, the male farmers do nothing but sit and drink wine. All day, all night, Maria. Two weeks after a farmer dies he turns into brandy. They bury them in casks.

Madrid.

Broad boulevards but Washington is much, much finer.

El Escorial, thirty miles out of town. Sensational! We are taken down a completely marble stairwell to see the tombs of the kings of Spain and all their relatives. A mile of white marble sarcophagi with the figures of the folks inside carved in white marble on the lids. One room houses the caskets of infants, all piled up like a white wedding cake.

In an octagonal room of brown marble are the caskets of the kings. No queens allowed! Most of the people buried here are relatives of the Hapsburgs.

Dinner at Boltin's, where, according to *Temple Fielding's Guide,* the knowledgeable order the house specialty which is the best roast pig in all of Spain.

It is nauseating.

They are struck dumb when we both switch to salad.

❊❊❊❊

Holy Madrid is blanketed in whores.

A fella named Carlo takes us to a house at night where naked girls are offered to us to do "Living History." It will cost us fifty cents a girl so we hire all twelve. In a hot, airless room smelling of sweat and cheap cologne, the Madam acts as 'narrator.' The three of us men are huddled in a corner, dying of the heat, the booze, the stench. The Narrator calls out, "Washington Crossing the Delaware!" The girls fall over one another to create a tableau, one posing heroically with an American flag.

We leave fifty cents more for each girl and rush down the stairs.

On another night we go to a place called "El Gitana." Girls do "Spanish dancing" for ten minutes and then walk out with the male customers. Holy Spain! Holy Franco!

Barcelona.

The way to get a maid at the Ritz is to take off your clothes. Two different maids will take turns opening the unlockable door.

Or, you can push the button marked MAID which is next to the bed. A man in a frock coat arrives and after you explain that you want the maid, he bows and leaves, and apparently quits his job. Nobody shows up. Ever.

In every Spanish hotel we've been in, the maids arrive every twenty minutes to count the rooms. They're followed by strange men who count the maids.

✦✦✦✦

More notes:

If a Spanish tart looks at you you get syphilis.

Conversation between Frank and a waiter in a restaurant . . .

Frank: Tortillas?

Waiter: Cerveza?

Frank: Tortillas?

Waiter: What?

Frank: Tortillas.

Waiter: Tortillas?

Frank: Yes.

Waiter: What?

✦✦✦✦

If you ask a Spanish doctor what's the matter, he'll tell you it's something you ate. He's right.

Barcelona looks very attractive from the roof of the Ritz, but up close it's not much at all. And we really did despise miles of the journey through poor, hot, hot countryside. To put it

181

another way, when we finally crossed the border back into France, we both got out of the car and kissed the ground.

❖❖❖

Some French notes:

The woman at the hotel desk in Avignon asked me if I wanted a room "with douche." I blushed 'no.'

So it had a tub but no shower.

Nice.

At the Carleton a man comes up to me and says he was a bouncer at the Copacabana night club in New York, but now he gives messages.

At six I get a call from Mitch Basker, who is a friend of my Uncle Mike and who handles the Astor estate in New York. The masseur told him I was here. He's having dinner with TV host and columnist Ed Sullivan, but I'm worn out.

A truly beautiful French gal picks me up and I tell Mitch about it. He asks if she has a dog, and I tell him yes. He says, "Henry, very soon after you meet a French girl with a dog, you'll find out that she's hungry, the dog is hungry, and she has an old uncle who isn't doing too good either."

Mitch was wrong this time. It wasn't her uncle, it was her Grandma. But they cost about the same.

36

(From my diary)

Went to Eden Roc in Nice to play a little gin and saw a really gorgeous young girl. She was seventeen or eighteen, and I was told that she's an up-and-coming movie star named Elizabeth Taylor. So absolutely, delicately stunning that I wouldn't want to so much as touch her.

She's on a wedding trip with Nicky Hilton, and I don't think he's much interested. He was playing gin and she wandered off to the jewelry shop on the premises. Soon she came back with a ring on her finger and held it out to him.

"Nicky, what do you think?"

He gave a quick glance and turned back to his cards.

"If you like it, buy it," he snapped.

She's such a nice little girl that I felt sorry for her. I don't give that marriage too long.

✿✿✿✿

Went back to Eden Roc the following day and took a bunch of francs from Ed Sullivan and Nat Pendleton. It's the only place on earth that caters to gin players who are worse than I am.

The terrace of the Carleton at Goofy Hour is a madhouse. The place is loaded with gorgeous hookers and their tiny escorts. There are Arabs in full burnoose who keep their

183

Rolls-Royces sitting just beyond the railing with the motors running! And they drink, these guys. A lot.

Amid the Arabs, Brazilians, Greeks, Italians and folks from Minneapolis, there are a few Frenchmen.

I meet an "André de la Roche" and his, ah, ward? They ask me to go water-skiing the next day and I do. She is, she says, a research biologist from Oran, Algiers, where her brother owns a clinic. André is noncommital.

(Marie Andrée will turn up again, you bet.)

The next day, as a matter of fact. La Roche phones and says he has to return to Paris, will I keep an eye on Marie Andrée? This is a puzzler. When a man leaves this area, he often turns over his girl to the next guy to feed and house. Is that what de la Roche means?

Nope. He says the girl likes me and has her own money.

Well, later on it turns out that there's more to it than that. A lot more. She wants to go to the States to attend Purdue, she tells me. Would I consider a marriage of convenience? We're sitting in the stern of a motorboat: she doesn't know me or what I do for a living or if I'm on the lam, and she wants me to marry her so she can go to Purdue? I was too startled even to be dumbfounded.

I find what's left of my tongue. I am obliged to her for asking, but I can't, I explain. I'm waiting for my divorce.

The following day I figure, what the hell. Frank isn't going any further with me, so I put Marie Andrée in the car and we set out to finish my trip.

Am I going too fast in through here?

A word or two about this girl. She wasn't beautiful but had a vibrant quality and a bright awareness that, combined with a sharp humor, made her very attractive. She hadn't been de la Roche's girl either, and she announced firmly that she would pay her share for the trip. (I didn't let her, of course.)

(I put that in to show that, no matter what I say, I'm really a helluva guy).

It is interesting to note at this point that she auditions for marriage anyway at the Villa Medici Hassler Hotel in Rome.

184

And I regret being married more than ever.

On the way to the Eternal City, Marie Andrée had suggested that we visit Portofino.

Let's leave the 'notes' for a moment so that I can tell you something. Portofino is one of the visual delights of the world. I've been back six times, most recently with my wife Karen in 1985, and the views from the Splendido Hotel are still a green-and-blue enchantment. The only thing that had changed was the hotel—and for the better, at that.

One clue to Portofino's charm is that a local law forbids anyone to build a house that can be seen from the harbor.

The last one to be built—and only one-story high at that—was erected on the irremovable remains of a concrete gun emplacement that had been built by the Germans during WWII. The town agreed that a small house was better than the ugly ruins.

✿✿✿✿

More notes:

My room at the Hassler has a terrace overlooking the city of Rome. They have Camel Cigarettes and Pabst Beer, it's cool at night and I am going to stay forever. I had driven to the Hassler garage early in the morning and asked the attendant if he spoke English?

"Momento," he said.

He returned with another fella. I asked him the same question. Sure he spoke English. What he said, with a bow, was "Gooda night."

I think I like Italians.

(Present day note: I *love* Italians. Oh, don't jump down my throat—you know what I mean.)

One night we go to the open-air opera at the Termi di Caracalla which is, or are, the sketchy remains of an old Roman bath house. The craggy walls create a sensational backdrop for the stage, and the opera that night is *Aida*. Boy, do they know what to do with that setting! *Including* elephants.

185

But the singing is third rate. After the performance I ask an Italian gentleman why this is so? He laughs.

"If they sing good, they go to New York!"

Capisce?

The next day we go to see the catacombs where, outside the entrance there are benches with signs reading ENGLISH, FRENCH, and so forth and you pick the language of your choice, sit down and wait for a guide. And guess who is sitting at English?

Nicky and Elizabeth.

The marriage has lasted longer than I thought.

We are perhaps a dozen people when our guide, an Irish priest, comes and signals us to rise and follow him, which we do.

At the foot of the steps we stop for a bit and look about. Bones, man, lots of bones in crypts. It's not a holy place, but everybody is solemn and thoughtful. It's an ill-lit tunnel and we are dead quiet.

Then our guide starts his spiel.

"Laydeez on ginlemun," he says, in a high-pitched voice loaded with shamrocks, "on yer royt yiz'll nawtice . . ."

The contrast between them dry bones in that dark and dismal tunnel and the squeaky voice of Dublin does us in. Nicky Hilton starts it, then I join him. We fight it, biting our lips and heaving, but at last we break up. It's hilarious! I mean, HILARIOUS.

Liz is all prim and noble and hissing at us. Marie Andrée, whose English isn't that good, hasn't a clue. The guide, though, *has,* and we get thumbed right back up the staircase.

Days later we go to Capri and have a lovely time, then back to Naples and head north, stopping on the way to have a look at Siena.

Siena:

Marie Andrée and I are standing on the rim of a kind of bowl that holds the lovely old Town Hall. A bit of dialogue, friends.

ME: Look at those paving stones, they seem to match the old buildings, and they're such a lovely color. Odd color. What color is that?

SHE: Siena.

ME: (blushing) Ah ha.

Look, folks, I'll give us both a break and leave out the rest of that trip. We DID Italy, and I can write ten pages just on Venice, but you've either been there or, if you haven't been, take my advice and never go. I've been back (1986) and it's a dreadful hassle. Too many tourists. It's so awful that the Venetians make the busses stop way the hell away from the city. And it's getting to be truly tacky. Or am I just a senior elitist?

So then it was back to Paris and a goodbye to Marie Andrée. I was to see her again, though.

Paid another visit to London. London afforded just one brief anecdote. Walking along a street one day I noticed a sign reading "The Cheshire Cheese." I'd read about that restaurant somewhere and thought I'd give it a try. After a lunch that wasn't too jolly, I ordered coffee. When I could catch the waitress's eye again I politely asked may I have a little cream?

She snapped at me.

"Don't you know there's been a war?"

It had been over for five years!

I didn't think of an answer until I was back at Claridge's. What I should have said was, "And did the nasty Germans kill all the cows?" Orrr, "Yes, I know. I was with the American Army that bailed you Limey's out of it."

❀ ❀ ❀

That winter, in spite of my *Red Channel* problems, through the courtesy of Fred Allen, my radio show was still on NBC—but we'll get to that (and him) later. Still, I was able to put by a few dollars and by summer I felt Europe again.

I flew to Wiesbaden to see Frank who was back with Philco, and working for them in Germany. I was queasy about Germany and the Germans but . . . oh, well.

Frank was out of town when I arrived, but had left word with "the boys" and they were simply grand to me on his behalf. They took me for what they called their 'personal' tour—a lovely drive alongside the Rhine. They stopped at a vineyard that had belonged to the Austrian statesman Metternich, and bought me a bottle of 'his' wine. Thirty bucks, way back then!

I regret to say that when they stopped for me to get out and look at the Rock of the Lorelei, the sirens whose singing used to drive sailors up the gunwales, I chipped off a piece. (When Frank and I were at the Acropolis there was a lot of loose marble but I didn't touch so much as a shard. There was a cop there.)

Frank got back to town and showed me around. Laughing, he'd point out where buildings had been bombed and the roofs replaced. He took me to a beer cellar which was under, of all places, the Town Hall. Whole families sat on long wooden benches at trestle tables facing a platform on which a guy with an accordion performed. Suddenly a fat-neck turned to me and without any hello or other preamble launched this missile:

"You know, Hitler was a great man, a great man. But he should not try to be a general. No. If he would not be a general, we win the war."

I was grateful for the information.

Which reminds me of the elevator at my hotel, the Vier Jahrezeiten, The Four Seasons. There was a nice cylindrical hole from roof to basement that a bomb had created. But more memorable was the sixtyish elevator operator. As I approached, he bowed and opened the door. At my floor, he bowed me out. I'm talking about a real bow, not a head-nod. It was disgusting and reminded me of Churchill's description of the Teuton.

"He's either at your throat or at your feet," the Great Man once said.

(In times gone by, Black porters assigned to the parlor cars on American railroads would, as you neared your station, kneel down to polish your shoes. I would refuse, I couldn't bear it, and would overtip.) When Karen and I first landed in Hong Kong, she wanted to take a rickshaw. I couldn't: I just couldn't have a man act like a horse. She said he needed the money, so I handed the man some money and we walked away.

❖❖❖❖

From Wiesbaden it was back to Paris and an interesting rendezvous.

I had known that Simone, since having left my bed and not inconsiderable board (I'd put her on 'salary') was living in Amsterdam with Miles Standish, her new husband. I'd phoned her from Germany and when I got back to Paris she was already installed at 'my' hotel, the darling little old Matignon.

A small divergence here for a word or two about this delightful place. In the small lobby was the stand-up desk of the concierge. You soon learned that whatever you wanted in Paris, this man was the key; he made my reservations at the Tour d'Argent and it was a window table. The window that looks out at Notre Dame, of course. If you needed a stamp, a dictionary, a lion, a Greek acrobat, Monsieur Didot would have it for you shortly. When you left he'd hand you a summary of what you owed, you'd add a nice tip, if you had any sense at all, and on your return to the Matignon you were an emperor.

The elevator was a visible cage-within-a-cage. Sometimes Didot would take you up, sometimes he'd just set up the buttons and you did the job yourself. "My" room and bath was on the Avenue and had French doors leading to a tiny balcony. The wallpaper was a dreadful bile—but then, I used the place only for sleeping.

End of divergence, back to Simone. She wasn't in my room but had the suite I'd asked for. It belonged to the owner who was never there in summer and it had a view smack up to Montmartre.

Now, it may seem that my invitation to Simone to leave Miles for a while was on the callous side. Still, like almost everything else I've done, it wasn't planned, it had just occurred to me. Besides, why did she accept? I really don't know. I'm not the most attractive of men and I certainly wasn't rich nor had any hope of being so. Nor was I easy to get along with nor was I a great man in, as we used to say, the hay.

Maybe she just needed a vacation.

At any rate, two days later, off we drove. To the gem of Italy, "my" Portofino!

37

If you think you've had it with name-dropping, just you wyte. What follows is surely a masterpiece of that particular art form.

The shorefront of the teensy harbor at Portofino is paved with cobblestones. In a rough arc facing the water are old two-story houses, each painted in a different, or so it seems, pastel. Folks live upstairs, store downstairs. Funny little shops and some of them are terribly expensive. This is the quaintest of towns but a lot of the visitors are rich.

Along shore one can rent a boat, and one day a local young man sailed us around a point of land to Frutuosa, a restaurant perched on a cliff. It is reached by a flight of old stone steps. The main dishes are seafood from the morning's catch.

Poor Simone, from sitting in the boat she'd suffered a slight sunstroke and after lunch we were half-way down the steps when she suddenly sat down and said she felt simply awful.

An old Italian fisherman making his way up, took one look at her, diagnosed the problem, and ran back down to dip his bandanna in sea water. As he dabbed the back of her neck he told us, in Italian, along with body language, about his voyages in a four-master to India. You know how you do—body twists, hand-pictures-in-air—we understood and had a lovely time. At last Simone perked a bit and the old boy, seeing his work accomplished, said good-bye.

A small power boat entered the minuscule harbor and in a few minutes a couple disembarked and started up the steps. They were Rex Harrison and Lili Palmer. It seems that Rex had a house in Portofino. At any rate, I was obliged to tell him that I'd come away from the Splendido with no money and owed three dollars for lunch. He said he'd pay it if I would swear on my mother's life to leave the money for him at the hotel desk.

I swore, he and Lili climbed upward, and another couple appeared from the harbor. Ronald Colman and Benita.

Simone began to look much, much better.

Colman remarked that since Simone didn't feel too well it would be silly to go back in the sailboat. Why didn't we go back with them, or the Harrison's?

Simone never looked better in her whole life.

I was impressed, if that's the word. If it isn't, how about 'unnerved'. How about 'numb'?

Wait. To make room in the Harrison boat, Rex said that his house guest, Jean Pierre Aumont, would be glad to move over.

Simone had roses in her cheeks, in her hair, in her ears.

I figured no one would ever believe me. But believe!

The trip back was slowed considerably because Rex had picked up a pair of local boys to help him look for an anchor he'd lost the year before.

"He's funny," Aumont said. "He's paying those boys half-a-dollar and using up a dollar's worth of gas to look for an old anchor he bought three years ago for a quarter."

Finally, without the anchor, although Rex had made the boys dive a dozen times looking for it, we headed back to Portofino.

Coming into the harbor we passed an enormous white yacht with a long, black streak on one side where the inept pilot had scraped a coal barge.

The five of us, Rex, Lili, Jean Pierre, Simone and I stood on the pier and watched Mr. Inept manoeuver himself crazy.

"Oh," said Rex, "it's he."

It was he indeed. The Prince of Wales. The Duke of Windsor.

"He travels incognito, you know," Rex said.

I don't know how anyone would ever have known he was

there. As we climbed the hill up to the hotel we passed an enormous, unattended station wagon. On both sides, in shiny brass letters five inches high, appeared the legend

H.R.H. PRINCE OF WALES

Simone's headache was of course long gone and, such was the attention that had been paid to her, Miss Palmer refused to say "goodbye."

She didn't, but Rex did.

"Don't forget to leave the three dollars at the desk," he said.

❖ ❖ ❖ ❖

When last we looked in on Marie Andrée she hadn't arranged the marriage that was on her mind, but in exchange she got an automobile ride.

What she got was a nice, long drive to Rome, to Berne, and then back home to Paris.

About a year later in New York I got a cable from her. Would I mind meeting her ship at the pier in Brooklyn?

I drove over in my Jeep. The ship was a sparkling new freighter and the captain was her uncle. Marie Andrée took me all over the boat to explain the mechanics, the fire-control system, how the navigator worked—many things in which I had, let us say, minimal interest.

At last I went down the ladder to the pier. There was something wrong. What was wrong was that my Jeep had been stolen.

"Well, not exactly," said the would-be-surgeon. "I had them raise the Jeep and put it in the hold. What you shall do now is get your clothes. We will then sail to France, and then go to North Africa, to my other home in Oran. My brother runs the clinic there. You will have your own cottage down by the beach where you can write all day. You are a writer, you know."

Funny, I hadn't known.

At long last they off-loaded the Jeep and I drove back to my townhouse on East 61st Street and set fire to my typewriter.

A year later I was spending the summer as usual at the Golden Apple, the small house in the dunes of Truro, Cape Cod. Little Roberta bicycled up my road and delivered a telegram from my brother who was taking care of my New York house. It said to call him, as some French lady had phoned from Baltimore where she'd just gotten off a freighter.

"Send her up here," I told him.

Marie Andrée arrived in Truro loaded down with the lore of the sea.

After she'd explained the effect of the tides on the shoreline, I popped the question. Did she still intend to marry me?

No. She had been to Abijan, Africa, and had made a fortune running a drug store there.

A drug store—for the natives?

"Oh, yes. They work for the French entrepreneurs, and they spend their money buying the pretty, colored glass bottles."

She was about to open a branch in Oran.

I had a call from Marie Andrée in New York five years ago. I hadn't seen nor heard anything in oh, say thirty years. On the phone she told me that she now owned a drug supply house in Oran and one in Paris. She was here on a business trip and didn't have time to see me. The cottage in Oran was still available: Just send her a cable.

A month later, from Oran, I received a box of dates.

Haven't heard anything lately though.

38

The Hinge of Fate

I was unemployed and, it was dawning on me, unemployable. Nobody in the business said anything to me but odd things happened. For instance, I went to my old boss at NBC, Bud Something, and suggested that I resume my old fifteen minute radio show. He laughed.

"Listen," he said, "you're way beyond that now. Besides, we just hired two guys from Boston who do your stuff. Ever hear of Bob and Ray?"

I hadn't. A few years later, though, *they* hired *me* to replace them for two weeks when they went on vacation. And very fine people they were, too.

I had moved in with a TV actress named Ruby. She was a dear, bouncy type and we got along fine. AND it was a Park Avenue address, AND I paid a token rent, which I got back by selling her [us] an air-conditioner I had in storage. She insisted on paying, honest.

One night we walked into Sardi's and Richard Condon, a failure, was standing at the bar planning to write *The Manchurian Candidate* in about fifteen years. Richard was a stutterer. He knew Ruby had quit her last job.

195

"Ah-hah!" he said. "When Morgan d-doesn't work, n-n-nobody works!"

Shortly, Ruby got a job on a show dreamed up by Pat Weaver of NBC and starring Arlene Francis. I went to work on WMGM radio, broadcasting a local show for three hours every midnight from a new restaurant on West Fifty First Street in Manhattan.

Hutton's was owned by Ishmael Dzurk. A slight, greying person with horn-rims, Dzurk was far from affable. He had the ingratiating smile of a consummate shit. But for the first week or so I couldn't really blame him because our audience consisted mainly of apathetic waiters who, dependent on tips, were starving to death. But even when things began picking up, Dzurk was still a shit.

Deponent testifies as follows:

Item: One morning at 12:30 Dzurk appeared with a party of guests. He seated them and then came over to my desk-podium and smiled a Dzurk smile.

"Look how it looks in here," he said. "Look at it. Nobody, maybe a couple of tables. I bring friends in, I'm ashamed how it looks."

I worked six mornings a week interviewing people, making jokes, talking my brains out and finally, at the end of about a month, there was actually a line outside waiting to get in.

I mentioned this to Dzurk.

First, the smile. Then, "It's the food, the food," he said.

Item: One night when Ruby was in Hutton's I asked her to read the commercial for the restaurant itself, which she did.

Dzurk liked it and asked if she'd do it again from time to time, which she did.

He never offered her so much as a glass of water. Never. Nothing was ever on the house.

Item: Once I asked him to sell me six raw steaks to take home. He didn't charge me for the steaks, he charged me the full price for six steak *dinners*.

Item: Whenever I ordered a drink for myself, I had to pay. When a guest of mine sat at a table waiting to go on, the guest paid for whatever he or she ate or drank. Broadway columnists,

NAMES, fellow restaurateurs (Toots Schor included)—they all had to pay. When I complained to the man he said all right—but if you don't want your guests to pay, then *you* pick up the tabs.!! One night Jimmy Stewart walked in off the street to be interviewed on the air. Yep, him too!

* * * *

Of the six million Jews in the United States, at least five-million-nine-hundred-thousand-four-hundred and five think of ourselves in this order:

1. Man (Woman)
2. American
3. American
4. As American as the Christmas tree.
5. Jewish.

But the gentleman doth protest too much!

Yes, in a strange way.

Perhaps because every Jewish-American knows in his heart that it *can* happen here.

Perhaps it's because whenever he sees a headline about a man arrested for "insider trading", for stealing from a nursing home, for embezzlement, for child abuse—he prays that the criminal isn't a Jew.

Perhaps it's because he knows that Germans are a highly civilized people, but when civilized people hit a depression, they can turn into dogs. And Americans are a highly civilized people, too.

Perhaps it's because he knows that White Supremacists are an iceberg tip; after all, "the Jews have all the money."

Perhaps it's because when he was a boy, he was told, as I was told, "You killed our Christ."

An old Yiddish song begins, "Es is sehr, sehr, schwer zu sein a Yid." (It is very, very hard to be a Jew).

And so easy to be an American.

If they'd only let you.

* * * *

Oh, we're fascinated by Israel. And, as you know, we take sides, too. We had hoped it would turn out to be in fact "A light unto the world."

What it *did* become should have been foreseen—just another proof that "A Jew is just like everybody else, only more so."

We understand that.

Do you?

＊＊＊＊

I used to think that only Jews had miserable thoughts until I got into a conversation with a gorgeous Irish secretary at the Boston radio station where I worked.

A big star at WNAC was Adrien (sic) O'Brien, a man with a swell Irish tenor.

One day I was talking with "alabaster skin" Rosemary Fallon and mentioned how much I liked O'Brien's singing.

Rosemary didn't like it. Nor him. Not a bit.

I asked her what was wrong with him? "Oh," she said. "I don't know. Well, yes, I do. It's that he's so—well, he's so—*Irish*.

(One day I wormed and wormed and finally, sullenly, Rosemary told me what her father did for a living.

"He's a bartender. An *Irish* bartender.")

On New York radio one night I'd used the word 'negress.' The second I was off the air the phone rang and it was a famous black piano-playing singer-songwriter whom I'd never met but whose voice was unmistakable.

"You know, Henry, what you said? Negress? I know you meant it all right, you meant it to mean 'colored woman.' But to us it means 'whore.' "

＊＊＊＊

But let's get back to Hutton's. People are waiting.

The show was booked by a young man named Chester Feldman who, working all by himself, booked fifty guests a week. They were all 'celebs' of one kind or another and sometimes it was a real coup, such as when he booked Tommy and Jimmy Dorsey—who hadn't spoken to each other for years—on the air at the same time and *with their father!*

Later on I was able to get Mr. Feldman the job of producer on *"I've Got a Secret."*

And I have to get back to Jimmy Stewart and the night he just walked in and sat down next to me and said, "Well, let's go!"

I asked him if he had always talked the way he did now.

The answer delighted me.

"Walll, naw," he said. "I used to talk the same as everybody else . . . the same as you do now. I was walking around Broadway trying to get into the acting business, but no soap. Then one day I read for a part in a play and I didn't really know what I was reading and so I sort of mumbled through it. Well, gosh, I got the job—and I've been talking like this ever since. Fact is, I can't talk the other way any more."

It was a lovely interview, right up there with the times Jackie Gleason would make an (unpredictable) appearance. Jackie would storm in and take over the room, the broadcast, the world. He was one of a handful of vastly amusing men who could also *think*, a rare commodity among 'comics.' Jonathan Winters is another, and he made one of his debuts with me at Hutton's.

About twice-a-week a short, moon-faced man with greying hair sat at a table right beneath me and stared. It transpired that he was Mark Goodson, producer of TV shows, and he was sort of weighing me for one of his new ideas, *"I've Got a Secret."* He decided to give me a shot at it, but there was a, uh, problem. It seems that he had hired a man for his other show, *"What's My Line?"* and the man turned out to have a . . . well, a bad record. In short, could I prove that I was not now nor had I ever been . . . ?

This, I think, is the perfect place at which to insert what we've all been waiting for. Please turn the page.

VINCENT W. HARTNETT
541 East 20th Street
New York 10, N.Y.
Oregon 4–8936
February 10, 1952

Mr. Henry Morgan
310 East 50th St.
New York 22, N.Y.

Dear Mr. Morgan:

As you know, I am the originator of RED CHANNELS.

As you also know, only a small portion of your record in connection with Communist fronts was given in that book.

A new and much more complete book is now in preparation. It is not my intention to create undue hardship for anyone. Above and beyond telling the truth, I try to make it a work of supererogation not to refer to the past records of those who had conclusively broken with the Communist or Communist front movement.

I am familiar with the background of your anti-Communist position taken at the TVA meeting at City Center Casino on Thursday, January 24, 1952. I am also familiar with the status of your former wife, Isobel, and can make due allowance for the influence she may have exerted on you.

I enclose a confidential memo listing reported affiliations on your part with Communist fronts and causes. Only a few of these were used in my former book. If you care, in your own interests, to comment on these to me before I publish them, I shall be glad to hear your side of the story. It is imperative that I hear from you before Thursday, February 14th, if at all. It is also necessary that this matter be confidential between us. Should you attempt to draw a certain fraternal organization (which is now endeavoring to "clear" people) into our conversation, I shall consider the matter ended automatically. I simply do not have time to dissipate in endless discussions with pressure groups.

I wish to make it crystal clear that I am tendering you this opportunity to comment not because I have any obligation to do so, but purely gratuitously and without any expectation or desire of personal gain of any sort. I am acting out of a wish to protect you from undue hardship, in view of your position taken on January 24, 1952, a position which was productive of patriotic gains in the entertainment industry, no matter how belated.

Faithfully yours,

(signed)   Vincent W. Hartnett

Red Channels was a 212-page paperback published in June, 1950, by a faceless, nameless person or group of persons described in the book as *"former* FBI men." (Italics his or theirs.)

It listed actors in radio and television who had, according to published (?) reports, appeared at dinners or attended rallies sponsored by alleged Communist front organizations. Or were members of organizations believed to be fronts.

We're coming to something amusing.

I am mentioned three times. Once for being a member of something called Progressive Citizens of America (not true), once for having spoken by recording at a rally called by The Stop Censorship Committee, and once for making a collection pitch at a rally for Veterans Against Discriminations. (true.)

That's not the funny part. (I'm assuming that you understand that if someone came to me today and asked me to speak out against discrimination or against censorship that I most certainly would. Even in full knowledge that once again, as in the past, some smart ass would decide ten years later that those were Communist fronts.)

The funny part is that I was, briefly, a member of something called the Duncan Parris Post of the American Legion. It took only two meetings of this group for me to discover, to my surprise, that it actually *was* dominated by Communists, so I quit. The funny part is that the wonderful *"former* FBI men" never even *heard* of this Post.

The secretary of the outfit, the one who kept the minutes, was a strikingly handsome girl, an ex-WAC sergeant named Ruth Cosgrove. She quit Duncan Parris when I did. Until her death a few years back she'd been Mrs. Milton Berle.

That's funny.

Oh, one other funny thing (you must be tired of laughing, hey?). There was a flurry in 1952 when it was revealed to the House Committee on Un-American Activities that Lucille Ball's father had been a declared Socialist and an admitted contributor to the Socialist Party. And Lucille Ball had a bit of red tint on herself, too.

What happened was that when these facts were revealed, the members of the Committee just shrugged, looked at one another and then laughed. I mean, after all, *Lucille Ball*, for chrissake. And that was the end of that.

I once said to a member of the American Legion Americanism Committee (coming up in a minute) "How the hell could I, one of the few really outspoken people in radio, want a government that arrests individuals, professors, doctors and dissidents? For crying out loud, they'd shoot me."

"Well," he said, "you ought to be more careful about what you say."

39

Kindergarten Kafka

"Mr. Morgan, I'd like you to meet Alger Hiss."

It is Toronto, 1975. On being introduced to Mr. Hiss I smile but I feel like laughing. Not, certainly, at the charming, polite and obviously decent man standing there, but at the "by George-ness" of things. Here it is late in the evening and we're backstage of the auditorium in which I've just done a broadcast and there's no time, nor is this the place to tell him the story and maybe he wouldn't think it funny anyway. But, by George, life sure is funny. It sure is.

In 1952 I got blacklisted officially (*Red Channels* had come out two years earlier, and I hadn't been working, but nobody'd told me why.)

I remember listening to the radio one day in the '60's while a famous Senator made a speech in which he announced that after intensive investigation it had been absolutely proven that there never was a blacklist in radio and television. It reminded me of the day I was called by CBS to appear in a new, experimental color TV program.

A lady named Rose Tobias called me. She was obliged to call back the next day to tell me that my name had gone upstairs and come back down marked 'unacceptable.' A few months before I'd been a star in great demand. Therefore I feel free in remarking that the Senator, like many others you can name, was either an idiot or a liar, or both, because I sure as hell was blacklisted.

Broke, I was taken in by that lovely girl named Ruby who lived in a new apartment house at 72nd and Park. She had her own TV hour-and-a-half on NBC. Her boss was an overbearing genius named Ted Cott who, among other decisions, changed her name to Eve.

After a while, Eve quit and there we were, tapped out, on Park Avenue. It was a cold winter and sometimes we ate breakfast on the outdoor terrace of the cafeteria at the Central Park Zoo. By ourselves.

I spent my business hours calling on all the people I knew in the business, trying to get work. Bud Barry was pleasant, Sylvester Weaver was pleasant, Bob Kintner was pleasant. Nowadays I think it would have been kinder of them not to see me at all. Like Bill Paley.

Well, sir, one day I had a phone call from a name I didn't know. He asked me to come see him about "your problem" and since he was with a big advertising agency, I went. Things had been getting too rough. There was the threatening letter from Vincent Hartnett. (A columnist named Jack O'Brian had given me a lot of space. He was a popeyed little golliwog and he had the intriguing habit of saving the country from Godless Red Communists by attacking, among others, me.) So I went to see Mr. Wren.

Jack Wren was little. He was spare and balding, pale and snowy white with righteousness. He moved and talked like an efficient senior bank teller. His Americanism was not to be questioned. And he was, it turned out, IT. His small office was stacked with copies of the Congressional Record, *Red Channels,* reports from God-knows-whom, memoranda from people who kept tabs on people like me . . . he was IT.

"I know you're not a Party member," he began, "so how do you explain the fact that you spoke at this (pointing to something on paper) meeting on veteran's housing?"

"Was that wrong to do?"

"That, my friend, was a Communist front organization."

After an hour or so of this kind of badinage it suddenly occurred to me.

"Mr. Wren . . . you said you know I'm not a communist. How do you know?"

"Your cousin told us. Your cousin Martin Berkeley."

"Martin? How the hell would he know?"

"Because Martin was the secretary of the Communist Party of California."

"*My* cousin Martin? When did he quit?"

"When the Germans signed a treaty with the Russians in 1939. He saw the light. Now he works with us."

Son of a bitch. My good old favorite relative in the whole world. An informer. Son of a bitch.

A light bulb lit in the balloon over my head. So *that* was why my wife had told me not to have anything to do with Martin! *He had left the Party.*

Later I learned that good old Marty was okay. He'd started to turn the bastards in when he learned that his agent, a Party member, had refused to accept assignments for him; his doctor, another Red, knowing of Martin's bad heart, had recommended that he play tennis. The Party tried to kill him. It was enough to ruin his faith, it was. He decided to kill them, that was all.

Mr. Wren then went on to explain that to complete my 'clearing' (for what I hadn't done) I would have to meet with 'certain' people. I was lucky, he said. "That son-of-a-bitch José Ferrer will never work again as long as *I* live," Wren told me.

Now began a time of what I can only call restrained humiliation. First, I was sent to a lady with an Italian name (which I've forgotten) who lived on East 23rd or 24th Street. She told me I had to talk to her or appear before the House Committee on Un-American Activities. I had to cooperate, she said, and cooperating meant that I was to tell her the names of all the Communists I knew. She assured me that she, and therefore "they," knew I wasn't a Party member nor a Fellow Traveler. So, what Commies did I know?

"Surely you must know some. Some you suspect, even?"

"But lady, if I wasn't a member, how would I *know*? And if I just 'guess,' wouldn't I be doing what's already been done to *me*?"

"Because," she said, "you owe it to your country. You love your country, don't you?"

"Yeah, yeah, I love my country. But I think that naming names is un-American."

My God she was mad. And she phoned me twice more to go through the same stupid routine.

Wren sent me to the Americanism Committee of the American Legion. The head man had a name something like Oscar Barshlag, or maybe that *was* his name. I remembered having read somewhere that he had been Very large in the Communist Party, or so I thought. Turned out I was right. He was now Ex- and was doing *his* bit for the American Legion. *He* was clearing *me*. He and Martin. Clearing me from what they said they knew I was not.

I can't remember how many places Wren sent me, or how many months went by, but I remember what happened near the end. One day, he sent for me and handed me a speech he had written.

"There's an AFTRA meeting Tuesday," he told me. "Phil Loeb was fired off the soap opera *The Goldbergs*. He wants AFTRA to do something about it. You go up to that meeting and read this speech."

To my everlasting shame, I didn't do it. What I should have done was go and read the speech and tell them where it came from. But I chickened. How the hell could I stand in front of my union and read something that started out . . . "This rotten swine . . ."?

Instead, I re-wrote it to say, merely, that since *I* hadn't brought *my* case to the union, neither should Phil. I still believe that. At any rate, a large number of my peers didn't agree and shouted me out of the hall.

The fact that I gave a speech made a nice impression on the blacklist folks, though, and they invited me to a party. I was led to understand that my appearance there would be "good for you" and a sign that I was a true *American*. (BBD&O put me

206

on their Conrad Nagel TV show to signal the industry. Nothing came of it, of course.)

The party (on Park Avenue) was a terror. Shoulder-to-shoulder, cigarette-to-cigarette and drink-to-drink stood every professional anti-Communist in the Western World. There were the people who made a living from it. There were perhaps a hundred and fifty of them, smug and creepy, and happy to be in one another's company. I had trapped myself.

I was so upset that I felt I had to say so, right then, to *somebody*.

I said to the man on my right, "Well, I'll tell you one person I really can't stand. Whittaker Chambers."

The man smiled and reached across me to tap another guy on the shoulder. A short, rumpled man turned toward us. The guy on my right said, "Mr. Morgan . . . I'd like you to meet Whittaker Chambers."

That's why I felt like laughing when I met Alger Hiss.

40

And now, friends, let us return to poor Mark Goodson, who'd been waiting to find out whether he was about to get stuck with another Commie or not.

Can you, reader, prove right now, today, that you've never been a member of the Communist Party nor a Fellow Traveler?

Well, I could and I did. (Whew!)

At the very beginning of the Second World War I had done a lot of overseas broadcasts for the Office of War Information. Before they gave me the job, the F.B.I. investigated me three times.

After the war, I'd won a trophy, if you want to call it that, awarded by our Army of Occupation In Europe. It's a carved wooden plaque in the shape of a shield.

THE AMERICAN FORCES NETWORK OF THE ARMED FORCES RADIO SERVICE PRESENTS THE FIRST ANNUAL KILROY AWARD

Underneath that on a raised oblong, a carved likeness of Kilroy (of the famous "Kilroy was here" catch phrase of the 40's) is leaning over:

HENRY MORGAN
Chosen Outstanding Comedy Program
By The Men of
The European Command
May 29, 1948

I'd found out, by luck, that the F.B.I. had investigated me all over again before they allowed the plaque to be delivered to me—two years later.

I got the job.

But I hadn't been told as yet and was still in thrall to the miserable Dzurk who, swooning at the marvelous business he was now doing, became even more unbearable.

Well, the time came. I mentioned it to the man that he was quite rude. He just smiled and shrugged. He was a bi-lingual shrugger, that one, and, recognizing my background, gave me one in English. In rough translation it said, "Business is great—who needs you?"

So I quit, and took a plane to Bermuda. An hour after landing I found myself in the King Edward Hospital with a fine case of pneumonia.

Friend, I hope that something as wonderful as happened to me, happens to you:

Two weeks to the day after my departure.

THE RESTAURANT FOLDED!

There is a God. There is a God. There is a God.

And I am more vengeful than He.

41

"I've Got a Secret"

The panel show I joined was chaired by Garry Moore and consisted of Bill Cullen, Faye Emerson and Jayne Meadows, sister of Audrey and, later, wife of Steve Allen.

The best looking of these people was Faye Emerson, a woman who, during the time I knew her, had been married, married the second time to Elliott Roosevelt, and thirdly to a sort of band leader named Skitch Henderson. She was vibrantly beautiful but her hips were much too broad (for what? for whom?) and she disguised them by dressing cleverly. She was fond of men but fought the strong ones and married the weaklings. She said to me once during a marital hiatus—for both of us—that the reason I didn't want to marry her was that she wasn't Jewish. Not so. The reason was that I loved her the way I loved a great guy. Faye's 'motto' was, "The good times are where *I* am," and she meant it. And it was so.

We both played in summer theater a lot, and once I told her what I thought was the clever way in which I handled actors who 'upstaged' me.

Faye's way was different . . . and more effective by far.

"When someone does that to me," she said, "I take him aside

after the show and say, 'do that again and I'll just stand there and *glitter*.'"

Which, of course, she could and did and it worked every time.

In a real sense nothing ever really worked out for her and she died in a lonely house far in the hills on the island of Majorca.

I doubt that she was as old as fifty.

Jayne was, and is, a charmer and a fine friend. She once thought me a possible match for her sister, but Audrey talked through her nose. Well, some of us are like that.

During my stay on "Secret" there were lots of pretty ladies. Larraine Day comes to mind, as does dear, delightful Betsy Palmer and a woman of whom we shall hear more, Bess Meyerson. (Boy, do I have a surprise for *you*!)

The most interesting of the lot was our leader, Thomas Garrison Moffit, a convoluted man who used a name he had chosen in a contest—Garry Moore.

Once there was a party for Garry in a large tent at the back of his house in Rye, N.Y. It was a kind of serious evening which included Republican neighbors, the minister who married Garry to Nell, announcer Durward Kirby, and me. After dinner, there were lots and lots of toasts. Durward, a tall, craggy-faced man made the last of them, a small, craggy toast.

"To Garry, a man I've known for many years. I think I may say that he often reminds me of St. Joseph." (PAUSE) "A small, undistinguished town in Missouri."

The preceding lauds had all been heartfelt, and they were not misplaced. The persona Garry used for TV was that of a considerate, kind, honest man, both fair and warm.

Inside all that was an additional Garry, a highly intelligent and well-read man who just happened to be in show biz.

I mention Republicans. Garry never said what his politics were, but after knowing him for too many years to *have* to guess, I'd guess that he was a Democrat who lived like a Republican.

One day he invited me for a cruise on his swell, old eighty-foot schooner, *Redwing*. You may know someone like him; the ship was rigged in such fashion that when Garry felt like it, and most of the time he did, he could sail her by himself.

On this voyage there were four of us. Garry, a man named Al Smith, who had taught him sailing, a writer whose job was to "cook" har, har, and me.

The other gents had bunks. I slept on the floor in a bag. There may have been a message there, no?

Just one highlight: It tells a lot.

On the second night Garry piloted his sturdy band of Lascars up a narrow Connecticut river and, with a lot of "Danforth" and "heaving the lead" and "make fast" and other hake-and-flounder talk, we stopped. The noble corsair put out an anchor fore and one aft because of the current, or the wind, or the cow in the field about forty feet away.

At three in the morning (six bells, Connecticut ocean time), I tried to turn over in my little bag but couldn't do it and the effort woke me. It seems (don't you just love "it seems"?) that the river only existed at high tide and our gallant ship was lying at a forty-five degree angle in the mud.

By five A.M. we had the vessel roped to some trees so that it stopped listing.

Hours later the tide changed its mind and we were able to horse the damn thing out of the mud and up on its feet, like.

All-in-all it was an experience I wouldn't have missed for forty, forty-five cents.

Once ashore, Garry and I went to his house to be greeted by a knowing Nell. In her presence, I called Garry "Peep."

"Why Peep?" Nell asked me.

"Short for 'people lover,'" I said.

She laughed herself into a fit, and we became friends.

One night I was doing my own local TV show and, in lighting a cigarette, I remarked that I was creating my *own* cancer. It didn't occur to me, of course, that "Secret" was sponsored by Winston, the w.k. cancer purveyors. But it did occur to a viewer, a well-wisher who got in touch with Winston-Salem so fast that they fired me at dawn.

Garry flew down to North Carolina and talked them out of it.

What can you do with a guy like that? More to the point, what can you do *without* him?

In his retirement on the Atlantic coast he was quite happy. He sailed, he told me, every day.

Not alone. He was the crew for an aged New Englander who brought his schooner south. "Not *Redwing*," Garry told me, "but she's okay."

Well sir, I had a job, so I rented a little penthouse with a grand view of the Hudson and I got off Ruby's back. She took umbrage, married him and removed to California. I stayed on West End Avenue for the next fifteen years, happy as a bachelor with a steady flow of bucks can be—give or take about forty lawsuits from the old-time Mrs. Morgan.

On "Secret" I played, ha, ha, the heavy. I was the Dorothy Kilgallen, but with laughs. One night I wore a striped seersucker suit to a party where Miss Kilgallen said, en passant, "Where'd you get the mattress ticking, Henry?"

"Gee, Dorothy," I said, "you know a lot more about mattresses than I do."

She never spoke to me again, and that was a very nice thing to happen to a young man.

I realize now that I had a number of hobbies: Girls, traveling, girls, the theater, poker, making train models and also girls—I had a quarter-of-a-century of fun. When *Secret* went off the air I was making, or, rather, being paid, one thousand seven hundred and fifty dollars a week. I did 'voice-overs' on TV and radio commercials on the side, played in stock and, in season, was a big help to various clubs and restaurants.

42

Ann Honeycutt, the woman who had introduced me to both Benchley and Thurber, came up with a poker game that took place sometimes at her house, sometimes at the home of Skip Randall, a tugboat captain who lived in the Village.

The cast varied but the regulars included Randall; John Lardner, the silent; Hazel Lardner, the merry; Nick Wolkoff, a detective; Charlie Samuels, Night Editor of the *Daily News*; John McNulty, a writer of short stories; Mrs. McN; Wolcott Gibbs, of the *New Yorker* magazine, Ann and me.

The names may not mean much to you, but to me they are pictures in the firelight. Talking pictures, at that.

How could I forget tall, dark, good-looking John Lardner's two years of silence, broken only by a monotonous "I raise."

Or his wife Hazel's two years of snapping, "What the hell do you mean, you raise? On what, for Chrissake?" And Mrs. McNulty betting whatever, and John M's turning to me and saying "That woman's a millstone around my neck." (They later divorced.) Or McNulty's spreading his hand out for me to see, and announcing, "Look, the Devil's Picture Book!" Or Gibbs, loudly humming away at Rodgers and Hart and, drunk, folding three aces. Or Charlie Samuels, trying to figure his chances while I kept up a steady stream of babble, forcing him to remark to Heaven, "You know, that kid is like a whole Jewish summer camp."

A person could drop three hundred dollars in that game. I know at least one who did.

Of course there were times when I won. And, though not a contestant, I sometimes won on *Secret*, too. For example, the time glorious Ann Sheridan was the celebrity guest. I should tell you that the program was 'live' in those days, and what went on happened precisely while the viewer was watching.

We hadn't guessed Ann's "secret", so Garry told her to tell the panel what it was.

"I'm going to the Belgian Congo. With Henry Morgan."

The producers had renewed my passport, had the necessary stamps in it, and a doctor was waiting backstage to give me my shots.

Here two of my pet hobbies came together, travel and girls!

There was a drawback. Ann seemed somewhat more mature than I. But naturally! She was just my age.

What I didn't know, but learned on the plane; was that her one real love had died recently, and the only reason she was making this trip was that ultimately Sabena Air Lines would take her to where she really wanted to go, which was London.

Poor, beautiful, red-haired dear. When we got to Brussels, our first stop, she didn't have enough energy even to see the town. I sat alone in the handsome old Square in khaki shorts and bush jacket (damn those producers!) with my naked knees sticking out into the cold November. The silly outfit was for the publicity picture-taking—which never took place.

We flew on to Port Said, Egypt, then to Leopoldville in the Congo, where we transferred to a small plane for our ultimate destination, Bukavu.

The 'small plane' just mentioned was full. There were twelve passengers. A tall man in a tarboosh, a jelaba, and no shoes served lunch: breasts of goat on white bread, and two figs. No water, but he said he'd open one bottle of vichy provided at least ten passengers asked. The entire trip from New York took forty-eight hours—propeller planes, all.

Which gave me barely three days to see the hell out of five inches of Africa.

My room at the Bukavu Hotel had a terrace overlooking gorgeous Lake Havasu and the Mountains of the Moon. Excellent start.

Belgium then still ruled the Congro (now Zaire) and I spent all the next day in the jungle with a Belgian jungle officer. He took me to the weekly open air market where old women sat on old blankets on old behinds and sold the usual: tiny, tiny silver fish, piled in mounds; earthen pots of palm oil; spare parts of alarm clocks; rags, rusty stuff, pieces of things, rags.

I had been there since just before sun-up and at about eight ayem two old guys in tattered brown togas came out of the jungle to watch the excitement. Each had a staff in one hand and stood on his opposite leg. The other was folded under his toga.

"Well, that's the way they stand," the officer explained.

We spoke in French. Make your kids learn it. It comes in handy in Zaire and also in Thailand, as I found out later. In France, too. Besides, the Japanese aren't really going to take over the world. Just the banking systems.

Late in the day this nice man loaded me down with native carvings and pottery that had been presented to his predecessor. He had just too much stuff because, he said enviously, his predecessor had been a very popular man. I, of course, was more than happy to schlepp my loot all the way back to the States.

Ultimately I gave most of it away. It's tiresome after a while explaining to people why you have a lion spear over the fireplace—especially when you got it the way I did. I still have a long knife in a carved wood case bound by thongs.

That night, at dinner with a Belgian family, I guessed that the natives, having walked out of the jungle every morning of their lives to wait on the Belgians and do their dirty chores, would one day throw them out. The Belgians were terribly pleased at my remarks, sold me some native paintings at a special reduced rate, and threw *me* out.

Six months later the natives threw *them* out.

I must have slept five hours altogether during the three nights I was there. I tried to cover all of Africa, naturally! I flew to Ruanda-Burundi, to Dar-es-Salaam, I rode a bicycle down jungle paths, I photographed naked mothers in the river with their kids.

I mentioned that I'm a professional tourist. What it really means is that you have antennae out all the time and I got the impression, which many travel writers have confirmed, that Africa is about twice whatever you think it is. On the return journey, for example, the pilot deliberately flew low. It was sunset and we could see over huge mountains what seemed a thousand miles through the clear, clear air.

If my ship comes in just one more time I'll go back there and do it right. The names of places I have yet to see go bonging around in my head like Big Ben; Serengeti—BONGGGG, Nrongorongo, BONGGG, The Valley of the Nile—BONGGG.

✿✿✿✿

Anyway, Ann flew on to London, I made it back to New York barely in time for the program—and I had my very own spot on the show. It lasted two minutes, thirty seconds. I stood up and took a bow in my jungle shorts and jacket.

Garry was amused.

Somewhere in here I did a year of commuting every week to Hollywood to do six hour-and-a-half West Coast TV shows, of which I was the host. I came back every Sunday for Monday's "Secret" and made this idiot arrangement possible by taping *two* shows every Thursday in California. There was no orchestra and no side-kick, just me, slaving away.

The series was a failure.

I have just saved you a whole chapter of tragedies.

At any rate I still had the panel thing going: nobody on the east side of the Rockies had seen my disaster, and, as a matter of fact, practically nobody in Los Angeles had seen it either. My record was clear—I was still an amusing fellow and was eminently employable.

Besides, I'm dying to talk about Fred Allen.

43

Fred

Fred Allen is one of the few heroes in my Pantheon. Fred, Joe DiMaggio and Winston Churchill, and that's about it. Franklin Roosevelt is on a supplementary list somewhere, and so are Renata Tebaldi, Al Hirschfeld, Thomas Jefferson and Señor Wences, the ventriloquist, but the top is the top. And Fred's the one I knew best.

He was twenty-one years older than I, but he never so much as hinted that we were anything but equals. He was a gracious man who had read a great deal, but his major resources, it always seemed to me, was his vast knowledge of people. That and the skewed, skeptical way of looking at the world that is the wellspring of the true comic mind.

He was the only person I ever saw who had bags under his eyes that looked as though he'd been born with them. He hadn't acquired them: they'd just aged along with the rest of him. The voice was a nasal, whiny rasp, if you can imagine such a thing. And he was more amusing off-stage than on.

His radio show didn't make the move to television easily, so he gave it up. The last TV work he did was as a panelist on *What's my Line?*, where he joined Dorothy Kilgallen, Arlene Francis and Bennett Cerf. The host was John Daly.

After he'd been on the panel for a couple of months I asked Fred what it was like?

"Well, it's odd," he said. "Do you know—Dorothy and Arlene *play to win!!?*" (Not money—just enmity. The panel couldn't win any money).

"And how do you feel about Bennett Cerf?"

"Bennett? Oh, he's just a tweed wastebasket."

I wish I had some way of telling you how *accurate* that was.

Fred came from some poor but Irish part of Boston. His name was John Florence Sullivan, and he began his professional career as a juggler on Amateur Nights around the town. Like some others before him—W.C. Fields, and Will Rogers (who did rope tricks) he gradually developed a patter to go with the juggling and then, on the advice of theater managers, dropped the juggling.

As a vaudeville monologist he traveled the country over, Canada, and Australia, and he seemed able to remember the names and hilarious stories about the house managers of every theater he ever played. None of the stories was complimentary. People who had heard any of them pleaded with him to write a book, and he wrote two, but none contained his flavor. Perhaps he tried too hard. The first of them was *Treadmill To Oblivion*. He gave me an inscribed copy

****

For Henry

You louse—wait until *your* book comes out. I won't buy *it* either.

Fred Allen.

P. S. The only surviving Morgan fan.

****

Well, Herman Wouk wrote briefly for Fred, and, later, for me. When Herman's first book came out (and he quit the show) he inscribed on the flyleaf, "For Henry M.—the best boss I ever had."

So there, Fred. Of course, between the time he worked for Fred and the time he worked for me, Herman had been a lieutenant in WWII Navy and was probably comparing me to Captain Queeg.

Off-stage, Mr. Allen had a peculiar hobby. He attended funerals. Anybody's. I ran into him once when he was on his way home from the service held for a vaudeville comedian, Willie Howard. Absentmindedly, I asked him how it was?

"Well, Milton Berle was there. I expected him to jump into the coffin. After all, he gets into everybody else's act."

One rainy evening we were standing at the entrance to Toots Shor's when a toothless old actor shuffled by and saw Fred.

"Hiya, Fred, remember me? The Great Harrington?"

"I sure do. Things a little slow, Irving?"

"Yeah, Fred, you could say that. Little slow."

"Listen, take this card. Here's the name and address of my dentist. I'll write on it for him to take care of you. Go get some teeth—on me."

"Geez, Fred, I don't need no teeth. I ain't had no teeth for years now."

"Go get some teeth, Irving. How do you know—one of these days you might want to laugh at something."

I ran into Fred one day just outside the New York Athletic Club.

"Hello, Henry. Say, I just came from a meeting of the National Council of Christians and Jews. Notice how *we* still get top billing?"

"Yeah. Where you going, Fred?"

"Over to the 'Y' to play a little handball."

"Why do you go to that dump. Can't you go to the New York Athletic Club?"

"Oh, sure. But I go to the 'Y'. I can always get a game. See, they know me there."

Absolutely sincere, he was, too.

When I first met him he'd been a big star on radio for many years, but he and his wife Portland Hoffa still lived in a hotel. I asked him why—why didn't he rent an apartment?

"Why? Because in this business you never know. You go and

sign a lease and bang! The next week you find you have to open in Montreal."

Interesting, because in *Treadmill* he'd written, "In the theater the actor had uncertainty, broken promises, constant travel and a gypsy existence. In radio, if you were successful . . . there was no travel and the actor could enjoy a permanent home."

Once a vaudevillian . . .

And he never did forget the hard times. He told me of a job he once had in New York.

"I opened the act on Monday matinee up at 191st Street, that theater there. That was the first show of the week, and the manager always watched that one.

"I was still juggling then and part of the act was, I'd throw a turnip up in the air and catch it as it came down on a fork I held in my mouth. I only had a split-week (Monday to Thursday) so I'd bought eight turnips and put them on the windowsill in my dressing room. I took one for the matinee.

"When I got off the stage the manager was standing there with my suitcase. He, Bailey, his name was, escorted me right out the stage door.

"I still wonder sometimes—what did the next act think when they came in and saw the seven turnips sitting on the windowsill?"

Fred was a kind of semi-lapsed Catholic. It was as though he was religious, to be sure, but not in any particular way. I ran into him one September after he'd spent part of the summer at a Maine hotel.

"I heard that there was this revival thing out in the woods," he said, "and I thought I'd catch the show. I sort of hid behind a tree and watched this clown peddling God to the natives. It was terrible. Suddenly, some young guy spies me there. He's carrying a stack of pamphlets. He says to me, "Brother, have you been saved?"

"'Get away from me, you pimply faced son-of-a-bitch,' I told him." And brayed a happy bray.

Fred did me many favors, including making NBC put my

(unsponsored) radio show on the air right after his. Mine went on the air this way:

"*The Henry Morgan Show,* sponsored by (PAUSE) *The Fred Allen Show!*"

On my program I had a (supposed) phone conversation with Fred every week, and the last line always was, "Yes, I know you did, Fred, and thanks a lot!"

At Christmas I gave him an Atmos Clock, a gaudy thing in a glass case that works by changes in the air pressure. Across the base I had the Jeweler etch:

I KNOW YOU DID, FRED, AND THANKS A LOT!

He phoned.

"Listen, I got that thing and it's made a mess of the whole apartment." The Allens had finally rented an apartment. I had to get the super to build a shelf for it and his tools are all over the place and wood shavings and paint and screws and God knows what. Geez, Portland had to leave the house."

I shall always treasure My Man's way of saying, 'Thank you.'

I was at home talking with a girl named Geraldine the night the flash came over the radio.

I started to bawl. She mumbled something to the effect that she was sure I wanted to be alone and she fled.

No, I didn't want to be by myself. And I couldn't stop crying, either.

44

Emily
or,
My Affair with Mrs. Lundgren

While I was ensconced on Park Avenue with Ruby, she had a maid who did a few little chores for her. Emily washed out a nightie or so, redded up—nothing much that I could see. But she was fast and immaculate and silent. Never said a word.

I asked the mistress, ha, ha, of the house where she'd found this treasure, and she said it was at the Finnish Employment Agency. All right, then Emily was a Finn. She wasn't, but I didn't know that for ten years. She was quiet, that lady.

Shortly after I was hired for *"Secret"* I moved to that peachy little penthouse on West End Avenue with a view of the known world. I spoke to Emily and she agreed to come for one half-day and one full-day-a-week for fourteen dollars. Nine for the full-day, five for the half.

Well, you could mail a letter for three cents, you know.

A long roll of Necco Wafers was a nickel.

Actually, Emily was sort of expensive. And greedy. Ten short years after she started with me she asked for seven-and-twelve . . . but what could I do? By then I was used to her.

It transpired that she had learned the basis of fine house-keeping when she worked for the Marshall Field family in Chicago. It also came to light (after a few years) that she was Swedish.

"I thought you were Finnish?"

She was horrified.

"No, no! I Swedish! Finland, yes, I live there—but the Finns, they carry knives! My hoosban tell me."

Her hoosban, she mentioned a few years later, was a construction worker who had built their house in New Jersey.

And when I moved to East 57th, she came right along from New Jersey even though it took her three busses to get there.

She was about forty-five when we met, already grey, very strong, very much against working for ladies. Why she'd put up with Ruby I don't know. I used to bring women home from time-to-time, and Em said nothing except to mention in an off-hand way that when I got married, she'd leave.

Get married and lose Emily? Good Lord! Insanity!

This is not a joke. And this adoring memento is appended because I don't believe you've ever heard the likes of it.

I never asked nor told her what to do. She knew much better than I, and anyway, it was done before I thought of it.

Get ready for Fantasy Island.

When the kitchen floor needed washing, she did it on her hands and knees. She did the windows (there were twelve) when she thought they needed it—about five-times-a-year. She cleaned the silverware on a regular basis. I had three thousand books, and she dusted them twice-a-year, every single, damn one of them. She looked over my suits and sent out whatever needed pressing. She washed my hairbrush. She vacuumed, she scrubbed, she polished and rubbed and hauled and buffed and she watered all the plants, both indoors and those out on the terrace.

When I was away for any length of time she came in all the way from Jersey to make sure the terrace was in good shape. She pinched buds and trowelled and transplanted and weeded.

There was a fireplace for which she would gladly have chopped the wood.

One of the few multi-syllable words in her stock was "exterminator," and this is how I found out.

I had answered the door and an exterminator wanted to know

just where to work, so I went to the terrace where Emily was pruning the roses (YES, roses!) to ask her.

"The exterminator is here, Emily."

"No," she said. "Not in *my* house."

Of course. The way she kept the place a church mouse, had he known, would have sent CARE packages.

It dawned on me one day that she never took anything from the fridge. I discovered that she brought a sandwich from home.

She would change the furniture around. Her taste was perfect—so much so that when I bought something new I'd be obliged to tell the dealer that my "wife" might not like it.

Once I bought a painting from an acquaintance, dancer Geoffrey Holder. It was of a couple of dancers, tall and graceful like Geoffrey. I thought it marvelous and, since it was six-feet-high I made a special place for it.

Emily arrived and said nothing—until I asked.

"Color not good," she said.

I took a good look. A long look. Geez! where did I ever get *that* sore thumb! And why?

Holder accepted my dreary explanation and was really quite nice about taking it back.

Time passed (Doesn't it, though?) and a thoughtful judge declared me in contempt (alimony) and issued a warrant for my arrest. Those things are effective in all of New York State, and not of much help in *any* State. I decided that, rather than go to jail or pay I would leave the country. My Cape Cod friend, Bob Eldred agreed to store some of my stuff and auction off (it was his business) the rest. The truck came and took just about everything.

Dear Emily, she had wanted one of the Chinese chairs and I hadn't known. Emily never talked when she was working—and she was always working.

Damn, I wish I'd known about that chair. All I could do was give her the air conditioners, the TV, the entire contents of the kitchen and a purse of gold. But you know, it still bothers me today that she'd would've rather have had the chair.

When it was time to leave, Karen and I were out in front of

the building and she said, "Aren't you going to say goodbye to Emily?"

You know, I couldn't go back and do it? I lost my nerve entirely.

I'm sorry, Emily.

It was just short of twenty years. Did you know that?

✳✳✳✳

I must confess that specific years don't mean much to me. If I seem to go forward and then back once in a while it's owing to the fact that I prefer to tell a story in its own, internal sequence. If a year seems to jump out of place, why, just let it. No harm done. For instance, the following account is of an event of the early Fifties and it's actually in its proper place. Have faith!

45

Borah

Remember the Harmonica Rascals with the little guy in cowboy chaps who got shoved around by the rest of the group? Borah Minnevitch thought up the act back in vaudeville days. When he retired it was to a marvelous, crazy house in Merrieville, about forty miles from Paris. He retired with a girl named Lucille, the wife of Deems Taylor. Mr. Taylor was America's foremost music critic and the composer of one of the first American operas, *Peter Ibbetson*. He did many years of music commentary on radio in a dry, pedantic voice which had, nevertheless, a great deal of charm. The charm apparently didn't quite get to Lucille who had moved to a large loft in Paris where she'd been living with an owl. Sorry, but that's the way it was. With a live owl.

I was spending the summer at the Matignon in Paris on the advice of "Fat Alfred" Katz, the manager of Anton Dolin and Alicia Markova, ballet stars who were currently touring Australia.

Fat Alfred knew everybody in the civilized world. At his suggestion, he and I took General David Sarnoff and his French wife Lizette to dinner a couple of times at La Table du Roi. Mrs. Sarnoff once asked me if I was working? No? Then she would speak to the General. It really wasn't my place to tell her I was blacklisted and down to my final two thousand dollars, now was it?

Once when we were looking up the hill of Montmartre, she told me, "Would you believe, Henri, when I was a little girl I lived up there with no shoes. No shoes!"

She was a charmer, that one.

We stray. Let's stray a bit farther. One night when we were leaving the Table du Roi the car wouldn't start. I saw a familiar face (and body) leaving the restaurant and called out, "Milton, c'mere."

The Great Berle approached.

"Milton, I need a push. Push the car."

"Cut it out."

"Milton, look at the back seat."

He did the only triple take of his life.

After all, the General was the head of RCA and the head of NBC-TV, and Milton *was* NBC-TV "Mr. Television." It is hard to say who would have pushed for whom, but in this instance, Uncle Miltie did the pushing. (It was a Hillman-Minx—very small).

So one day Fat Alfred and I were invited to a party at Borah's farm in Merrieville. It wasn't hard to find because, following directions, we stopped at the local bar there at which the Central Casting fat patronne in black perked up when I mentioned the name Minnevitch, cranked up the phone, and a car was sent to guide us. They loved Borah not only because he was crazy but he was also the Fire Chief. He had given Merrieville its new fire truck.

We arrived at about noon and forty guests were already there. Out in the barn I played table tennis with Art Buchwald, a writer for the Paris *Herald-Tribune*. A waiter in a battered top hat kept circling us with trays of wine but Buchwald, intent on beating me, kept saying to him, "Pas encore, pas encore!"

Borah showed me the house. I can't go into it too much because you'll think *I'm* trying to be funny. Example: All the johns were lined up in a sort of wing and they faced a small trout stream. Each stall was provided with rod, reel and net. See what I mean?

At dinner we all sat on either side of a long table which didn't quite accomodate forty and ended at a window. Outside the window at an additional table all by himself sat the great French comic, Tati.

It was uproar time because we all kept jumping up and down to see what Tati was doing. Occasionally, he'd hop into a Jeep, drive up to the kitchen window, knock on it with a fishing rod and solemnly ask for more coffee, please.

There's no future in this. All I can tell you is that it was one of the best parties I've ever been to, it lasted until four in the morning, and I'll never have the strength to go through anything like it again. Not to worry. How could there be anything like it again?

One last note. Borah took me to meet his hermit. Borah raised watercress for market and to one side of the vast cress bed was a rock outcropping. As he instructed, I knocked on the rock with a stick and a raggedy, scraggle-bearded old man appeared at the mouth of a cave, said, "bon jour," took the hundred francs which Borah had ready, and retired.

Borah assured me that he had the only privately-owned hermit in France. He was too modest to say "in the world."

The last I saw of Borah and Lucille was a year or two later when they were sailing back to France from a visit to New York. They had come over to get a couple of wooden Indians that Borah owned and had kept stored in the basement of the "21" Club.

The happy couple were wearing fighter-pilot helmets because, Borah said, they had to take a helicopter from Le Havre to Paris to be back in time for the opening of his new bar on the Isle de la Cite. He had to make sure that the records for the jukebox had arrived.

I later was told that they had indeed arrived and that all Paris was singing the new songs from Borah's cafe.

They were all in Yiddish.

Only a few people had come down to see the couple leave New York. Among the handful was another old friend of mine, Deems Taylor, Lucille's husband.

46

A Short Muse

It occurs to me that this souffle contains more than the usual garniture of 'names.' As chef, may I assure you that this continues until you have, at last, cleansed your palate, paid the check and tipped the girl in the cloak room.

The reason is that I have always been in show biz, by choice, and a kind of bum-about-town. Also by choice. I had staunch friends among the laity, but even they weren't all that lay. Will Glickman and his wife Hortense—well, Will was a comedy writer for many people, from Stoopnagle and Budd to Sid Caesar.

Valentine Sherry was a diamond seller, but at any party he gave one met the absolute cream of the Broadway theater, together with sundry writers and wandering creatives of all kinds. Val and Will owned a power boat named the SRO, show business term for Standing Room Only. Late in life Val married a woman who was the manager-agent of Sly Stallone. When Will and Horty moved to San Francisco, they were taken in hand by Frank Crennan. And so it went.

And, as it was going in, say, 1951, I was invited one evening to Val's apartment to meet a new girl of his, and a friend of hers, Joanna Simon, age eighteen. I was forty-one. But when I asked Joanna what she did, she said, "I'm an opera singer." And she had blonde hair down to her waist. What would you?

235

I hate people who settle old scores in an autobiography don't you? It's so, ah, cheap and vulgar.

Now, Joanna wasn't exactly an opera singer—yet. She was a student at Sarah Lawrence College.

I was at her graduation ceremony.

Well, it transpired that Jo had a father, Richard, a publisher, a young brother Peter, and two sisters, Lucy and Carly. Joanna told me that Carly had a better voice and was more musical than she but "she has some kind of fuzziness in her throat.

I imagine that by now Carly Simon is over the 'fuzziness.'

The Simons lived in a sprawling, yummy house in Riverdale, a suburb immediately adjacent to the City, and the house was, to me, exactly what a home should be. It had a leathery den, it had a music room (everybody played piano, everybody); there were trees and bushes and a stone wall and a live-in cook and a wonderful, elegant-but-salty grandma (who was smart enough not to live there).

There was another house in Stamford which was exactly the country place you've always wanted. It, too, rambled, and there was a pool and cabanas, tennis courts, huge vegetable gardens (taken care of by the cook and her husband) and a fifteen mile view.

I went with Joanna for years and I suppose the romance was nurtured in part by the fact that I needed a family. And I was invited to both homes quite often.

One day at the Stamford house I had a nice talk sitting under a tree with Jackie Robinson, another friend of the family's. (Mrs. Robinson was wont to make a lemon meringue pie that made people cry.) Jackie had been asked to give a talk somewhere in the South and was angry because they had, stupidly, sent him a speech. He was, after all, a graduate of UCLA, Stanford. A real graduate, if you get my drift.

Shortly after Jo's father died we took a trip to Round Hill, Jamaica. On our first day we took a survey walk. Coming toward us was a couple with a young girl, who suddenly shrieked "Joanna!", and the two girls clung together. The male parent stepped forward and held out his hand.

"Hello, Henry, I'm Bill Paley and this is my wife."
Yes, *that* Bill Paley. He had CBS tattooed on his forehead.
The word on mine was CRADLE SNATCHER.

❖❖❖❖

Each summer, "Secret" went off the air for thirteen weeks—
during which we were paid anyway. Yes, God takes care of
drunks and fools and I was on His short list.

So it was paid-for-summer again and I had nothing to do and
the money to do it with, so when Joanna got a singing job in
Italy and asked me to drop by, I did. She was working for
Menotti in Spoleto, but she'd had time to get to Florence and
find a hamburger place. It was my first time in Florence and I
was delighted to be shown the town . . . a hamburger place.
(No rolls. Rye bread.)

When her gig was up we drove to Nice and were having a
drink on the Carleton terrace when Frederick Loewe came by.
He had some news for me. First, he had a (rented) yacht in the
harbor. Second, his partner, Alan J. Lerner, was broke. Alan
broke?

"Oh, yes. Your cousin was taken for everything by his wives
and he's in debt up to here."

It sounded to me as though they were no longer partners.

It also turned out not to be true, but sometimes Fritz could
be as inventive with a lyric as Alan was.

(As I told you earlier, My mother's maiden name was Lerner,
and Alan was the son of one of her first cousins, but we all called
one another 'cousin'. Mom's cousins, Mike, Joe and Sam owned
the Lerner chain of dress shops. Alan couldn't be broke even if
he went broke, if you see what I mean.)

Another wealthy summer, and I took Jo to my favorite hotel
in Paris, the Prince de Galles. The man at the desk announced
that for little more than the ordinary rate I could have a suite on
the top floor. I was delighted. What he forgot to tell me was that
the top floor had once been the the quarters for staff members,
who, in French terms, were not part of the human race.
Therefore, the roof was made of thin tin. It was July. Joey went

237

off to audition at Glynedbourne and when she got back I weighed eighty pounds.

By previous arrangement, we met up with my dear Mamma who had saved, from the pittance I'd send her, and had made the trip on her own. (Another year, when she was in her seventies, she went to Japan . . . also on her own.)

Dear Mamma resented Joey (and every other girl I ever knew) and was such a damned pest that Jo usually took her off to lunch so that I could rest up.

There's a lot more Joanna I could add to this gumbo, but since I prefer to keep the main lines of a piece connected, let me tell you how we finally came to a tearless farewell.

One day I had the feeling that Jo's mother, Andrea, wasn't quite as friendly as she'd been for the past few years and I asked her about it. Well, she said, she'd been thinking. And the conclusion?

"I think," she said, "that you're not the perfect couple. It's not that you're too old for Joanna, not at all. It's just that she's, well, too *young* for you."

The logic was more than perfect so, gradually, we just tapered off.

As of today, a flock of years later, Karen and I are friends to Joanna and Gerry Walker, married now about ten years or more. Carly Simon is still turning out blockbusters, everyone seems to be reasonably happy and if there's a message or a moral here—please send it to me for inclusion in Volume Two.

47

Thule (too-lee) Greenland, anyone?

Thule is the farthest north permanent settlement in the world. I thank you.

Thule is an Army post, an airfield, the home of an early warning system, and a consummate pain in the ass.

I had to go there as a part of singer Gretchen Wyler's "Secret". I suppose you know it but just in case—the secrets for the celebrities were arranged by the producers of the program, and that's why I put the word in quotes.

A whole entertainment unit went with us in another forsaken propeller plane—with a stop for dinner at Gander, Newfoundland. The damn trip took a damned twenty-three hours.

Thule had been an Eskimo fishing village until the brains (sometimes referred to as "Washington," sometimes as "the Pentagon," sometimes as "the world's senior collection of horses' asses") decided that if we built a huge structure with an enormous radar installation on the site, we could spot enemy missiles in time to give fifteen minutes warning to the folks at headquarters—in Texas. This was deemed necessary at the time because it was common knowledge among common people that the Russians, to name a few, could wipe each of us out twelve times while we could do the same to them only

239

fifteen times. This meant that if they started first, they'd have a jump of at least one time and maybe two times, leaving us all dead twelve times, them, thirteen times.

Therefore, even though Greenland belongs to Denmark, we moved the Eskimos thirty miles to the north.

Just the highlights, please!

Fine. Everything in Thule is built above ground because of the permafrost. Not just the mean little buildings but all the piping, all the wiring, all the sewerage, everything; otherwise, if there were any heat in anything, it would sink through the icy ground.

Except that it is all surrounded by dead white. It looks a lot like what you see when you leave New York City and are making your way along the Jersey turnpike.

I'm not going to describe the main building because it may be classified or, out of boredom, the boys may have blown it up. It is sufficient to say that the place is below-freezing cold, all day, all night, Mary Ann.

It is ugly beyond ugliness.

That's not much of a highlight, hey? But a guy *did* take me up in a tiny chopper shaped like a glass bubble, flew me twenty miles out over the ocean of ice, and I got out and walked on the surface of the moon. A white, white, frigid moon, with ice-hills and nothing more. It went out to the horizon in every direction. I walked behind a berg, and the chopper disappeared. I was alone. It was scary and it was exhilirating.

It is so cold that everyone, without question of rank, takes heated taxis from one place to another, free. Young Danish drivers commit themselves for two years, take their money in a lump and go back to Denmark and pay for college or open a business.

As I say, I hated the place—but not nearly as much as did the poor bloody men who were stationed there. (Tenses have changed on me but it seems right, somehow.)

Oh. Comedian Rich Little was on the trip. He's okay. Or was.

❖ ❖ ❖ ❖

Speaking of flying, I forgot to tell you about something that happened when I was commuting to L.A. for the TV show that failed. I always flew TWA because it had the best 'on-time' record, and on my fifth trip in the all-but-empty First Class, a gentleman came down the aisle and introduced himself as Mr. Tillinghast, the President of the airline. He had been told that I flew out and back every week and asked if I had any complaints? Yes, I told him, I was tired of the excess of food—wasn't it possible for the line to serve something light, even though it was a six-hour trip?

"Just write down what you want," he said, "and I'll attend to it."

I wrote out a rotating menu for myself which included such delicacies as a corned beef sandwich every fourth trip.

For the rest of the nine months I did this painful slogging, TWA punctually had my stuff on board. It was a slow year for the airlines, and sometimes I was the only passenger in First Class. I had the unique thrill of hearing the head stewardess inquire, at the start of each trip, "Is Mr. Morgan's lunch here?"

When I finally quit the job, I forgot to tell the airline, and I sometimes wonder if, after all these years, TWA is still putting Mr. Morgan's corned beef sandwich and two bottles of Budweiser on board—just in case.

✿ ✿ ✿ ✿

Another tale about flying—or, rather, *not* flying.

It is midwinter and Kennedy Airport lies asprawl in a blizzard. There are hundreds of us depressed persons in the TWA Building staring out at the swirling whiteness, no place to go but home—and no way to get there.

Suddenly, a strange man rushes up and kisses me. I try to be unflappable, and do fairly well most of the time, but this time I am unnerved. The man stands there and looks at me with his beautiful eyes and it takes me a couple of moments to recognize that it is Montgomery Clift. We have never met, but I suppose that I was, perhaps, the most attractive port in the storm.

He has a thin young man with him, and the three of us kill an hour in the bar. At last, Monty makes up our minds. He has, may the blessings of the Lord be upon him, told his limo chauffeur to wait, and, by heaven, the car is still there.

He has a townhouse furnished in orange crates, I am not joshing, and we kill two bottles of scotch and I pour myself home.

A month later Monty phones and invites me to bring a girl to dinner, and I call Mary Deane Pulver, the only one I can think of who is attractive enough, charming enough and poised enough to handle him.

The scene is a remote room in a lovely French restaurant. Monty's date is a handsome and endearing lady in her sixties. Monty's condition is that of a man with beautiful eyes who is lurching drunk.

Mary Deane is wearing a smashing, simple dress of clear yellow jersey. Suddenly Monty decides that she MUST come around to his side of the table and sample his frog's legs.

"No!" I said.

Mary Deane looks at me reproachfully, gets up and goes around the table. He holds out his fork, and manages to dump a greasy frog's leg on her clear yellow dress.

She comes back and sits down and a waiter rushes to get some cleaning fluid. Monty just stares. After a minute or so he cradles his head in his arms on the table and starts to cry.

Shortly, Mary Deane and I leave.

This was in 1966, the year he died.

48

Bess Myerson and the Greek Islands

Some time ago Bess Myerson was acquitted of trying to bribe a judge to reduce the alimony of her boyfriend. Bess, a former "Miss America," was a panelist on *I've Got a Secret* and she was a good friend.

The last time I was in alimony court my case was heard by the same judge, a superior person named Hortense Gabel. (She's not the one who ordered me to alimony jail—that was an inferior judge named Justine Wise Polier.) Judge Gabel had ruled that I should pay my professional sue-er ten percent of my income until further notice. Well, here's the further notice: I won't.

Would you throw YOUR money into a suer?

The Bess I know is as even-tempered and talented a woman as a man could wish for, and the man who wished for it at the time of which I write was Arnold Grant. Arnold was a wealthy lawyer, art collector and admirer of the good life.

Bess deserved Arnold. Her first husband was her manager and not a nice man at all. I'm afraid to say more because I don't know if he's still around or not. But not nice doesn't even nearly cover it.

Well, Bess became friendly with Joanna—so much so that

she and Arnold invited the two of us to be their guests on a two-week tour of the Greek Islands on a chartered boat—just the four of us.

So here I was, back with my favorite hobby—going someplace with girls.

Some of us never learn. For instance, I wasted a good part of my life driving top-down convertibles with pretty girls in the sunshine. I did it until they stopped making convertibles. I should have been making something of myself, hah? And I spent years collecting chess sets. Sold them all the year before Bobby Fisher made them priceless. And I used to have season passes at the Metropolitan Opera House. Dear me. I did an awful lot of wasteful reading, too. Books, you follow me? Just for enjoyment, darn it.

Where was I? Oh.

Jo and I met the Grants in Athens and the first night we sat on the roof of the Hilton snapping at a few brandies and watching the play of lights on the Acropolis. The next day we went to Piraeus, the port for Athens.

We will not shift tenses, women and men, as the four spoiled-rotten corsairs troop aboard the *Pandora*, which carries a crew of five, a cook, and a chubby girl interpreter.

Chubby says the captain wants to know which way to go—out into the Aegean or go round to the Ionian Sea? Arnold, a splendid host, leaves the decision to me. Chubby says the captain wants to go Ionian but I choose the Aegean. No local snip of a sailor is going to dictate to me, right?

Wrong. Quite wrong. Chubby has neglected to tell us *why* the marster wants to go the other route. I have made a bum choice as those of you who opt for the trip will shortly see.

Summertime, and the sailin' is easy. The weather is fake. Day-after-day, the whole damn thing is a series of picture postcards. The sun shines, the air is cool, the food is good, the booze is plentiful, the cameras are working, the islands are unbelievable.

The guide books are accurate: the donkey drivers on the islands are pests, but know their business and the ruins are so enchanting I suggest that they must have been imported. The whole thing takes on an air of fakery, if you know what I mean. It's as though we have planned a marvelous party and we're actually having a marvelous party. Perhaps a touch too much perfection—good talk and laughs and the real world is back there, somewhere.

And then we discover what Chubby has forgotten to mention. It's called "the meltemmi"—it's a storm that hurls itself out of the Aegean at just this time of year with no warning of any kind; there are no clouds. It's just another bright and lovely day, and the four innocents are cruising along under sail (including the main, which the captain has been most reluctant to raise) when it hits like a terrorist attack.

We have been sunbathing in the stern on a sort of raised platform and as the waves grow bigger, we have to curl our arms around the balusters of the railing. The waves grow faster and faster, and the wind begins to shriek.

Quietly, almost nonchalantly, Arnold says, "What do you think?"

"Maybe we should get inside the cabin?"

By now the pitch is so steep that every time the bow goes down we are hanging by our arms and the sea is straight between our toes. As the ship struggles to right itself we make a mad dash for the cabin and slam the door.

"I wonder," Arnold says thoughtfully, "I wonder if they should take down the mainsail?"

C-R-R-A-C-K!!

"Why no," says the smart ass who chose this route, "No. I think it's down already."

It is in pieces, shreds, all over where we've just been sunbathing. It all happens in perhaps fifteen minutes.

"Tell the captain," I say to Chubby, "tell him to lower the rest of the sails, turn on his kicker and head for the nearest port whether it's on our schedule or not."

I lead Jo down the steps and suggest that what we should do is lie in our bunks and hang on to the sides, which we do.

Five minutes later the door of the medicine cabinet flies open and the bottles of perfume, the lotions, the whatever, hurtle across the cabin in a straight line and smash against the bulkhead.

"Can this kind of ship sink?" Jo's tone is the one she uses to ask if I want my back rubbed.

I guess that it can't sink, but if it turns on its side we should stay with the flotsam and hold on to something. I explain why, if we hear the engine stop, we should rush topside immediately.

That little engine "could", it really "could", and in five hours FIVE HOURS, we chuff into a tiny harbor where, after making suitable remarks to a beneficent God, we go to sleep.

The next day there is only half a storm, so we blunder and roll and slide until we get to Crete.

It is still rough out there, and we're to go to the island of Rhodes. I suggest we *fly* to Rhodes, and let the crew take *Pandora* over. Yes, but the only way to do it is to fly back to Athens, and from there fly to Rhodes. Which we do, and I get sunstroke.

When old *Pandora* staggered into Rhodes we were sorry for the crew, a raggedy bunch of worn-out men with red eyes and barely the strength to smile. It seems that right after we left another meltemmi hit them.

Summation: yes, take the trip. You can use public steamers, and people who've done it that way tell me it's just fine.

****

Back in Athens we wave goodbye to the Grants and fly to Venice where, through a nice sequence of breaks, we get seats for the first opera to be performed in the white marble courtyard of the Doges Palace since before WWII. It is *Othello* and stars Tito Gobbi.

Earlier I mentioned another hobby of mine. Opera.

This arena, because of the permanent white marble setting, is impressive indeed.

Oh, yes. The best restaurant in Athens is, surprise, in the Hilton Hotel. Others have confirmed this as recently as 1993.

Even though this chapter is headed, "Bess Meyerson and The

246

Greek Islands" there's little of Bess in it. The reason is that this memoir is full of stories about things that happened and with Bess, nothing happened. She created no fusses, she was amiable at all times, she was, well, passive. To put it more correctly, she was pleased. It's dreadful for the reader, I know, but in my *next* book I'm going to tell some awful, law-suit-type, rotten things about some big names, you bet. Sex, too. You know what I mean. Best-seller stuff. Watch for it

Meanwhile . . .

49

Wha' Happen?

Garry Moore had been doing both *I've Got a Secret* and a variety show on CBS-TV when a New Boy became President of the network. His was a puffy ego, this one; he pushed staff around, he hired inept cronies, and, worst of all, he didn't like Garry's variety program and he cancelled it. Disaster number one.

Disaster Number Two. Garry quit *Secret*. After all, he had been co-starred with Jimmy Durante at one time, and had had his own show on CBS every day for years. To be dumped by the new twit was just more than he could take.

Disaster Number Three. Garry was replaced on *Secret* by Steve Allen. For fifteen years Garry had played host to the panel. Steve, on the other hand, thought the panel's function was to be 'straights' for his personal ideas of what was funny. This approach was so wrong, and the chaos so complete, that the show tumbled rapidly out of the top ten, where it had been for the past twelve years, into the unforgiving darkness of TV death.

At the wake we members of the profit-sharing plan were given some money and I, the real-estate authority, sensing the imminent demise of West End Avenue and 76th Street, bought a small penthouse on East 57th Street. I had been paying three hundred a month 'uptown.' That same apartment sold recently for four hundred thousand dollars when it went condo. (When I had to sell at 57th Street I lost money—of course!)

I took to full-time shabby employment such as doing 'voice-overs' for TV commercials. The voice-over is the one you hear but don't see. The possessor of the voice gets the job by auditioning for people whose average age is eleven. These persons make tapes of forty or fifty middle-aged men and forward the results to more knowledgeable folks, people who are pushing twenty. These, and the clients, make the final decision.

I offer you a typical example of the material with which we are (I still do this kind of work) confronted. After you read it you may worry that I am burning some bridges—what if, after all, a CLIENT sees this? Not to worry. CLIENTS can't read.

This comes from Ogilvy & Mather:

> Equal with NutraSweet.
> The taste you never outgrow.

NOTES: The creative team is looking for a voice that is not too animated, not too flat . . . but ju-u-u-u-s-t right. Warm, simple, with a smile—to complement the humor of the campaign, which is celebrity voices being lip-synched to by children on-camera. You know, the Whoopi Goldberg, Joan Rivers, Robin Leach campaign. The new flight in this campaign is a bit more ambitiously shot—on film, with the characters interacting, the humor a bit wicked. The voice should *acknowledge* and *complement* the humor, BUT DO NOT CHUCKLE OR GIGGLE. Be as real as you can, be yourself, and sell the product without self-consciousness. But don't try t-o-o-o hard. Good luck.

50

Karen

Back in the days when Merv Griffin was piling up his first billion he ran a talk show on television. The oddest thing about him was that he had no particular wit and no particular charm, but he had an assistant, a sort of girl-of-all-work, who had both. Karen Sorensen was a sort of blonde, sort of not, with a cute nose, wonderful big blue eyes, a generous, sweetly curving mouth, a pretty figure, and the kind of directness that one finds even today only in girls from the Midwest. That's a blanket statement, and if you want to take issue, take one on me. Karen came from Iowa.

We'd been going together only a short time when we started on what became a trip around the world. In ten short years after that we got married. You are invited to the wedding in about twenty minutes of further reading.

But first a word from Draper Lewis.

Draper called me one day out of the wild blue yonder—it was exactly twenty-five years since I'd said bye-bye to him at the Miami Beach branch of the Air Force. Now, a quarter-century later, he was involved in a typical type of television trash called *Dating Game*. I knew this to be an afternoon pastime in which a celebrity of some sort questioned some hidden, off-stage, girls, and then chose one to go on a trip. It was an absurd show, aimed at the young. He wanted me to go on as a celebrity guest.

I explained to Draper that I'd aged up a bit since Miami, but he said not to mind, he'd have me on with older women. Besides, I'd get a trip abroad as a prize.

Aha! He'd made me an offer I couldn't refuse.

From the women on the show I picked (blind, remember) a bimbo we'll call Kathleen. (Her bimbo-ness wasn't immediately apparent but—you'll see, you'll see.)

The prize was a trip to Tokyo. Hot suchi!

On the agreed-on date, off we flew, bimbo and I, together with a female chaperone! House rules. But. I mean, man, I was fifty-three. Kathleen . . . well, let's just say that she'd been out to the barn a few times. She was and is an actress, and I just looked her up in the *World Almanac*. At the time of our trip she was forty-eight. Been out to that barn maybe a thousand times.

A carful of English-speaking Japanese men picked us up at the airport. In a loud, clear voice, Kathleen started telling jokes from the scrap heap of common G.I. trash left over from WWII. I sank in my seat. Before I slid to the floor I stage-whispered that the guys in the car spoke English. But the "slant-eyed bucktooth" material never stopped.

I don't know how this whole affair was arranged but it was done very well. On day two, for example, we are taken to lunch by one of the same charming guys, Yuki, who had picked us up at the airport. It's an indoor-outdoor restaurant on the edge of the city, with an enormous park-like area and a pagoda in the middle distance. On the lawn a wedding party is being posed for photographs. The bride is wearing an old-fashioned "do" with the obi, and her piled up hair is lacquered. Her attendants are in graceful kimonos and the gentlemen, on a narrow wooden platform in back of them, are all in formal Western attire.

Suddenly, Kathleen hops out in front of the group, assumes a "funny" pose, and demands that our photographer take her picture.

"NO," I bellow. I also growl a small suggestion to our photographer that if he makes a move I'll smash his goddamn camera. He grins. The bimbo is furious.

Later I take the ladies to a department store in the Ginza. (I'm curious; they are not.)

An old, old lady in kimono is bent over a counter examining some jewelry. The chaperone has a camera and, at signal from her, Kathleen takes the old Japanese lady's head between her hands and turns it toward the camera.

The clerk behind the counter is looking at me with no expression on her face. The reason is, she can't see me. I have invoked my magic powers and become invisible. All that remains of what was me is a deep blush which hangs in the air.

Evening, same day. Yuki has invited us three to the oldest tempura restaurant in the city. It's in the ancient part of Tokyo down near the waterfront.

At the door, Yuki rings the bell, the door opens and there on a mat is a maid, kneeling.

I swoon.

The ladies push right on in.

When I come to, we are in a gorgeous room of glowing old wood in various patterns. In the center is the only furnishing, a low table. We sit on rush matting with our shoeless feet sticking down into a kind of depression in the floor.

A waitress slides back a partition, kneels, and asks us for our order. Yuki and I ask for scotch, the actress orders scotch too, but when the chaperone demands Coke, the actress decides she needs one too. For her scotch.

Yuki translates and says the establishment will send out for Coke—it'll be a matter of half-an-hour. The missies make little moues of displeasure, and the actress surveys the walls, the magnificent carved ceiling and says acidly, "Well, what can you expect?"

I take the liberty of looking inside her head. There, sure enough and all lit up is the word, "WOG."

Dinner is served in an adjoining room by a cross-legged, enormously placid, live Buddha. He faces us across two vats of hot coating and with a pair of tongs, dips and serves, dips and serves—for two hours.

The chaperone is, of course, a vegetarian, so she refuses the fish, the shrimp and the beef. Fortunately for her, there are also at least twelve different vegetables.

Boy, how I wish Karen were there instead of these two pachakas. Or Herbert Hoover or Attila. Or even just Yuki and I and a polar bear. Still, it is one of the grandest meals I've ever had.

The next two days I wander around Tokyo by myself with a newly-bought tape recorder. First, I tape a parade, but I haven't been able to play the tape in years. They don't make that kind of equipment to play it anymore. Of course. Then I wander the streets.

There are hundreds of little snack bars in the side streets, and the first thing I notice, early in the morning, is that every inch of every shop and the sidewalk out front is washed with soap and water. New York wasn't that clean even when the Indians ran it. No problems with ordering, either. There are vitrines out front just loaded with wax models of what the place offers. You motion a waiter outside, point, smile, and you're home free.

Since the women are going north, I pack my things and head south. But first I cable Karen to meet me a few days hence in Hong Kong.

I pronounce the name of the railroad station very carefully to the cab driver, and sure enough, we arrive. It's not until I'm inside that I realize I told him the wrong station. Here I am, a sturdy little figure of a Westerner, with his two bags and his one-thousand-pound tape recorder, sweating like a dragon, twelve thousand miles from home, surrounded by twelve thousand identical Japanese people rushing in all directions. I have (zero) joyous thoughts.

A man leaning against a wall kindly looks at my ticket and says, "Tokyo." I point at the floor, *this* is Tokyo. He shakes his head no and points to, maybe, Alaska. A dim bulb begins to glow inside my dim head. There must be a *station* called "Tokyo."

I'll spare you the rest and just get there, all right?

On the proper railroad, the Tokkaido, the ticket has the time, your seat number and even where to stand on the platform. The train arrives on the nose, the doors open, and there's your seat, just where it's supposed to be.

Japan built this railroad soon after they lost the war—and they were broke. We had all the money in the world, so we threw our systems into the sewer and replaced them with trucks. Aren't we lucky?

I am off to Kyoto in a comfortable seat on an unbelievably quiet train, traveling smoothly at a top speed of one-hundred-fifty-miles-per-hour. At various scenic points a melodious chime introduces a soft voice which gives the salient facts. It's depressing. Trains are another of my hobbies, but not in the States, Jack. The phasing out of what was the greatest network on Earth was economic hooliganism. Did you know that the steam locomotive was the cheapest way to haul? The only thing that cost less was river barges . . . but let's not wrangle. The United States of America was built by steam railroads. Period.

The Tokkaido runs for the most part along the old roadway that the local daimyos travelled on their way to pay their semi-annual respects to the Emperor. They brought along their retinues—the caparisoned horses, the carriers of lamps, the outriders and the chests and pennons and musicians—oh, it must have been a brave sight.

Today the tracks seem to go through New Jersey because this is the industrial coast of the country. And Mount Fuji is hidden in a cloud as we go by. And the girls who roam the aisles and sell snacks are loaded down with tofu. Well, I've never won the lottery either. But it's a fine trip.

51

K-K-K-Kyoto

An American breakfast firmly in place, I take a short walk. Down the street is a handsome building, very Japanese-y, and what with one thing and another I realize that it is an inn, a ryokan. I stop and stare. I breathe a lot. I think about how you sleep in a futon on the floor. I think about pretty Japanese girls walking on your back. I think about a Japanese girl helping you to take a bath. I think about a lot of things. I lose my nerve.

Back at the coward's hotel where some English is spoke, I hire a car and chauffeur and ask the dispatcher to tell the driver to take me to take me to, (A) an antique shop and (B), to the deer park at Nara.

Parts of Kyoto look the way the place is supposed to, according to me—and according to you too, I bet. Once outside the town it's even more so. I wish I had Karen's arm to poke.

After a bit the driver stops and gestures. It's an antique shop, right enough. I take off my shoes, open the door and pad inside. Nice, musty old place with lots of things on glass shelves, lots of little corners, everything small and comfy and a bit loony—but no people. Until I round a corner, and there are two old gentlemen on a mat with their legs folded under their kimonos, between them a bucket of charcoal and a little kettle sitting on a grill. They are drinking tea from tiny cups. They have been waiting for me for a-hundred-and-fifty-years.

One of the gentlemen fills a third cup and offers it to me. I hunker down on the mat, drink my chai, and the three of us start babbling. We have no way of knowing what we're saying but we are having a very nice time, anyway.

After a suitable period I lumber to my entire five-feet-ten-and-a-half inches and pad over to a shelf. There's a beautiful, odd-shaped saucer-like affair with a bright red bird baked into lovely white porcelain. The minuscule proprietor explains it to me at great length in Japanese. It is very old, he says. (Well, I'm guessing. I assume he's not telling me it's the worst piece of trash in the shop.)

He sees the lust in my beady blue eyes. He closes in for the kill. Nine dollars, American money.

We settle the deal over another cup of tea, and the two tiny old men accompany me to the door, see me into the car, and, as we drive off, they stand there smiling and bowing, smiling and bowing.

The sequel is easy to guess. When I got back to New York I took the little saucer to Sotheby's (Park-Bernet at the time) where it fetched (things 'fetch' at the big auction houses) it fetched, I love the word, two million four hundred and eighty three thousand dollars. It was bought by the Metropolitan Museum of Art and they built a little house for it in Central Park.

If you want to know what the Deer Park at Nara's like, it's gorgeous. Sorry, that's the best I can do. But I should warn you that lots of school children are brought there to see the deer and the enormous reclining Buddha. Don't go if clusters of oriental black-eyed dolls annoy you.

I had another day in Kyoto and r'ared back and passed a vow that one day my junk would come in, and I'd come back for a month.

My junk is still at sea.

52

Hong Kong

The airport sticks out a little above the water level at the foot of a mountain. One day Karen and I sat on top of that mountain and watched the planes come over the top, circle, and then let down over the harbor and head back inland. Tricky.

I met her at the airport and we went, for what reason I don't remember, to the Miramar Hotel. The first room they showed us was noisy so when Ms. Ng showed us the Bridal Suite for a-hundred-a-day, we took it.

All three large rooms overlooked the harbor; a bedroom with a box bed completely surrounded with pink nylon, very Chinese; a large, comfortable living room, very Chinese; a dining room seating eight (Bridal Suite?) separated from the living room by a long, sliding folding screen in the Chinese style; a bar a few steps up, in the *bedroom* with a sensational view. I had seen the view many times before in a watercolor by Dong Kingman. It hangs just behind me as I type this.

The ceilings were all cut up into gilded groins, the lights were brass globes with fringes, there were two oversized bathrooms all in marble, a refrigerator, and hundreds of switches which did amusing things: the switch for the living room draperies operated the curtains in the bedroom, etc. There were three very large closets.

Home.

Next morning in the English-language paper we saw an article by one Scarth Flett. Ten minutes later in the lobby, Ms. Ng introduced us to our taxi-driver-guide, Kelly Ho. Kelly Ho, meet Scarth Flett.

Kelly drove us up into the hills to see a restaurant floating on a lake, but since we didn't seem to light up, he led us away to a stone path which led farther and farther up. It ran along a mountain stream, all carefully stoned in, the water pouring in a succession of cascades into little pools and then out of the mouths of charming stone heads. At the top of the stream a branch had been built which sent water down the hill through small fish markets where it flowed in and out of tanks of fish. There was no tourist junk for sale anywhere. Just different kinds of food. But there were no shoppers. Why, Kelly?

"Oh, tourists don't come here. Nothing to see, nothing to buy. It's just for Chinese. They come on weekends."

By George, he *understood* us!

He explained the shacks and the new apartment houses which climbed toward us. The people in the shacks could afford the thirty-a-month apartments, he said, but they didn't like to leave the old neighborhood.

Hong Kong apartment houses meant for the Chinese are mostly variations on a theme. Each floor has a balcony that circles the building. The balconies contain drying laundry, flowers, chairs, lanterns, people, dogs, children of people, children of dogs. On the street level it's all shops, and on every roof, a school! And, from a short distance, it all seems to be a perpetual party of some kind. Kelly Ho was fine, but let me tell you about Wally Kwok.

One day in San Francisco a few weeks back I'd run into columnist Herb Caen having lunch with the Editor-in-Chief of the *Christian Science Monitor*. When I said I was going to Hong Kong the editor told me to be sure to look up his old friend, Wally Kwok. Well, I don't do things like that. It's an imposition. Now, keep in mind that I had no idea of exactly *when* I'd be in Hong Kong, or at *what* hotel.

On the morning of our second day at the Miramar, Mr. Kwok called *us*.

Our first taste of the mysteries of the Orient.

Wally'd been born in Shanghai to what must have been money because he was a graduate of M.I.T. When the government of China fell, he'd gone to Hong Kong and done well. I asked a lot of nosy questions and he told me that he had the Asian distributorship for Parker Pens. Well sir, he also had a small yacht in the harbor and he took us for a cruise. Everything was fine except that after a while Wally couldn't stand my coughing and sneezing any more and asked me if I'd mind going to a Chinese doctor? At that point I would have gone up the mountain on my knees to consult a disbarred gypsy. When I get a cold it lasts two months. Always.

Wally radioed and when we came ashore his chauffered Cadillac was waiting for us.

Let me change tenses, please.

The doctor owns a tiny open-front store that sells corn flakes, shoelaces, sun glasses, brooms and sundry sundries. On one side of the shop. On the other side is a wall of drawers surmounting shelves of glass jars. The doctor and his wife and two children (we can see them doing homework) live in the rear.

Now for the examination. The tiny man sits opposite me at a bit of a table. He takes my wrists in his hands and stares into my eyes. Then he touches each of my temples, touches my hairline, then bends my fingertips back and forth. Then, through Wally, he asks me to stick out my tongue. Examination over.

The doctor picks up a slender brush and writes out the characters for the medicine. It takes about ten minutes because there are five columns of ideograms. (I still have the prescription, of course).

At this point, three men appear from nowhere. Number One reads out the recipe; Number Two reaches into (unmarked) drawers and bottles and weighs the ingredients on a hand-held scale; Number Three wraps each item neatly in brown paper and marks it, then adds up the costs on an abacus.

At last there are exactly twelve packages on the counter, and Number One sweeps them all into a shopping bag.

Now it's time to pay for the two examinations. (Karen was jealous and demanded her *own* examination, and then felt hurt because there was nothing wrong, ergo—no prescription.) Wally wants to pay, but there's the doctor's time, the twelve ingredients, plus the salaries and overhead; I insist.

One-dollar and seventy-five-cents.

Out on the sidewalk Wally confides that he thinks it was a bit high.

The huge Cadillac appears in the narrow street (how summoned?) and drives us down to the pier. Wally claps his hands and his yacht appears. On board I sneeze, groan, gasp, blow, wipe my streaming eyes, and then we're on the other side and Mary is waiting for us.

Who is Mary? How was she summoned? How did she know she was to take the medicines home to brew them? How did she know to come to our room that night with a pint thermos of piping hot bitter junk that she made me drink before she'd leave?

In the morning my cold was gone.

The Chinese have been fooling around with bark and herb medicines for six or seven thousand years. Do you suppose they're on to something?

Once when I was a radio monologist, I mentioned the town of More, Utah. It had two doctors. This led to the famous ad which begins, "More doctors recommend . . ."

Karen and I had a lovely time in Hong Kong, but go and see for yourself. Instead of hanging around the lobby, do what we did. We walked the crooked streets, ate in the outdoor markets, window-shopped and, come night, we jumped around in the festivals of light.

We did the best we could and our time was up. Then we decided to extend the trip ("I mean, as along as we've come *this* far . . .")

We got on a plane for Pnom Penh.

53

Angkor Wat

You go first to Pnom Penh in Cambodia to see if you can pronounce it; from there you take a plane to Siem Riep, which a lot of people can say. You get a concrete room with a ceiling fan at the Auberge des Temples. You do all this at night so that you don't know where the hell you are, except for a hunch, and, if you're like me, you get bursitis.

If you have bursitis, you need a painkiller, and if you need that as badly as I do, your fainting French revives long enough for you to get hold of a boy who brings a decanter of water and two glasses so that you can drink the J&B you bought in Pnom Penh, if you can pronounce it.

At six in the morning, I open the shutters—and shout! There, a couple of hundred feet away with the sun coming up behind it, stretching for a quarter-of-a-mile, is the largest religious structure in the world. And that includes, friend, the enormous church a nut is building in Africa with money stolen from "his" people.

We walk across the road and down the long stone causeway with enormous stone cobras as railings on either side. Every inch of every wall is carved into fanciful animals and people.

We find ourselves all alone in a huge courtyard, alone with a million dragonflies glistening in the early sun. It's very much like floating in a dream of marvels.

263

We clomp around other temples too, mostly in the jungle. Men have to slash back at the growing stuff every single day or the jungle takes everything back. The place is like a textbook. Man refers to himself as a "higher form" of life. Yop. Man talks, but the horseshoe crab doesn't listen. The tadpole can't use a dictionary, but it doesn't get cirrhosis, either.

You can't hardly get thoughtful stuff in an autobiography like that any more.

I booked a one-hour elephant ride for the following day. It rained, so I switched from the nine o'clock to the ten o'clock elephant, and we swayed around seeing the sights. One sight was a sign stuck in the ground: FUTURE HOLIDAY INN.

They didn't know that the Khmer Rouge was waiting out there in the bushes. We didn't either, of course, but we were among the last visitors to Cambodia even till now (1994).

That night inside Angkor there are costumed dancers acting out the classical stories to the music of a gamelan orchestra. It sums up what we hoped for just fine.

The next day it's back to Pnom Penh.

54

Phnom Bloody Penh

My bursitis was killing me and I just couldn't wait all those hours at the ha, ha, airport, so a taxi took us, through deafening streets, to the "best" hotel in the city.

We got lucky. Our room was the one with the air-conditioner in it. The first one ever made. There was also a sink in the room with a cold water tap and a hole for what might have become, some day, a hot water pipe. This really was the best hotel in town, so I imagine there were toilet facilities somewhere.

The noise from the street drowned out even the "air-conditioner", and to make it even more attractive, someone kept knocking on the door. A guy trying to sell us a tour.

Karen went to get me something to eat, and came back with two dried things in cellophane and a bottle of, maybe, beer. I took the cellophane off the stuff and bit into it. I asked Karen what she had asked for? She said a chicken sandwich. In what language? English. We will never know what we ate.

We go for a walk. The people are short and thin, the young ones quite handsome. The main business seems to be the operating of empty pedi-cabs, a kind of box-on-two-wheels with the driver sitting behind on a bicycle wheel. When it rains, he throws a cloth over the box—or, as in many cases we saw—he doesn't. The shops are all open to the street and sell what seems

265

to be an amalgam of plastic junk, toilet bowls, and things stolen off of trucks.

The city on the whole is street-after-street of things falling apart. When, in 1976 the "Reds" ordered Phnom Penh evacuated, the people had nothing much to leave behind. The few natives I spoke with in my acrylic French seemed to think that "things" had been better under the French. They most assuredly couldn't have been any worse.

We went back to the hotel and sat at a scruffy table on the sidewalk, and it was there that we learned about the division of labor. One man took the order for beer, another took the bottles out of a chest, a third brought ice cream and a fourth brought the check. Old China?

People go by . . . an old man with a pole across his shoulders. Suspended from either end are panniers containing skimpy vegetables, fish, fatty meat, all for sale. It rains. Poor, poor souls shush by in the wet. (No sewers). The place reeks of poverty and it seems to be in the lower depths of Calcutta, but this is the *best* hotel on the *best* street in the city.

It's not possible to understand why the West was astonished by the dread that hit Cambodia. I am most certainly not worldly wise, but the clues! In downtown Phnom Penh there are chickens pecking between the parked cars, such as they are. There are loose pigs wandering in the side streets. From what we saw in the shops and on the sidewalks, the populace is living on nothing, mixed with a few grains of rice and leaves. On the way back to the airport we proceeded down the Boulevard of the Soviet Union and then into the Avenue of Mao tse-Tung. We passed people working in paddies under weather-beaten Esso and Shell signs. Something had to happen.

It is possible that one system of government is better than another. The question is, for whom? If we were to send our President and all of Official Washington to Cambodia, they would just naturally lie down and die. By the same token I don't believe that the Supreme Soviet would last eight minutes in the United States. (Lately, it doesn't last in Russia, either.)

Let's take a break. I just found the business card of the man who directed us to the swell hotel and then came around to break the door down to try to sell us a tour. Remember this man!

OU-SENG HOR

Head Office;	*Mailing Address;*
88 Vithei Prey Kokor	C% Mrs. Sar-Thach
Phnom Penh	Pharmacie Angkor
Tel: 2 3776	34,V. Charles de Gaulle
C.T.S. Pchentong Airport	Phnom Penh

At the airport the only plane is obviously ours, but the officials claim it isn't. How we got us and our stuff on it in time is so bothersome that I think I'll let you off the hook and pass on it.

From Phnom Penh (say nom pen, and spell it as you will) to Bangkok via Viet Nam Airways is twenty-five minutes. Two doll-faces in sensational Ao-dais, slit up to the neck, serve us cocktails, champagne, excellent hors d'oevres, pastries, coffee, brandy—all of this—and as the plane is taxiing one of the doll-faces forces us to have a "farewell" drink. A twenty-five minutes flight.

55

Bursitis In Bangkok

Wally Kwok had recommended the Oriental Hotel and we blessed him for it. We were ensconced in a fine living room with a big picture window on the river, steps up to a large, oh, sleeping loft, I guess, too well done to be called a loft, but there you are. Built-in air-conditioning, fine restaurant up on the roof—Hey, Wally, look at us!

The traffic on the river keeps us glued to the window. The largest freight carriers look like oversized Dutch wooden shoes which are towed by strange looking tugs. Smaller craft seem to be modelled after drawings in old books about the Far East. When we finally got out on the river, we found the water so full of mud, rotting vegetables and expired wild life that it was amazing to see how many people bathed and brushed their teeth in it.

An American I knew, Jim Thompson, had been a Major in the OSS during WWII and had fallen in love with Bangkok. After the war he returned and organized Thaibok, a silk company, and he made up designs for the native weavers. He did well. A true believer, he bought six native houses and put them together in a single structure, which he filled with Thai sculpture which he'd dug up in the hills. Jim visited some people "upriver" for dinner one evening, went out for a walk, and was never seen again.

Everybody went looking for Jim: the U.S. Army, the British, the French and the Thais. His sister even hired a famous Dutch "seer" who said that he knew where Jim was, but after running through a few thousands of sister's money he gave up.

We asked around for Jim's house, but kept getting steered back to his shop. There they told us, finally, that the house was open to the public, but only on Fridays. Our flight left on Thursday, and since it was only a once-a-week deal, we were dead. When we got back to the States Jim's niece said, "Oh, dear. You should have told me you were going. Friends of the family are allowed to *stay* at Jim's house." Exciting news indeed.

✧ ✧ ✧

About my Bursitis. I'm in such pain that I fortify myself with lots of J&B before the hotel directs us to a hospital. It is night, and after we give the driver the hotel-prescribed five baht and not a baht more, he lets us out in the dark. There are some low wooden buildings, and it's only after we find a door with a light over it that we are sure it's the St. Louis Hospital. We wander along the wooden porch and run into a barefoot nurse. She steers us inside to a lit room, goes off and comes back with a Chinese who I guess to be a doctor. I trot out my miserable French, and he says "You can speak English with me. I interned at Montefiore Hospital in the Bronx."

I lie down on a wooden table under a plodding ceiling fan, and the doctor's assistant, a barefoot Thai, gives me the injection and the needle hits the shoulder bone. The doc goes out to bring Karen in off the porch to survey the drunk who has or has not passed out but, also, may be dead. (I ask Karen about this years later and she says, "Oh, yes, you looked like Scarlett O'Hara's mother's corpse.")

The hospital refuses to take any money on the grounds that foreigners are guests of the country. They call a taxi for us, hand us some painkillers and a bunch of Gelusil, and off we go, jouncing in the ruts through the hot night, me full of both booze and streptomycin, vowing to build them a new wing and not even put my name on it.

In the morning the arm works, so we hire a car, and a law student guide who hates the Government. He is one well-informed man, but we just don't have time to learn the entire background of each piece of mosaic in the Wat Po Temple—which covers an entire city block and is exactly what you go to Bangkok for. He starts leaving out some of the dates. Exactly what you go there for? Yes, until you see the Reclining Buddha.

Gentle Reader, I know that landing on the moon was hot stuff in its day, but this Buddha is one-hundred-and-sixty-feet long, and has been there since forever. The soles of his feet are inlaid with mother-of-pearl. Along his full-length are small figures of the Buddha in gold leaf, with extra leaves sort of just stuck on (like votive candles?) and each sits on his own altar, each alter covered with fresh flowers. Little kids follow us around—to hear spoken English, we found out.

From Karen's Notes:

Temple of the Emerald Buddha. H. said, "Like Disneyland done with real money." No cameras allowed, Temple of the Ramas open only on special days, and this one. Breathtaking, really breathtaking entrance. Enormous rooms of gold and mosaics with tiny bits of glass scattered throughout, shining like millions of jewels. Separate temple in the center, gold figures all over the place. Yards and yards of exquisite ceramics around the walls: painted story of King Rama and the Monkey Soldiers on cloister walls for about a mile. Checked shoes and went into temple.

Service in progress, but guide says they like to have foreign visitors. Which is just us. Monks chanting behind altar, people on floor on rugs and mats, praying, eating, talking, but atmosphere is serene, reverent, human. Babies are feeding or sleeping. Not solemn and stuffy like some of ours. HUMAN.

In center of altar, high on a column is the Emerald Buddha. Guide apologizes that it is "only jade."! The King of Siam (himself) changes Buddha's garments three-times-a-year, which

271

only he may do. Why three times—how many season are there? "We have two. Dry hot and wet hot."

Somewhere on grounds people buy colorful little birds in cages. Once out on the sidewalk, they set the birds free! A religious act of some kind.

On The Phraya River

Ferries, long, flat-bottomed boats with roofs of canvas and little outboards go up and down picking up people at tottering piers. Women poling boats with flowers and plants for sale.

Weathered and battered gingerbread-trimmed houses next to new ones built the same way. Rich new temple next to lean-to. Houses on stilts with steps leading down to river. Poppa in sarong reading newspaper inside open house. Kids, grownups, bathing and washing in the dirty water, how do they keep so clean? Kids hitching rides on tow ropes. A tiny motor boat pulling three huge houseboats and some baby boats.

Royal Barge Shed. Guide lets us climb all over magnificent Royal Barges with golden dragon prows. Seven kids stacked up in tiny rowboat, one falls out.

Impossible skyline. Pagodas, steel bridges, modern signs, falling down houses, cooking, swabbing.

H. says spoken Thai sounds like a Swede speaking Japanese clearly. Temple guide teaches us "crai"—upward inflection means 'farther', downward means 'nearer.'

✿ ✿ ✿

Thank you, Karen.

I try to buy a colorful shop sign man says no: people are used to it, but he'll make me an exact copy. No time, plane leaving for Copenhagen. Bangkok to Copenhagen? Yes, Scandinavian Airlines flies every Thursday. A Chinese lady told me about it in Hong Kong.

Pilot says in thirty-five minutes we'll see Mt. Everest. Too cloudy.

We think it's a non-stop, but no, we put down at Tashkent,

Russia, for refueling. To go from the plane to the airport building, about seventy feet, between ropes, a grim Russian takes our passports! I buy some Russian cigarettes and a lapel pin of the Hammer and Sickle. On the way out, Karen forces one of the armed Russian soldiers to smile back at her.

You can read about Copenhagen elsewhere—it was my second time, and I enjoyed it even more with K along. And so to London, about which I have only two snippets. In order to save a buck we went to the new Cavendish. Don't. We stayed one miserable night and then (for me) back to Claridge's for the fifth time. Two things did or didn't happen to K:

Didn't. She was upstairs when I saw, in the lobby, an old, old guy creeble out of the dining room. The maitre d' said to him, "Good afternoon, your Grace," and your Grace shook hands with him. K would have curtsied, I bet. (I saw her curtsy, and not kidding either, to Helen Hayes.)

Did. K had her butt pinched in Westminster Abbey right next to Edward the Confessor.

✵ ✵ ✵ ✵

A funny thing happened in New York after we got back, I had this crumpled mass of used ticket stubs and illegible receipts etc., and on a whim I took the stuff over to Japan Airlines and asked the nice girl at the desk if someone could go through it and see if I'd missed anything. A week later they sent me a refund of six hundred dollars. I gave it to Karen to give back to the guy who'd lent her the money to get to Hong Kong in the first place.

On what was really no more than some old friend's whim, or perhaps, hunch, my new friend and I had gone around the world. And the trip was, you may admit, a doozy.

Thank you, Draper Lewis. Thank you.

56

Canada

In order to avoid alimony jail (my cousin Alan, often divorced, had recommended one in Queens) I prepared to take off for Canada, and Karen announced that she was coming with me. I argued, using a weak tone.

We went around the corner from my house and bought a small station wagon right off the show room floor, drove it home, and piled it with stuff. Simple as that.

It was late May and I thought it would be nice to say goodbye to the States by spending the summer in dear old Truro, Cape Cod.

By a set of curious chances we were the first (and last) to occupy the bay-front house of—oh dear, please step back, I'm obliged to drop another name on you—the house of the famous painter Edward Hopper. Like little David it was small, but oh, my! The easel was still in the living room! The house was on a dune with the empty beach stretching away for miles.

Back of the easel was a twelve-foot arched and mullioned window framing a thrilling view across ten miles of harbor to Provincetown. There was a bitty kitchen and a bathroom which, there being no space for a door to swing, was separated from whatever by a plastic curtain. But there was a tiny room up under the eaves where Karen could sleep to the soft music of the rain on the shingles. Pure water from the well, a heater in the basement that roared tamely during the bad nights—what else on Earth *is* there?

September, that's what.

We had the small wagon, some clothes, and a few thousand dollars worth of bonds which Karen carried in her bra. At the Canadian border I was inside the office so long that Karen knew I was under arrest, but for once she couldn't think of how to cope. The poor thing had no way of knowing that the Canadians had recognized me, and were advising me on how to get my furniture cleared when it arrived, how to apply for a work card—and telling *me* jokes.

We crossed into Canada and, yes, Niagara Falls is better on their side.

I am obliged to state that whereas it's been mentioned previously how much I enjoy girls and travel, this wasn't my idea of one of the great voyages of the century. In the simplest of terms, we really didn't know what the hell we were doing.

We went to Toronto. I had a vague idea of finding work with the American TV people who made films there (because the unions charged less), and perhaps I had some other brilliant ideas, but I doubt it.

We drove to a hotel, unpacked, and made careful plans for the future. Well, no. We went down to the bar.

From the start it was perfectly clear that we weren't going to be able to live very long at the expensive Four Seasons Hotel in the Park.

Tom Kneebone is a fine actor. Karen knew him somehow and somehow he found us a place to live. I tell you for no urgent reason that the name of the family in the next apartment was Ilk. Mr. and Mrs. Ilk and baby Ilk.

After a bit I got a radio job doing a five-minute humorful commentary every day. It was humorful to me. It was sort of humorful to the management. But there wasn't much chuckling and thigh slapping among the general run of Toronto listeners. They, like us, don't appreciate outsiders who think there's anything particularly amusing about their country. Another problem is that Canadians don't have too much of a sense of who they are, and people who are without that kind of, oh, *security*, find it impossible to laugh at themselves.

The problem, as we saw it during the four years we spent there, was a compound of attitudes. Some of the people feel inferior to, and/or jealous of, the U.S. "We're taking you to a good restaurant—but not like New York, of course," etc. Some Canadians think of themselves as basically British, and some think they are French, while others, in British Columbia, for instance, and in Newfoundland, seem to believe that they are separate entities entirely.

Their interior debate about how the removal of trade barriers between our two countries would diminish their "culture" is corroboration of this, I think.

To put it another way, there definitely *is* a Canadian culture, but many of the Canadians don't seem to have a grip on it. Americans certainly can't possibly define *their* "culture", but they have an sort of "feel" for it, whatever it is. My God, I'd make a dreadful social scientist, to be sure—but aren't they all?

Marshall McLuhan ("The Medium is The Message") invited me to address his graduate class at the University in Toronto. The subject of "culture" came up, and he announced firmly that Canada had none. I asked where was culture, after all? "Harvard" he said. He was, in Canadian terms, "sending me up"—pulling my leg.

Did you know that ninety-one percent of Canadian investors send their money to the U.S.? Yair. More than the Brits, more than the Japanese.

Montreal is where I refined my dislike of the Quois, as they call themselves. For one thing, they say they are French-speaking. Har har. "Horse" is 'cheval', hah? Not to the Quois (from 'Quebeçois'). They say 'zhoual.' And that's only the beginning, folks. On my Cape Cod, when the owner of a motel hears that accent, he jacks up the rate so that when the Quois get through arguing, it's back down to where it *should* be. At Truro's Blacksmith Shop Restaurant a party of them had dinner one night and left the waitress a five-cent tip. Karen was bartender there. She told me.

These here Quois, when they feel mistreated, refer to themselves as "The Jews of Canada."

Odd. I'd always thought of the Jews as a lively people.

Lively Canadians? In Quebec? Listen, Jack, Montreal is just like Omaha, Nebraska, but without the excitement.

Our social life,—well, "life" is an exaggeration. Karen is the charming, outgoing one of us, but even she had a rough time of it. We were invited to dinner a number of times, but the people we were introduced to turned out to be either clannish, cloddish, or simply in awe at meeting someone they'd seen LIVE on the telly. We were saved from complete insularity by a grand couple, Fletcher and Dorothy Markle. Fletcher, that handsome, kind, intelligent and amusing man is gone, dammit, and Dorothy lives in Pasadena in their big old house, trying to avoid her mother.

Here is our beloved Dorothy. An attractive, penny-bright and charming woman, she has the kind of humor that is rare, rare. One example: It is a day or two before Christmas and Dorothy is driving the four of us to the theater. An oaf in another car suddenly cuts her off. Dorothy maneuvers quickly, pulls even with him, grinds down the window and yells, "You dumb fucker!" Then she turns to us and, with the smile of a partly contrite but amused little girl, says, "My! That wasn't very Christmassy, was it?"

The sales manager of the station where I did my stint was Ray Purves, and he and his family were our other bastions of sense and fun. Neither clannish nor cloddish, they, too, helped to save our minds.

Canadian television does not permit stars. This keeps talent from demanding money, therefore the only hope of a future in TV is in the U.S. Viz: Lorne Greene, Peter Jennings and many others. There is a Hollywood colony of ex-Canadians of which the one most visible at present is Alex Trebek. (The first to leave was Mary Pickford).

How does it feel to live, as we did, so near and yet . . . Well, one way to explain it is that I did an occasional quick run into New York to do a guest shot, and worried constantly that someone would notify someone. But I looked forward to those trips, not because I was going home. It was because I was going *somewhere*. Everything about Toronto was blah; the restaurants, the tiny bit of theater, even the seasonal Stratford Shakespeare Festival. We met, in all those years, *one* Canadian who seemed to have a feel for living. His name is Clair Westcott and he was the right-hand man for the Premier of the Province of Ontario. He was fun for us, and after we left we were glad to hear from him that he'd become the Commissioner of the Toronto Police.

Yes, Toronto is physically attractive. The Royal Ontario Museum is just fine, and there are other municipal attractions which you can count on your elbows.

We were often reminded, and I mean OFTEN, that the streets are clean and that one can safely walk them at night. My inevitable and accurate answer endeared me to none.

"Yes, you can walk them at night. But where would you go?"

It's a great place to visit.

✿ ✿ ✿ ✿

Here is a rough idea what Canadians say they think is funny. Stephen Leacock is their one (1) famous humorist. This is an excerpt from a book of his, chosen at random.

> Trout, as everyone knows who is an angler, never rise after a rain nor before one. It is impossible to get them to rise in the heat and any chill in the air keeps them down. The absolutely right day is a still, cloudy day, but even then there are certain kinds of clouds that prevent a rising of the trout.

Pull yourself together!

I was invited to host and address the annual dinner that celebrates Leacock's birthday. We gathered at a motel some fifty miles from Toronto, lined up before the dinner in our proper places, and a pipe-band played us in.

I must tell you that a band of pipers pipes you in almost everywhere. I was embarrassed to go to the john.

The main point of the party is that the papers carried not one word about it. It seems that they objected to the host. An *American*, God save the Province!

A stand-up comic in Toronto is a different guy in the same sweater you saw the last time. He makes remarks about how it is on the farm.

A note here to give you another point of view. The "Celebrity Club." This is an old wooden house that was somebody's home a long time ago. The kitchen has been enlarged and a sign hung or hanged outside. This decrepit sag is immediately across the street from the headquarters and studios of the Canadian Broadcasting Corporation, the CBC. On almost any business day you can spot among the celebs, chawing away at the slumgullion in the former living room is the Second Vice-President in charge of the boy in the mail room, the Coordinator of Floor Numbers, and the Head Buyer of Ink.

Oh. A radio producer, some little priss with a British accent, hired me to appear twice-a-week on an interview-talk show "just to ad-lib," he said. I was on for a couple of months when one day he called me at home and, in his his abominable imitation of the upper classes informed me that I was "ripping him off."

"How?"

"Because I want an opening, a middle and a close. Don't ramble on."

The following day I went on the air with the interviewer and told the story, somewhat. I said that I was now doing the opening. When I got to the middle, I said it was the middle. Finally, I said, "here we are at the end, as instructed. This is the end. I quit."

The CBC was horrified and instantly cancelled the repeat of the show, which was destined for other parts of the network. Papers picked up the story even in the States. One of them asked for the opinion of a failed Canadian who was running a shlock show on U.S. TV. A guy with approximately half the, ah, talent of an Ed McMahon. What did he think of Henry Morgan's conduct? "Why," he said, "he only went to Canada so he could say bad things about the United States." Fella named Monty Hall.

Funny thing. As soon as word got out that I could no longer appear on the CBC, a different talk-show host, *same* network, called and hired me to be on *his* radio show. I spent many a pleasant half-hour with him. Alex Trebek.

As I noted before, the first show-biz Canadian with talent to leave for the States for whatever reason was Mary Pickford around 1900 or so. Trebek, for my deflated dollar, has talent, and to spare.

So much for our amiable neighbors to the North.

Aside from the Purves family and the Markles, the only fun we had in the four years we spent in Canada was the two weeks we spent in Acapulco.

57

The Little House on the, Uh, Dirt Road Up the Hill.

While still in Canada I had managed to pick up a dollar here and there, 'there' being Hollywood. I'd fly every two weeks or so to be in a TV series called *My World and Welcome to It* starring an unusually pleasant guy named Bill Windom. I still ducked into New York occasionally to do a bit of "guesting" while worrying that some funny guy would have told the cops that the notorious alimony ducker was in town.

Now, when I use the term "money" I am sort of ad-libbing. We didn't have MONEY. Just the same, we were thinking more and more about how to get back to a country we understood. That meant money in hand, because I couldn't go back to New York and make a living.

Karen and I began to talk about buying a bit of land on the Cape. She had a sum of money because she worked all the time. In fact, she had enough for a down payment. On *something*. We hoped.

We had left word with an old buddy to let us know if anything came on the market in Truro, and one night he called. Karen and I promptly had one of the two fights of our lives together about Lord-knows-what. Still, somebody had to go look, and she was afraid of the responsibility, but I yelled louder. "GO!" I shouted, "Go ahead and look!"

She went.

Came The Call. A tremulous little girl's voice said, "It's five acres. I was up there at night. I could see the lights of Provincetown. I bought the land."

Well, orally, of course. Subsequently, what with this and that, and the First Gullibile National Bank of Cape Cod, my roomie came up with the deed to the property. Real, live land.

Acreage can prey on the mind. It just sits, know what I mean? It sits and sends messages about how it is lonely and it would like a house or something.

In Toronto, I asked K to search for some balsa wood so that I could make a model of THE HOUSE. (One of the things that drove us crazy in Canada was that we could never *find* anything. For a simple hard maple kitchen serving table I was obliged to send to Brauner in N.Y. When it arrived I had to pay forty-something dollars duty to Canada for a one-hundred-ten-dollar item.)

K found some balsa and some graph paper, and I asked her what was the first thing she wanted in a house? A fireplace in the kitchen, she said. So I laid out a ground floor, fifty-by-a-hundred (the easy way) with a fireplace in the kitchen. Then with the balsa I built a two story house, one-quarter-inch to the foot.

We had seen Del Johnson's daughter's new house and we thought it was the best we'd seen on the Cape. It was BUILT, and we prevailed on its builder to come to Toronto and take a gander at the balsa.

He came, he saw, he estimated, and we shook hands.

He used just four men in addition to himself, and about eight months later it was done. Done!

If you've lived all your life in an apartment you will understand why the ceiling downstairs was ten-and-a-half-feet above the floor. Upstairs it was nine-and-a-half. Three bedrooms and three baths, for goodness' sake. A kitchen the size of a small restaurant, *with a fireplace* built into an all-brick wall, and a bow window large enough for the round mahogany table a guy sold us. He and his partner were selling off their motel to the

National Seashore and, so it shouldn't be a total loss, we bought his flagpole too.

Listen, we had an upper porch from which we could see all the way from Provincetown to the beginning of the Cape—say forty miles. (The Cape is much longer than that, but the bay curves, right?) From the upstairs hall you could see, in the opposite direction, a sliver of the Atlantic.

Next to each of our bedrooms there was a workroom. Mine had a built-in work table for my model-making. The downstairs guest room and bath was near the kitchen so they could feed at any time. Full basement with obligatory workbench, of course. AND a sound-proof room for recording my programs for Canada.

Karen promptly put in a vegetable garden over *there* and a flower garden over *there*. We had a lawn put on top of the sand. We put in a gravel driveway and a line of cherry trees and some log fencing and a Sears tool house—oh, man, did we (the BANK) put in.

To get to this mansion you took two lefts out of town and then one more up a dirt road.

We had it made.

Or the bank did.

We commuted back and forth from Toronto until, I dunno, one day we just decided not to go back.

We sent for the rest of our furniture and had the fun of watching an enormous tractor-trailer get stuck on our road in the snow, back down, twist sideways, and have to get dug out by some of the local boys that, thank God, we knew.

The first time we left the house together the alarm went off. The local police were there in a shade under four minutes. Karen made them coffee. They all kissed her, shook my hand, and wished us all the best.

Home. A *safe* home.

I had to revise my Toronto joke about how you could walk the streets at night, but where would you go?

We had no streets.

✦✦✦✦

Truro was and still is a lovely town. Our one problem was the long winters because we saw only the same old faces. And there were only three of them. And to see even them, we had to go to the post office. People who were born in, or chose to move to the town (wash-ashores), aren't very big on visiting. When I felt that I needed a riotous time I'd drive twenty miles to the diner and talk to the chef.

Karen went to work at every job she could find. For a while she was a guide on buses that brought old folks down from Boston, and one of the stops was at a place called Sealand. You will hear of Sealand and its dolphin show in a page or two. Uh-, as the kids say, real!

Oh, why wait! Karen and I had been talking by now for ten years. One day she said she thought we ought to be married. Now, even if we didn't see people often, we sure knew a lot of them pretty well, maybe two hundred. Who to invite?

Karen loved the dolphins at Sealand—there were three adults and two kids. She decided that she wanted to get married with just the dolphins as guests and, Ladies and Gentlemen, one brisk March day, that's exactly what we did. It was off-season so there were just Karen and I, a local magistrate, Mr. and Mrs. King, who owned Sealand, and a cheerful chorus of beings as intelligent as, and more graceful than, anybody we knew. After the vows we all had cake together while some of the guests snorted and yipped and then, by golly, tail-walked across the pool.

It had taken me twenty-two years to get up the courage to marry again. Twenty-two years and Karen.

It was on my birthday, too.

✦✦✦✦

One evening after dinner in our peachy fire-placed kitchen, my wife suddenly started to cry. We'd been together for years by then and I had never seen her cry. Why now? Well, she had always handled the money and it seemed that, what with the rise in the cost of oil, the fact that I was no longer recording my monologues for the station in Toronto, with the endless payments to the bank—one thing and another, let's say—we could not afford to go on. We had to sell the house.

Friend, if you've ever tried to sell your home you know, without my belaboring the point, which I will anyway, you discover that:

A. The market is at an all-time low and
B. Interest rates for a new owner would be double what you've been paying the bank and
C. According to the prospective buyers, the kitchen's in the wrong place, the house should have been made of concrete, the view is on the wrong side, the dog won't be happy here, the flowers are too short, the basement should be upstairs, the hill is too high, the stove should burn coal.

❖❖❖❖

I learned the hard way that most people who are "looking for a house" aren't looking FOR at all; they go around looking AT houses. It's an inexpensive hobby. The agent who shows them around senses this but he figures, hey—ya never know.

Meanwhile Karen has found a nice old four-story house in New York City that's divided into two apartments. The landlord has the downstairs apartment and the back yard with the trees in it. Karen rents the top apartment. Two floors. Fireplace in living room.

Small terrace through the French doors. Free view of the trees. Great!

We still live here.

The wisteria now goes almost all the way around the terrace. Thought you'd like to know.

❖❖❖❖

Oh. After we left Truro our agent called us to say that the house had finally been sold. He didn't mention the buyer but we found out a year or so later.

Now I have to use a phrase that I never thought I would but here 'tis. "Trust me." Ready?

The house was sold to a branch of the followers of the Reverend Moon.

There were Moonies in our garden.

58

City Boy. Again.

On our first evening back in the much-more-flawed-than-I-remembered-it Apple, we went out for dinner and stopped at the first restaurant we came to. We'd been seated for about five minutes when a sightly woman jumped up at another table, yelled "Henry!" and rushed over to us.

It was darlin' Joan Harris, a good old buddy who had been Garry Moore's secretary for many years. From that night on she became so close a friend that a couple of years later she and Karen took a trip to Rome together. In fact, Joan read the first draft of this book and, like the loyalist she is, was noncommital.

Through Lois Korey, an old friend, I was hired to be the head of the radio department at a huge advertising agency. Since they did no radio advertising I smoked a little more than usual while I read the *Times* and did the crossword puzzle.

In a little less than a year a new man took over the agency and of course decided to trim costs.

I went back into an old trade of mine, TV commercial voice-overs. "Things" improved in the next couple of years so Karen and I took a trip to Leningrad. It's now back under its old name of St. Petersburg, and all I can say is that if the poor Russian people ever pull themselves together—go there.

We lived in the "best" hotel and the food and the service were abominable—but the city itself is worth it, no matter what. Go to the Hermitage, of course. You won't see many of the paintings because the place is too jammed with tour groups, but look at the rooms—no two of which are even remotely alike. Each of them must have cost, in present-day terms, two million dollars. They are grand, unreal, kitschy-to-death, and wonderful.

See the Winter Palace. Take a trip on the canals. Talk with the people—they love trying out their English.

From St. Petersburg, take the boat to Stockholm. The boat, which is Finnish, has five restaurants and real food. The trip itself, the entrance to the harbor, the beautiful little city . . . oh, boy!

✧✧✧✧

Travel note. Karen has been to Rome and Venice six times, four times with girl friends. After all, I'd been there twice before we even met.

Some day we're going to take one of those barge trips along the rivers of France.

Wait for the book.

59

July 4, U.S.A.

Here is a column I wrote for a New England paper a while back. After you've read the piece allow me to tell you how it came about. The whole story is a kind of Agatha Christie knock-off—but it's also true.

The Glorious Fourth!

Now, if I'm to believe even half of what I read these days, there's nothing to celebrate. Our poor old U.S.A. is falling apart, its cities in ruins, its countryside chopped up. Its children can't read nor write, TV is rotting everybody's brains, the few remaining farms are giant corporate enterprises owned by British billionaires, and drinking water, milk, grapes, orange juice and celery too, probably, are all poisoned.

Our appliances all come from Japan—which dislikes manufacturing such junk, so they contract it out of Taiwan. Our politicians are either thieves or crazy, or both: our last few dollars are being spent to convert underground Utah into a new target for Russian missiles: our foreign policy is either non-existent or revolting. Everybody in the world hates us, and it's all terrible, terrible.

Is it possible to celebrate the Fourth of July?

We arrived at our friends' house in Plymouth on the third of July. Yes, Plymouth-where-the-rock-is.

On the morning of the Fourth, our host and his Number Two son loaded the family pump-organ into a pickup truck. The organ is made of oak and is pretty old but it works all right. At least for Number Two son it does.

I drove with Pop and son in the truck while the ladies walked through the woods . . . oh, say, half-a-mile; there's a bowl-shaped small clearing with a flagpole sort of near the middle, and we drove up pretty close to the pole.

It was a quarter-to-ten. By five-of, everybody was there who was going to be there—about sixty, sixty-five people. They were all friends and relatives of our hosts, and it was what I suppose you would call a cross-section of one particular kind of New England summer-folk, the kind that own their own cottages—probably by inheritance. There were little-bitty kids, people with grey hair, in-between, nice-faced people. And, of course, the two dogs. I say "the" two dogs because there are *always* two dogs at this kind of thing.

Betty passed around the song sheets. It was the first and the last verses of *The Star-Spangled Banner*. Betty has never trusted people to get the fourth verse, her favorite, right.

At ten sharp, Number Two son played the introductory chords on the old organ, and we all sang both verses.

The people started raising the flag, slowly, so that it would reach the top at the end of the singing. As it practically did. Well, let's say it really did—anyway, it *was* awfully close.

Then everybody automatically sat down on the grass because they've done this each and every year for many and many a Fourth. Betty's elder brother, who has a fine, strong voice, read the Declaration of Independence, and once again everybody marvelled at *what it actually says*. He read off the names of the signers, too. It sounded grand.

Elder Brother read the Declaration from the same book as his grandfather had read it right here in this very clearing, seventy-five years ago.

Then, as she does every year, Betty read a poem that grandpa had written for that first celebration long ago. It was sort of funny and everybody, including Betty, knew that. Grandfather's world wasn't very big, you see. Each verse ended with the eagle screaming "from Plymouth to Buzzard's Bay!" The bay is, oh, thirty miles from Plymouth.

Afterwards, people stood in little knots talking and patting their children's heads and looking nice-faced and happy. Number Two son and I got back in the pickup, Dad turned it around, everybody waved and we took the old oaken organ back home.

Nobody mentioned "next year." Nobody had to, of course. The only thing different about next year is that it will be the seventy-sixth in a row, that's all. And of the Republic, the two-hundred-and-fifth.

THE CAST

Betty: Betty Steinway Chapin

Dad: Schuyler Chapin

Number Two Son: Theodore Chapin [actually one of twins (Sam)].

Elder Brother: John Steinway

More Anon.

Son *Theodore* married a girl named Joanna. They had a daughter whom they named Anika.

Right.

Well, one year Karen and I were asked to spend Christmas Eve with as much of the family as was in New York. Subsequently, we started spending a couple of days each summer at the family compound at Long Pond, near Plymouth, Massachusetts.

Thus the column for the paper.

It gets easier to follow from here on.

One Christmas eve when Anika was about three, we were at Theodore's apartment and Joanna handed me a Christmas card. She smiled in what I can only describe as a "mysterious" way and told me to read the handwriting inside.

"Will you accept being godfather to my next child who will be born in August?"

Of course the professional cynic choked up.

But that's how Karen and I became godparents to wonderful, gorgeous, adorable, brilliant, amazing Zoë.

Among other splendid times, we spend every Christmas and Fourth with our family.

Then there's the case of my newest child-by-a-godchild. It will be birthed by Jennifer Konecky Wheelock and, according to a series of photos Jennifer has shown me, it won't be much of anything, really. It's only a few months old, true enough, but we're living in amniographoscopic times, are we not? Well, we is, and amniographoscopy is us. (But Jennifer is so good-looking that the child will pull itself together in time for the real world.)

Which brings us to another godchild, Susan Feldman. Remember her father, Chester, who used to book ten people a night for me? Susan is pregging around too—but she has her own, definitive point of view. No pictures. No marriage. No discussion. No nonsense. She's my kid, see, and she has been for thirty-nine years.

You got a problem with that?

60

If You Knew Karen Like I Know Karen, Oh, Oh, Oh What a Girl!

One of the despairs common to ladies I knew and still keep in touch with is that Karen is so good-looking. About five-seven, she has a slightly uptilted nose, a classic forehead, swept back hair that is a gorgeous gray-blonde, a peachy figure—and a lovely disposition. She also has brains that work, humor, and great taste in just about everything.

(What I've said so far may seem overdone, but keep in mind, please—she can also read.)

Item: K does embroidery, at which she is very good. She is also a cartoonist, a good cook, and comes from Iowa.

Item: On one of my birthdays I arrived downstairs at about ten. The phone rang . . . it was an old friend I hadn't heard from for years. I was terribly pleased. About half-an-hour later there was a call from another old buddy. And about every half-hour after that until the evening. It seems that K had spent over a week in tracking people down, and *assigning* them times to call.

Item: Another birthday. K said we had to go to a special place for lunch at one o'clock. Okay. But to the Long Island railroad station? Yes. The special place was a bit out-of-town. We took a train and she said we had to change at the first transfer point. Okay. We got off, crossed the platform and K said we had to get on the train that had just pulled in. Last car was best, she said, so we got in the last car. Turned out it was a private car, with bedrooms, kitchen, the lot. In the comfortable sitting area were five of our favorite couples. There was a waiter and a headwaiter who passed around booze and wonderful hors d'oevres as we got under way. At the end of the trip the private car was put on a turntable, spun around and hooked to a train going back to the city. Only this time, I was in the locomotive, at the throttle!

But the day wasn't over. Back in the city we said goodbye to the folks, got into a taxi and K announced that dinner was at "21." It certainly was, with our friends the Dong Kingmans as hosts.

We take you now to November, 1992. K had had trouble swallowing and, after a biopsy of her esophagus was sent to a surgeon, Dr. Yeoh. He made a decision and I spoke with him. "What are the chances?" I asked. He looked directly at me. "It is a very difficult operation," he said. And that's all he said.

Frank Crennan has saved a letter I wrote to him in early December of 1983.

Hi.

Had the idea of writing to you about an astonishing woman. With me, to think is to shirk, but it's Sunday and I've finished the *Times* puzzle. So . . .

When Karen learned that she was going to the hospital, the first thing she did was "arrange." She made lists. She checked on her insurance, she went to AFTRA to make sure about what was covered and what was not. She picked up the required forms.

She made out lists for me as to what needed to be done day-by-day. A separate directive told how to heat each different frozen thing in the fridge, including the shepherd's pie and the tomato pie she baked and left for me. When to pay the housekeeper. How to refill my pill container (it holds a week's worth, laid out by days). She bought Christmas presents for her West Coast family and sent them all.

She left a check for apartment insurance and directions. She paid the next month's rent in advance.

The morning of the day she went in she left early to get the last of my stuff from the laundry.

When I walked into Intensive Care on the first day, a voice buried in tubes and wires said, "I could get up and walk down the hall if I wanted to."

When she came home she stood in the center of the living room and looked around.

"I love every piece of shit in this room," she said.

On Friday, during the worst storm in the history of the city we went to have her badly infected tooth extracted. Luckily, we had rented a car and driver. It took an hour-and-a-half to go two miles.

When we left in all the wind and rain, some of the streets had been closed off. The car was impeded unbelievably. Wind shook us. Rain whipped. As we slowly, slowly passed an out-of-town bus that had managed to park outside a hotel and unload its newly-arrived visitors, K holding an ice-bag to her cheek, lowered the car window, turned in the direction of the frozen bus-driver who was painfully unloading the baggage and said, "Welcome to New York!"

She may have told you that her left hand isn't much help because some nerves stopped working for awhile because her arm was partly under her for eight hours. Yesterday, December 19th, she went to luncheon with her oldest friend, and before she left she said, "I got my pantyhose on with one hand!"

As of now she truly intends to visit friends on the eves of the 22, 23 and 24. What the heck, she's already wrapped a hundred gifts, sent a hundred cards and done the tree. Ergo.

A thoughtful doctor has already been kind enough to tell her that, because of the painful arthritis, she probably will have to undergo a hip replacement. Yes, doctors do things like that.

And every morning she remakes my bed, and every evening she "does" it the way they do at the Pierre.

Well, after all, she's been home since Dec. 3rd and this is the 30th. Nobody wants riff-raff hanging about.

On January 6th she starts a month of daily radiation.

I send real love. And guess where I learned about it.

L'Envol

When I was a kid up on Washington Heights and would run into another specimen on the street he would say, as was common at the time, "Well, whadda ya know for sure?"

I've had a while to think about it, and I'm neither sorry nor happy to have the answer, at last.

"Not very much."

The only things I know have been said much better long, long ago by much better thinkers.

A few notes:

From George Santayana, "Skepticism is the chastity of the intellect."

From Alistair Cooke, who, in this passage, is quoting something Charles Chaplin wrote as an old man. "Procreation is Nature's principal occupation, and every man, whether young or old, when meeting any woman measures the potentiality of sex between them. Thus it has always been with me."

Me too, Charlie.

Herbert Spencer said, "You might gauge a man's intellectual capacity by the degree of his intolerance of unnecessary noises."

And from Thoreau. "If a man does not keep pace with his companions, perhaps it is because he hears a different drummer. Let him step to the music he hears, however measured or far away."

And my dear old Mencken said, "No one ever went broke underestimating the intelligence of the American people."

Which leads in beautifully to this mot from Bertrand Russell. "Men fear thought as they fear nothing else on earth—more than ruin, more even than death."

Russell was far from alone. Luther Burbank, (who is remembered today, if at all, as a TV studio in California) is on record with "Less than fifteen percent of the people do any original thinking on any subject . . . The greatest torture in the world for most people is to think."

Which reminds me of what Goethe, without knowing it said

of Ronald Reagan—"Nothing is more terrible than ignorance in action."

And this one is an Armenian saying: "He who speaks the truth must have one foot in the stirrup."

The best, of course, is last. It's from Hugh Walpole.

"The world? A comedy to those who think; a tragedy to those who feel."

May I add one of my own? "If it is true that God created Man, by now he surely has laughed himself to death."

And I'm not sure about any of the above, either.

"Grow old along with me, the best is yet to be."
—Robert Browning

"Bullshit."
—Henry Morgan